Oh Garden of
Fresh Possibilities!

Oh Garden of Fresh

 DAVID R. GODINE · *Publisher* · BOSTON

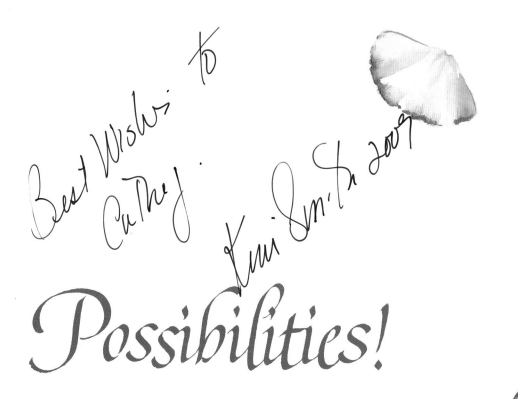

Possibilities!

NOTES FROM A
GLOUCESTER GARDEN

Written and Illustrated by

Kim Smith

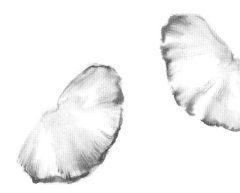

FIRST PUBLISHED IN 2009 BY
DAVID R. GODINE · *Publisher*
POST OFFICE BOX 450
JAFFREY, NEW HAMPSHIRE 03452
www.godine.com

Library of Congress Cataloging-in-Publication Data
Smith, Kim
Oh garden of fresh possibilities! : notes from a
Gloucester garden / written and illustrated by Kim Smith. —
1st ed.
p. cm.
Includes bibliographical references.
ISBN 978-1-56792-330-8 (hardcover)
1. Gardens—Atlantic Coast (U.S.)—Design.
2. Gardens—Poetry. I. Title. II. Title: Notes from a
Gloucester garden.
SB473.S562 2007
712'.60974—dc22
2007006326

FIRST EDITION
Printed in China

For Liv and Alex

Contents

List of Illustrations ix
Introduction xi

Part One: Creating the Framework

CHAPTER ONE
A Pair of Pear Trees 3

CHAPTER TWO
Flowering Trees for the Romantic Garden 9

CHAPTER THREE
Planting in Harmony with Nature:
Combining Native and Ornamental Trees and Shrubs 21

CHAPTER FOUR
Plum Trees for Plum Street 33

CHAPTER FIVE
The Narrative of the Garden 41

CHAPTER SIX
Through the Moon Door 47

CHAPTER SEVEN
Scented Lilacs 53

CHAPTER EIGHT
Hydrangea paniculata 'Grandiflora' 61

CHAPTER NINE
A Note on Hollies 65

Part Two: Candidates for the Borders

CHAPTER TEN
The Fragrant Path 73

CHAPTER ELEVEN
The Narrative of the Garden: Part Two 83

CHAPTER TWELVE
Oh Garden of Fresh Possibilities! 93

CHAPTER THIRTEEN
Fragrant Herbaceous Peonies 103

CHAPTER FOURTEEN
Roses for the Intimate Garden 109

CHAPTER FIFTEEN
Flowers of the Air 123

CHAPTER SIXTEEN
A Summer of Fragrant Yellow Daylilies 133

CHAPTER SEVENTEEN
Terrace Plantings 143

CHAPTER EIGHTEEN
Late Summer Splendor in the Garden 153

CHAPTER NINETEEN
Exquisite Flora in Autumn 161

CHAPTER TWENTY
A Note to Spring Signed Autumn 171

CHAPTER TWENTY-ONE
My Grandmother's Gardens 187

CHAPTER TWENTY-TWO
The Memorable Garden 191

Appendix
Coaxing Winter Blooms 197
Favorite Flowers for Butterflies 202
My Mother's Garden 206
Bibliography 207
Acknowledgments 211

List of Illustrations

COVER – *Compositae*
HALF TITLE – Handful of Shirleys
TITLE – Picotee Poppy Petals
DEDICATION – Pink Poppy
CONTENTS – Summer Butterflies
LIST OF ILLUSTRATIONS – *Viola* 'Etain'
INTRODUCTION – *Papaver rhoeas*

CHAPTER ONE

Goldfinch and Pear Blossoms 3
Two Pears 7

CHAPTER TWO

Peach Blossom Sprig 9
Magnolia stellata 'Water Lily' 11
Apricot Blossoms 12
Prunus persica 'Belle of Georgia' 14

CHAPTER THREE

Summersweet 'Ruby Spice' 21
Canadian Tiger Swallowtail 22
Philadelphus 'Innocence' 25
Chaenomoles 'Toyo-Nishiki' 28
Rhododendron viscosum 31
Red-spotted Purple 32

CHAPTER FOUR

Falling Plum Blossoms 33
Prunus cerasifera 'Thundercloud' 37

CHAPTER FIVE

Oriental Lily 'Casa Blanca' 41
Maypop and Honeysuckle 44

CHAPTER SIX

'Silver Moon' Clematis 47
'Silver Moon' Seed Head 49
Long-tailed Skipper 50

CHAPTER SEVEN

Syringa 'Wedgwood' 53
Paeonia 'Rockii 57
Lilac Smudges 59

CHAPTER EIGHT

'Peegee' Hydrangea 61

CHAPTER NINE

Cardinal and 'Dragon Lady' Holly 65

CHAPTER TEN

'Variegata di Bologna' Buds 73
Oriental Lily 'Sorbonne' 75
Alpine Strawberry 77
Oriental Lily 'Olivia' 82

CHAPTER ELEVEN

Moonflower 83
Stephanotis floribunda 88
Campsis 'Madame Galen' 90

CHAPTER TWELVE

Handful of Shirleys 97
Monarch and *Tithonia* 98
Pink Poppy 101

CHAPTER THIRTEEN

'Roselette' 103
Peony Petals 108

List of Illustrations

CHAPTER FOURTEEN

Sweet Briar Hips 109
'Variegata di Bologna' 114
'Frederick Mistral' 119
'Aloha' 122

CHAPTER FIFTEEN

Two Orange Sulphurs 123
Great Spangled Fritillary 125
Apple Blossoms and Spring Azure 128
Red Admiral 131
Pearl Crescent and Nasturtium 132

CHAPTER SIXTEEN

Hemerocallis dumortieri 133
Hydrangea 'Endless Summer' 136
Chinese Bellflower 138
Hemerocallis thunbergii 140
Hemerocallis citrina 142

CHAPTER SEVENTEEN

Gardenia Bud 143
Brugmansia 'Charles Grimaldi' 145
'Tea Breeze' Blossom 146
Ficus carica 'Lattarula' 148
Meyer Lemon Sprig 150
Gardenia 152

CHAPTER EIGHTEEN

Lilium speciosum 155
Red Lily Beetle 156
'Blue Star' Morning Glory 157
Peacock Orchid 158
Lily-of-the-Valley Seed Capsules 160

CHAPTER NINETEEN

Korean Daisy 161
'Nanho Blue'/Tiger Swallowtail 164
Compositae 169

CHAPTER TWENTY

Convallaria majalis 'Rosea' 171
Narcissus tazetta 'Geranium' 177
'Red Riding Hood' Tulip 180
'Spring Green' Viridiflora Tulip 186

CHAPTER TWENTY-ONE

'Heavenly Blue' Morning Glory 187
Alcea rugosa 188
Rosa eglanteria 190

CHAPTER TWENTY-TWO

Hollyhock Seed Capsule 191
Philadelphus 'Belle Etoile' 196

APPENDIX

Narcissus 'Chinese Sacred Lily' 197
Chaenomoles 'Toyo-Nishiki' 200
'Frederick Mistral' 206

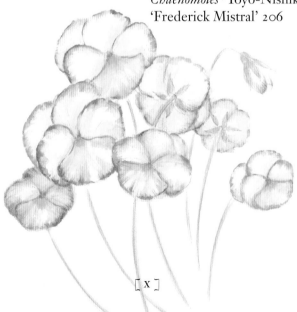

Introduction

We all carry within us the image of a home to create and a garden to tend. Perhaps you dream, as I do, of a welcoming haven to foster family bonds and friendships and to rejoice in life's journey. The garden and the home to which it belongs becomes a memory catcher to weave a life's tapestry.

To imagine a garden paradise, one must live in one's home and listen to its own particular music. Gradually, by degrees, the idea of the garden will grow. A home and a garden should look as though they had grown up together and *will*, when one takes the time and necessary thought. A garden cannot be hurriedly created. Delicious, blissful pleasure is derived from the garden's use as a continuation of the home.

Our gardens provide a safe harbor from hectic lives, a place to celebrate life and an opportunity to express our creativity. The garden is an inviting sanctuary to guide one through the rhythms and harmonies of the natural world. Planted to nurture the imagination and hearten the soul, a "new" cottage garden is a whimsical, exuberant intermingling of scented flowers and foliage, fresh fruit, and savory herbs.

As a designer, I believe I am here to channel ideas for the benefit of many. This book is my communication of a profound desire to share with readers the immeasurable joy gleaned from creating a personal paradise of one's own making.

The illustrations are of flowers, songbirds, and butterflies I love to draw and to paint, and selected because they only become more beautiful when intimately observed.

A poetic world lies waiting to be discovered. Let us open the garden gate and take a step within.

PART ONE

Creating the Framework

CHAPTER ONE

A Pair of Pear Trees

SUMMER SHOWER

A drop fell on the apple tree,
Another on the roof;
A half a dozen kissed the eaves,
And made the gables laugh.

A few went out to help the brook,
That went to help the sea.
Myself conjectured, Were they pearls,
What necklace could be!

The dust replaced in
    hoisted roads,
The birds jocoser sung;
The sunshine threw his hat away,
The orchards spangles hung.

The breezes brought dejected lutes,
And bathed them in the glee;
The East put out a single flag,
And signed the fête away.

— EMILY DICKINSON (1830–1886)

W E TREASURE OUR CHARMING old house, despite the never-ending tug-of-war between working on its restoration and our full lives. The earliest part of the house is a side-gable, two-rooms-over-two constructed in 1851, and fortunately many of the nineteenth-century details remain intact. Wrapping around the front is the original farmhouse-style porch lending a friendly air to the facade. The windowpanes are early crown glass, replete with waves and bubbles, the door and window moldings deeply carved in the classical Greek Revival style, and the ceilings decorated with floral plaster center medallions. The last time the house underwent a major renovation was during the 1930s when a "modern" kitchen was added. The kitchen floor tile is laid in a checkered design of buttery cream yellow and French blue six-inch square linoleum, with a one-inch-wide, hand-cut border in the creamy yellow. Despite its general state of dilapidation, we knew the house had great bones, and we enthusiastically forged ahead.

The house's architecture and interior details called on us to interpret the design of the landscape. We sought to make the garden a continuation of the house, to create a series of outdoor rooms for living, fragrant corridors, and a garden rich in useful and edible plantings. The ideal of the garden began to take shape, and we hoped it would be as friendly and unpretentious as is the house. A "new" cottage garden for a modern family (with an eye on the practical grandmother's garden), planted luxuriantly, with touches of whimsy added here and there, would suit our home and lifestyle.

From the previous owners we inherited two pear trees (*Pyrus communis*) growing in the rear yard. Along with several evergreens overwhelming the front dooryard and a withered patch of an heirloom lemon-scented yellow bearded iris (*Iris germanica* 'Honoribile'), these were the last remnants of a long-forgotten garden. Despite years of neglect, the two old pear trees had survived admirably, standing side by side, their limbs trained to grow in an arc toward each other. Considering how carefully they were shaped, it was clear they were thoughtfully maintained at one time. That first summer they produced a motley, distorted, and diseased crop of fruit. The following fall we pruned branches that were weak or dying, and, attempting to grow a lawn, tilled and fertilized the hard, compacted soil beneath and around the trees. With only this slight attention, those trees miraculously perked up.

Next spring they were clothed in clusters of deliciously scented white blossoms and visited by a single Baltimore Oriole. Each year we have gained a bit more knowledge on how to rescue old fruit trees. With the aid of a local Orchardist, we learned that our trees are the old garden variety 'Beurre Bosc.' The European pears are buttery smooth, sweet, and fragrant as exemplified by the familiar 'Bartlett,' 'Anjou,' and 'Comice.' The 'Beurre Bosc' has golden russet skin with honey-sweet tender flesh.

While traveling through northern New England, I became familiar with another heirloom pear tree growing in the sheltered garden of the former manse of a New England sea captain. As was the 'Beurre Bosc,' the 'Flemish Beauty,' originally known as 'Fondant de Boise' or "sweetmeat of the woods," was first introduced into this country in the early 1800s. The fruit is large, rounded and pale yellow with rose-blushed cheek, and like that of the 'Beurre Bosc' is sweet and aromatic. Interest in growing pears in America peaked in 1820 and continued for the next fifty years. Eastern Massachusetts, and especially the Massachusetts Horticultural Society, was the epicenter of this enthusiasm.

> *He who plants for pears*
> *Plants for heirs*
> — an old saying

Pyrus communis, or common European pear, is not seen growing in the wild. The cultivated pears as we know them today are thought to be derived from *Pyrus nivalis* and *P. caucasia*. Few pears ripen well on the tree and that may be one reason they have not been grown as extensively in America as apples and peaches, although apple and peach trees are not as long lived as pear trees. A healthy pear tree can live and bear fruit for several centuries. The trick to harvesting pears is to pick them as they are ripening, while they are still quite firm. If you wait until the flesh yields with pressure on the outside, the fruit will be rotted inside. Each individual variety of pears has an estimated ripening date from when the tree blooms. Note the date when the tree begins to flower and count the days forward to the approximate ripening time.[1] The quality of the soil, where the tree is sited, as well as changes in the weather from year to year will influence the number of days until the pears are ready to be harvested. Bearing in mind that this is only an approximation, begin monitoring the fruit closely as the day approaches. Nearing the correct time of harvest, the color of the fruit will begin to change. For example, the 'Beurre Bosc' begins to turn a light golden yellow beneath its russet skin. Carefully hold the stem of the pear in one hand and the fruit-bearing spur in the other hand. Gently twist with an upward turn. Remove the pear and stem, not the bumpy, fruit-bearing spur. It takes several years for a spur to develop, and if damaged or accidentally harvested with the pear, the crop will be significantly decreased the following year.

Stack the fruit in the coldest section of a refrigerator and store for several weeks. After two to three weeks, remove a pear or two and let it ripen at room temperature for several days. At this point the pear will ideally be fully ripe and ready to eat. Depending on the cultivar, pears will keep for weeks to several months when kept well chilled.

During the tree's dormant period, after several hard frosts and before the buds begin to swell, roughly through the months of January to February, is the ideal time of year to prune pear trees. Remove vertically growing shoots from the tops of the trees. They will develop into strong leaders. Branches that are growing back into the tree and smaller branches crossing more vigorous limbs should be cut out as well. The lateral limbs that grow perpendicular to the trunk bear the greatest amounts of fruit. These should not be removed, unless they become damaged or diseased. Bear in mind it is best for the good health of an older fruit tree to practice pruning by degrees, never removing more than one-third of the old growth per year. All tree branches have a distinguishable collar at the base of the branch at the point where they extend from the tree. There are natural healing agents in the collar. When pruning, cut through the outer edge of the collar at an angle to allow rainwater to run outward, away from the tree.

Very early in the spring before the flower buds become plump, spray the trees with horticultural oil to suffocate overwintering pests and refresh the compost at the base of the trees. Pear trees do not require a fertilizer containing nitrogen. Nitrogen promotes the growth of an abundance of tender foliage, attracting both pests and diseases, with little added fruit.

We added a border of fragrant crocuses, early jonquils, and lily of-the-valley encircling each tree, edged with a ring of smooth oval stones scavenged from the beach. The stones were troublesome initially because we had not buried them in the soil deep enough, and the children and pets knocked them about. We re-dug and realigned them all, and it was worth the extra effort, for now the edging always looks tidy even when the flowers do not.

HORTICULTURAL OIL SPRAY

Full-leaf Solution – to a one-gallon container add ⅓ cup canola or saf-flower oil. Add a few drops of dish detergent. Fill with water to make one gallon. Use this spray when the planting is in full leaf. When the solution is applied to a tree in its dormant stage, in late fall or early spring, before the buds break, make a slightly stronger solution by in-creasing the amount of oil to ½ cup. Horticultural oil is also referred to as superior, summer, or supreme oil.

A Pair of Pear Trees

The arcing branches of our two pear trees create a perfect place to hang the hammock. Our daughter adores curling up with a book in this delightful shady bower, and my hard-working husband has been found there asleep. Our son spends hours climbing the pear trees as does Cosmos, the cat.

We are blessed with the many gifts provided by our pair of pear trees, the dancing interludes of sunlight glittering through their leaf-net canopy, fragrant blossoms and fresh fruit, and the lilting songbirds attracted to their sheltering boughs.

ENDNOTES
1. *Taylor's Guide to Fruit and Berries* (New York: Houghton Mifflin, 1996).

Stella Otto, *The Backyard Orchardist* (Maple City, Michigan: Ottographics, 1993).

CHAPTER TWO

Flowering Trees for

the Romantic Garden

THE BLUEBIRD

Before you thought of spring,
Except as a surmise,
You see, God bless his suddenness,
A fellow in the skies
Of independent hues,
A little weather-worn,
Inspiriting habiliments
Of indigo and brown.

With specimens of song,
As if for you to choose,
Discretion in the interval,
With gay delays he goes
To some superior tree
Without a single leaf,
And shouts for joy to nobody
But his seraphic self!

— EMILY DICKINSON

SEEKING TO CREATE A HARMONIOUS composition in form, scale, and texture, we have designed the framework of our garden by planting both small flowering trees and large flowering shrubs. Plants are not static elements and are continually fluctuating. We nurture the successes and find new homes for, or discard, plants that are not able to thrive.

Oh Garden of Fresh Possibilities!

Our trees provide a welcome sense of shelter with the shifting light and shadows filtering through the ever-changing ceiling. They are a haven for the chorus of songbirds gracing our garden. I look out the kitchen window to see nearly a dozen goldfinches feathered in brilliant cadmium yellow, lunching at the thistle feeder hanging from our 'Beurre Bosc' pear tree. Perched on its upper branch is the genteel Mourning Dove, preening himself after the passing thunderstorm. From the limb of the weeping cherry tree hangs a pagoda-shaped copper bird feeder, where we often hear a noisy battle between the House Finches scrapping at the near-empty tray. The descriptions of their exquisite tree-beauty – their unfolding romantic floral fragrances, the merry scents of the orchard fruits, and the birdsongs they attract I hope will pique your interest and encourage you to plant a tree-garden.

Magnolia stellata

The bark of the star magnolia is a striking shade of warm gray silhouetted in the cool gray of winter's light. Throughout autumn and winter it is covered with downy sage green, pussy willow-like buds, full of the promise of spring. The star magnolia is the tree that flowers first in our garden; with the earliest waves of warm southern breezes, it unfurls its delicate fingered petals. In early spring, on one of those rare New England days when the weather is warm enough to let us open the windows wide, their fragrance floats freely into the rooms adjacent to where the tree is planted. There are few flowering trees lovelier to plant close to dwellings than the star magnolia. And so begins the spell cast by spring's emergent beauty.

The starry blossoms range in shades of white to pink, which are sometimes, but not necessarily, fragrant. When choosing a star magnolia, I recommend visiting your nursery while they are in bloom. Our magnolia is only lightly scented. A friend has two mature heirloom star magnolias growing on either side of the entryway leading to his eighteenth-century brick office building. One is washed in shades of soft rose and is penetratingly fragrant, the other, not at all. I believe that the scented cultivar is 'Waterlily' because of its exquisite coloration and rich lily of-the-valley perfume. I only wish our tree were as highly scented, hence the suggestion to purchase one of the many hybrid *Magnolia stellata* cultivars while it is in flower. Although they are usually described as fragrant, scent is mutable, subjective, and altered by a variety of conditions.

M. stellata is native to central Japan, where it is found growing wild on the slopes of Mount Fujiama. It is one of the oldest of the imported Japanese trees, introduced directly to the United States in 1862, when Japan was as yet unwilling to establish trade with foreign governments. Scores of plants, which are now common to every garden, followed as trade relations with Japan improved. *Shidekobushi*, meaning "Seed of the Warrior Fist," is its Japanese name, an accurate description of the interesting fruit shape resembling a tightly clenched fist.

Magnolia stellata is a fairly fast growing, multi-stemmed, rounded shrub or tree usually reaching a mature height of no more than fifteen to twenty feet when planted in cooler climates. Blooming prodigally while still very young, it is naturally graceful in shape and requires minimal pruning, making the tree ideally suited for an intimate garden setting or as part of the framework of a garden room. Ours is planted along the fragrant pathway close to our home to better enable us to observe its transformations through the four seasons.

M. stellata prefers a cool, rich, and fertile soil, planted in an area protected from strong winds. A light dressing of compost, applied early in the spring or late in the fall, is the only additional maintenance necessary to grow a healthy and vigorous plant. The roots grow close to the ground surface; therefore caution is advised when cultivating the soil around the base of the tree. Beneath our tree's canopy and spilling over the brick path are growing sweetly scented narcissus and jonquils, azure bearded iris (*Iris pallida* subs. 'Dalmatica'), with a fresh perfume like wild grapes, Oriental lilies, and species daylilies – planned to create a sequential progression of fragrance.

Oh Garden of Fresh Possibilities!

Prunus armeniaca 'Harglow'

The genus *Prunus* evokes a multitude of images of picturesque spring flowering and summer fruit-bearing trees. The wands of branches shrouded in five-petal blossoms hold their color high up while the floor of the garden is carpeted in companionable tulips, jonquils, forget-me-nots, and lily of-the-valley. Falling blossoms swirling like snow sift their fragrant petals through the floral carpet, clinging and scattering along the pathways.

The apricot tree (*Prunus armeniaca*), *abricocke* as it was known of old, may seem like an odd selection of fruit tree for a garden in the northeastern region of the United States. Apricots are generally considered more suitable for a warmer Mediterranean climate, though several cultivars are hardy through zone five! *Prunus armeniaca* was formerly thought to originate from Armenia, therein the name *armeniaca*. There is little doubt that its original habitat was in the temperate areas of Asia. Never having seen a living apricot tree, nonetheless we were inspired to grow *Prunus armeniaca* from an old photograph of one pictured in an enclosed garden setting, as well as by our desire to make apricot tarts from our own tree-ripened fruit.

With its ornamental round-headed silhouette and broad, oval leaves, it is a tree of graceful beauty. The sweetly scented pure white flowers issue forth from plump violet colored sepal-enclosed buds. The two colors of violet and white are visible while the tree is leafless and in bloom and, from a distance, create the illusion of a delicately pale pink flower. We sited our apricot tree at the top of our fragrant path to savor the lilting honey scent of its blossoms.

The apricot buds swell at the earliest hint of warm air and are the first fruit bearing trees to flower in our garden. Unfortunately the flowers, and therefore the fruit crop, may be damaged by a late spring frost. Spring in New England is predictably unpredictable; some years the tree sets fruit and some years it does not. Nevertheless, the apricot is a worthy specimen for the beauty of its blooms and branches alone. There are several varieties of European apricots that are suitable to grow in a northern climate. We chose 'Harglow'. Named varieties beginning with 'Har' ('Harval,' 'Hargrand,' Harcot,' and 'Harlayne') were developed in Canada at the Harrow Research Station. For the most part, these cultivars are resistant to fungal and bacterial diseases caused by exceedingly damp, wet springs and humid summers. They are an ideal choice for a garden in a temperate zone where the growing season is shorter than a Mediterranean climate and are grown extensively in the Pacific Northwest.

Apricots are also a sound selection for the urban garden as they are less affected by air pollution than other fruit trees. 'Harglow' is a perfect cultivar for the small garden. They are self-pollinating and grown on a semi-dwarf rootstock, ultimately reaching only fifteen to eighteen feet in height. For four seasons of beauty I encourage every gardener who lives in a suitable climate, including those with only a wee bit of space, to consider growing the elegant apricot tree.

When planning where to site an apricot tree, choose a sunny, sheltered location out of the path of drying winter winds. Plant apricot trees in loose soil with excellent drainage. After the first hard frost, cover the root area with several inches of compost. Water apricot trees deeply, once a week during the growing season and more if you are experiencing drought-like conditions.

Standard and semi-dwarf apricot trees require regular pruning to maintain their height for ease of harvesting fruit and to allow light and air to penetrate the interior of the tree. Most fruits are borne on one- to three-year-old spurs that look like short, stubby branchlets. To best see the overall shape of the tree, prune in late winter or early spring, just after flowering, while the tree is leafless.

Apricots are plagued by many of the same pests as peach trees. Be on the lookout for signs of the Oriental fruit moth and peachtree borer. Peachtree borers burrow into the bark of the tree, leaving a gummy exudate of sap and tree-dust. To prevent this problematic creature from destroying the tree, wrap the trunk of a newly planted tree with strips of brown paper up to the first lateral branch. Cultivate the soil four inches deep within the drip-line of the tree, being mindful of the tree's root system. With its distinguishable black body banded with vermilion or yellow, the adult peach tree borer moth is easy to detect, and unlike most moths, this one flies during the day.

From the first indication of an infestation of Oriental fruit moth, one will observe the new growing tips have a drooping and wilted appearance. Caused by adult moths burrowing into the tips of the tender new shoots, the subsequent generations of larvae will then burrow into the fruit. Cut (and discard) the infested twig tips back to healthy growth. Again, working the soil at the base of the tree will help to destroy the pupae and therefore any future attacks by the Oriental fruit moth. The adult Oriental fruit moth is a mottled gray-brown with a relatively small wingspan (½ inch).

At the first sign of disease or pest problem, cut out the infected growth. Practicing good housekeeping and growing disease-resistant varieties may be the best remedies for growing healthy, strong fruit trees. Weak and stressed plants are at a much greater risk than those that are healthy and vigorous.

Apricots are ready to be picked when all traces of their green color have disappeared and they turn a glowing golden yellow. Gently grasp the fruit and pull with a bit of an upward twist. As with pear trees, do not pull the fruit off vigorously. The fruit-bearing spurs may be damaged, thereby reducing next year's potential harvest.

The Persians referred to apricots as "seeds of the sun." Some cultivars ('Stark Sweethearts' for example) produce fruits with large and edible sweet pits inside the stone fruit. And since apricots and almonds are closely related, the edible pits taste characteristically like an almond.

Prunus persica 'Belle of Georgia'

Cultivated by the Chinese for thousands of years, the peach tree is grown for its fruit as well as for its exquisite flowers and gracefully shaped branches. To better understand the significance of the peach tree in the Chinese culture, it is worth noting that the development of the Chinese garden, with its *yin-yang* symbolism, was essentially Daoist in origin.

Daoists believe the peach tree is the Tree of Life at the Center of Paradise. The peach tree is also believed to be the Tree of Immortality growing in a garden guarded by Hsi-wang Mu, the Mother Empress of the West. Men and women alike must meet her standards before they are granted immortality. Hsi-wang Mu is usually portrayed in paintings and sculpture as a stately matriarch holding one of her peaches.

The peach tree is a symbol of longevity, wealth, spring, youth, and marriage. Peach stones were considered apotropaic and were beautifully carved and were kept, or worn, as amulets and talismans.[1] Sprays of blossoming peach branches were at one time placed above the front door to prevent even the strongest evil from entering into the home. Today's custom is to use them decoratively inside the house.

While the Spaniards brought the peach to North America in the sixteenth-century, Native Americans are credited with moving the peach westward, planting seeds as they traveled.

'Belle of Georgia' is an older cultivar of peach tree, bearing heavenly tasting white-fleshed peaches. The fruit is pale creamy white-blushed gold and rose. It was reportedly first propagated by Lewis Rumph in Georgia in the 1870s from seeds of the 'Chinese Cling,' which is also the parent of the well known 'Elberta' peach, a firm, yellow-fleshed fruit with a crimson blush. Both the 'Belle of Georgia' and 'Elberta' cultivars are hardy through zone five and are adaptable to a variety of soil conditions, though well-drained and sandy soil is their preferred growing medium.

The blooming period of our 'Belle of Georgia' overlaps with 'Harglow', arriving elegantly dressed in warm rose-colored blossoms. Ours has proved to be quite resilient as well, despite being planted in the path of the cold North wind gusting up from the harbor. At the top of our fragrant path leading into the garden we have planted on one side the peach tree, and on the opposite side the apricot tree, framing the view beyond and thereby creating the illusion of a greater depth of space.

Growing fruit trees in the home garden can be tremendously rewarding, though at times frustrating. It is advisable to try to anticipate pest and disease problems early on. Our young 'Belle of Georgia' was plagued by nearly every conceivable difficulty its first year after planting. We now know what to look for and manage to control the problems effectively with preventative monitoring using organic deterrents. The advice provided to combat pests for apricot trees is identical to that for peach trees.

Early spring is the appropriate time of year to fertilize fruit-bearing trees and refresh the compost at the base of the tree. Before the buds break, spray the peach tree with a three percent solution of horticultural oil. Spray weekly throughout the growing season with an organic fish- and seaweed-based foliar feed (Neptune's Harvest, for example) for an added boost of nutrients and an extra weapon against unwanted pests. In addition, treating the peach tree with a weekly dousing of lime, applied by sprinkling the powdered lime through an old flour sifter, will help to control the Oriental fruit moth.

With fruit-bearing trees in particular, it is of the utmost importance to maintain vigilant housekeeping all year round. Remove, clean up, and destroy any fallen fruit or diseased and pest-ridden foliage and fruit.

Our 'Belle of Georgia' peach tree sets fruit heavily so that we have to thin the young fruit after the naturally occurring June drop. Remove fruit that looks damaged, choosing the healthiest and largest of the crop, and prune to a distance of a fist between peaches. When the boughs become heavy with rose-gold burnished ripening fruit and are draped in long-ellipses of verdant foliage, *Prunus persica* is the picture of summer's bounty.

Prunus subhirtella 'Pendula Rosea' ⁓ *Weeping Higan Cherry*

Located in our community is an enchanting nineteenth-century brick town house surrounded by a small grove of weeping Higan cherry trees. Tucked beneath the trees is an inviting seating arrangement. The blooming time of cherry trees is fleeting, lasting but a few short days in early spring. Occasionally, I have had the good fortune to be in the neighborhood while the weeping cherry trees are in full bloom. The cascading branches covered in pale rose-colored blossoms envelop the home and garden, shrouding it with a whispering veil of ethereal lace.

Prunus subhirtella are native to Japan. They are cultivated extensively and are also seen growing wild on plains and mountains in the countryside. For more than ten centuries, and continuing with no less enthusiasm today, cherry trees and cherry blossom time have been a cause for joyful celebrations deeply integrated in the culture of Japan.

From ancient times, during early spring planting rituals, falling blossoms symbolized a bounteous crop of rice. Beginning with the Heian period (794–1185), when the imperial courtiers of Kyoto held power, the preference for graceful beauty and the appreciation of cherry blossoms for beauty's sake began to evolve. The way in which cherry petals fall at the height of their beauty, before they have withered and become unsightly, and the transience of their brief period of blooming, assumed symbolism in Buddhism and the samurai warrior code.

The delicacy and transience of the cherry blossom have poignant and poetic appea, providing themes for songs and poems since the earliest times. The motif of the five petal cherry blossoms is used extensively for decorative arts designs, including kimonos, works in enamel, pottery, and lacquer ware. Cherry tree wood is valued for its tight grain and is a lustrous reddish brown when polished. The wood is used to make furniture, trays, seals, checkerboards, and woodblocks for producing color wood block prints.

In the Japanese language the cherry is called "sakura," which is generally believed to be a corruption of the word "sukuya" (blooming). Poets and artists strive to express the loveliness of its flowers in words and artistry. Called the flower of flowers, when the Japanese use the word "hane" (flower) it has come to mean sakura, and no other flower. Since the Heian period "hanami" has referred to cherry blossom viewing; the term was used to describe cherry blossom parties in the *Tale of Gengi*. Aristocrats wrote poetry and sang songs under the flowering trees for celebratory flower viewing parties. The custom soon spread to the samurai society and by the Edo period, hanami was celebrated by all people.

In modern times the advent of the cherry blossom season not only heralds the coming of spring, but is also the beginning of the new school year and the new fiscal year for businesses. Today families and friends gather under the blooms and celebrate with picnicking, drinking, and singing. The fleeting beauty of the blossoms, scattering just a few days after flowering, is a reminder to take time to appreciate life. In the evening when the sun goes down, viewing the pale-colored cherry blossoms silhouetted against the night sky is considered an added pleasure of the season.

The tradition of celebrating cherry blossom season began in the United States when, on Valentine's Day in 1912, Tokyo mayor Yukio Okaki gave the city of Washington, D.C., 3,000 of twelve different varieties of cherry trees as an act of friendship. First Lady Helen Taft and the wife of the Japanese ambassador, Viscountess Chinda, planted the initial two of these first cherry trees in Potomac Park. Today cherry blossom festivals are celebrated annually not only in Washington, D.C., but in Brooklyn, San Francisco, Seattle, and Macon, Georgia.

Cherry trees are long lived in Japan. There is one specimen over a thousand years old with a circumference of thirty-two feet. *Prunus subhirtella* 'Pendula' are among the most decoratively beautiful of the ornamental flowering cherry trees. We could fit but one weeping cherry in our own postage stamp of a yard. Our *P. subhirtella* 'Pendula Rosea' receives a good half-day of sun. The tree would bear more blossoms if it were planted in full sun, though with the passing of time it has come to fill out and bloom satisfactorily. Weeping cherry trees prefer a moisture-retentive, well-drained soil, though they will adapt to average garden soil. Our cherry tree is sited to view from the dining room, framed by the window sashes, and can be seen in the background from the street, looking down the garden path.

Oh Garden of Fresh Possibilities!

The long waving wands of delicate foliage allow for shade-tolerant plants to grow and thrive beneath its airy canopy. Suggestions for under plantings might include 'Annabelle' hydrangea, honeysuckle azalea, columbine, forget-me-nots, lily of-the-valley, Peacock orchids (*Acidanthera murielae*), species lilies, and species daylilies.

It is said that the true lover of cherry blossoms considers the season is at its height when the buds are little more than half open – for when the blossoms are fully opened there is already the intimation of their decline.

When cherry blossoms begin to fall heavily, the flurry of blossoms is called "cherry snowstorm." The following is a traditional Japanese song that has been passed down for generations. The definition for the Japanese word "yayoi" is the third lunar month, coinciding with March to April.

SAKURA

Cherry blossoms, cherry blossoms
As far as you can see.
Across yayoi skies
Is it mist? Is it clouds?
Ah, the fragrance!
Let us go, Let us go and see!

Cornus florida and *Stewartia pseudocamellia*

Imagine looking out through a window onto a dreamy garden setting of two flowering dogwood trees, one covered in white flower bracts, the other in bracts shaded pink, their level branches growing horizontally toward each other. Upon purchasing our new home, we set about to create just such a picture. The American linden tree on our neighbor's property partially shades our rear yard, creating what I had read to be ideal conditions for cultivating a pair of dogwoods. Or so I thought. The vast majority of information regarding growing flowering dogwoods suggests part shade and does not differentiate between gardening in the north versus gardening in the midwest or northern Florida for that matter. If one lives in sunnier areas south of New England, yes, it is possible to grow a healthy *C. florida* in partial shade.

The first spring after we planted our two dogwood trees, *Cornus florida* and *C. florida* var. *rubrum*, hoping to achieve this idyllic picture, there were a few flower buds. The following spring there were none. And by the third spring both trees were dead.

Dogwood anthracnose is a lethal disease caused by the aptly named fungus *Discula destructiva*. It will typically kill an untreated *Cornus florida* within two to three years. If we look to nature for an answer, the native flowering dogwoods growing in the fertile, moist, friable soil of the Northeastern woodlands, as understory trees, are the trees most affected by anthracnose. *Cornus florida* growing in an open, sunny location are far less afflicted. What we can clearly learn from this lesson is to choose a location that has good air circulation and full sun. By providing the tree with a thick blanket of mulch, encircling the tree from the trunk to the drip-line, and with occasional watering during very dry spells, these precautions will help to prevent drought stress. What we know is that *Discula destructiva* requires high humidity for infection; therefore trees planted in mesic sites in the shade are more susceptible than trees growing in xeric sites.

As our shady backyard has become ever shadier (for our neighbor's centuries-old great American linden has grown ever healthier and more vigorous, enjoying the water and nutrients provided by our tending the rear yard), we determined there simply wasn't enough available sunlight to grow a healthy *C. florida*, including the disease-resistant cultivars of *Cornus florida*.

The disappointments of one failure in the garden are offset by the possibility of experimenting with something different. We are now growing a *Stewartia pseudocamellia*. The tree has a desirable oval-head shape with ovate and glossy bright green foliage. Less than one year in the garden it has yet to flower, but thus far looks content. Hopefully it is receiving enough sunlight for more than a few flowers.

Stewartia pseudocamellia is native to Japan, growing in the cool mountainous regions in fertile, lime-free soil. *Stewartia pseudocamellia*, known also as the Japanese stewartia, is a member of the Theaceae (Tea family), which includes camellias and the native Franklin tree (*Franklinia alatamaha*). *S. pseudocamellia* flowers in early July, well after the glory of spring flowering *Prunus* and *Malus*, when one is longing to see the season of trees in bloom extended. The pearlescent buds form along the leaf axles of the level branches, and, as the name infers, the flowers of *Stewartia pseudocamellia* resemble a species camellia, single and white with a tuft of vivid orange-yellow anthers. The leaves turn sunset tints of gold to crimson in the autumn. During the winter months, in shades of mourning dove-gray, the peeling bark adds to the beauty of the winter landscape. Of note, and even though they are slow growing, it is advisable not to purchase a large Japanese stewartia. They resent transplanting, and one will enjoy greater success planting a smaller tree. Unlike *C. florida*, *S. pseudocamellia* is not much bothered by disease, but that may be because there are so few planted.

Oh Garden of Fresh Possibilities!

The following list is a collection of flowering trees well suited for creating the framework of a small garden. With their relatively smaller size at maturity, they are more easily kept within bounds and have the added benefit of flowers, some of which are fragrant, and attractive foliage.

Eastern redbud (*Cercis canadensis*)
Pagoda dogwood (*Cornus alternifolia, C. alternifolia* 'Argentea')
Disease resistant varieties of dogwood (*Cornus florida*)[2]
Kousa dogwood (*Cornus kousa*)
Smoketree (*Cotinus obovatus, C. coggygria*)
Franklin tree (*Franklinia alatamaha*)
Silverbell (*Halesia diptera*)
Laburnum (*Laburnum* x *watereri* 'Vossii')
Oyama magnolia (*Magnolia sieboldii*)
Star magnolia (*Magnolia stellata*)
Saucer magnolia (*Magnolia* x *soulangiana*)
Sweetbay magnolia (*Magnolia virginiana*)
Fruit trees: peach, apricot, plum, apple, pear, crab, cherry
    (*Prunus, Pyrus, Malus*)
Japanese stewartia (*Stewartia pseudocamellia*)[3]
Fragrant snowbell (*Styrax obassia*)

Fragrance, flowers, the shelter they provide, form, and texture of the leaves are not the only attributes of a tree garden. During the winter months there is the elegant beauty of pure line, "the beauty of the branch" (Jessie Vaughn Harrier, the poet, speaking of her garden Boisfleury).[4] Our gardens abound with myriad designs not visible during the months of lush summer foliage. In late autumn, after the trees lose their leaves, the architecture of the garden is then revealed. The patterns of the stones and lattice, the architectural details and the beauty of the bare limbs become visible, an imprint of time spent and time to come in the garden.

ENDNOTES

1. Jean C. Cooper, *Yin and Yang: The Taoist Harmony of Opposites* (Wellingborough, Northamptonshire: Aquarian Press, 1981).
2. Disease resistant cultivars include *C. florida* 'Spring Grove' and 'Sunset', *Cornus florida* x *Cornus kousa* hybrids 'Constellation,' 'Star Dust,' 'Ruth Ellen,' 'Stellar Pink,' and 'Celestial'.
3. Although they are slow growing when planted in part-shade, *Stewartia pseudocamellia* may eventually grow to forty feet or more when planted in full sun.
4. Virginia Tuttle Clayton, *The Once and Future Gardener* (Boston: David R. Godine, 2000).

CHAPTER THREE

Planting in Harmony with Nature

COMBINING NATIVE AND ORNAMENTAL TREES AND SHRUBS

Season follows after season, after winter the spring,
   after summer the harvest-laden autumn.
From bud to blossom, from flower to fruit, from
   seed to bud again, the beauty of the earth unfolds.

— from *A Harvest of Gratitude* by PERCIVAL CHUBB
(1860–1960)

THE IDEA OF A GARDEN PLANTED in harmony with nature is to create a loosely mixed arrangement of beauty combining native and ornamental flowering trees and shrubs. This informal style of a woodland border or bucolic country hedge is not new and is what the French call a *haie champêtre*. Perhaps the country hedge evolved because it was comprised of easily propagated, or dispersed by wildlife, native species of plants and perhaps as a revolt against the neatly manicured boxed hedges of formal European gardens. The country hedge is used, as is any hedge, to create a physical and visual boundary, but rather than forming the backdrop for ornamental plants, it *is* the show. By planting with a combination of native and ornamental trees and shrubs, whether developing the framework of a new garden, designing a garden room, or extending an existing garden, one can create an interplay of plants drawing from a more widely varied collection of forms, textures, and colors. The framework is the living tapestry of foliage, flowers, fruit and fauna. Working and living in our garden rooms, we are enchanted by the creatures drawn to the sheltering boughs, blossoms, and berries. And by choosing to plant with a combination of companionable fragrant ornamental and fragrant native North American trees and shrubs, designing a garden planted for a well-orchestrated symphony of sequential and interwoven scents is decidedly easier.

We tend to be more familiar with ornamental trees and shrubs because they are readily obtained through the nursery trade. With the accessibility to resources available through the internet we can design with an increasing selection of native species.

Magnolia virginiana ⌒ Sweetbay Magnolia

Located in the heart of Ravenswood Park in Gloucester on the lovely peninsula of Cape Ann, Massachusetts, there is a stand of *Magnolia virginiana* growing in the Great Magnolia Swamp. It is the only population of sweetbay magnolias known to grow this far north. I took one look at the native sweetbay magnolia and breathed in the fresh lemon-honeysuckle bouquet of the blossoms, fell in love, and immediately set out to learn all I could about this graceful and captivating tree.

Returning from a trip to visit my family in northern Florida, I had tucked the bud of a *Magnolia grandiflora* into my suitcase. I was dreaming of someday having a garden large enough to accommodate a *Magnolia grandiflora* and was elated to discover how similar *M. virginiana* is to *M. grandiflora*. For those not familiar with the Southern magnolia, it is a grand, imposing specimen in the landscape, growing up to fifty feet in the cooler zones five and six, and one hundred feet plus in the southern states. *M. grandiflora* is the only native magnolia that is evergreen in its northern range, flowering initially in the late spring and sporadically throughout the summer. The creamy white flowers, enormous and bowl-shaped (ten to twelve inches across), emit a delicious, heady sweet lemon fragrance.

In contrast, the flowers of the sweetbay magnolia are smaller, ivory white, water-lily cup shaped, and sweetly scented of citrus and honeysuckle. The leaves are similar in shape to the *Magnolia grandiflora*, ovate and glossy viridissimus green on the topside, though they are more delicate, and lack the leathery toughness of the Southern magnolia. The lustrous rich green above and the glaucous silvery green on the underside of the foliage creates a lovely ornamental bi-color effect as the leaves are caught in the seasonal breezes.

Magnolia virginiana is an ideal tree for a small garden in its northern range growing to roughly twenty feet compared to the more commanding height of a mature Southern magnolia. *M. virginiana* grows from Massachusetts to Florida in coastal freshwater wetland areas as an understory tree. The tree can be single- or multi-stemmed. Sweetbay is a stunning addition to the woodland garden with an open form, allowing a variety of part-shade loving flora to grow beneath the airy canopy. The leaves are a larval food for the Eastern Tiger Swallowtail butterfly. Almost immediately after planting we began to notice the swallowtails gliding from the sunny borders of the front dooryard, where an abundance of nectar-rich flowers are planted specifically to attract butterflies, around to the shady border in the rear yard where our sweetbay is located.

Garden designs are continually evolving. Part of our garden has given way to a limited version of a woodland garden, for the shady canopy created by the ever-growing ceiling of foliage of our neighboring trees has increasingly defined our landscape. We sited our *Magnolia virginiana* in the center of our diminutive shaded woodland garden where we can observe the tree from the kitchen window while standing at the kitchen sink. Gazing upon the tree bending and swaying gracefully in the wind, displaying its shifting bi-color leaves, provides a pleasant view when tending to daily chores.

Ilex verticillata 'Winter Red'

Surrounding the sweetbay magnolia in our shaded border is a collection of indigenous and ornamental shrubs. The native summersweet, honeysuckle azalea, and winterberry were planted as they are butterfly, moth, and songbird attractants. Growing against the wall in fairly dense shade is an *Ilex verticillata* 'Winter Red,' resplendent in brilliant red berries held well into winter (hence the common name). If by early spring the ravenous starlings haven't devoured the berries, they are a nourishing treat for the robins.

Common winterberry grows in moist woods from Nova Scotia and Quebec and west to Minnesota, along the eastern and central United States to Arkansas and the Florida Panhandle. 'Winter Red' slowly matures to about eight feet tall and equally as wide. *Ilex verticillata* will produce greater quantities of fruit when planted in full sun and moist, acidic soil, though the shrub will tolerate shade and less than adequate soil. If the soil is too alkaline, the leaves will yellow and drop off. Both male and female *Ilex verticillata* flower, though only female plants bear fruit. To insure pollination and therefore a good crop of berries, a male cultivar ('Southern Gentleman' is a good choice for the female 'Winter Red') must be planted within fifty feet and flower at the same time as the female. Pruning the decorative branches during the holiday season will not affect the yield of berries for the following year, as winterberry flowers on the current year's growth.

'Winter Red' is an outstanding specimen of winterberry for the high yield of berries as well as dense branching growth habit providing cover and nesting spots for a variety of birds. Throughout the seasons we observe Cedar Waxwings, Mockingbirds, Cardinals, Gray Catbirds, and American Robins seeking shelter and nourishment from this handsome shrub.

Clethra alnifolia ⌒ Summersweet

Alongside our winterberry bush is a *Clethra alnifolia*, more commonly known by its many descriptive names of summersweet, sweet pepperbush, and honey-sweet. In Gloucester, Massachusetts of old it was described as "sailor's delight." A large stand of *Clethra alnifolia* grows along the shady lanes of Gloucester's easternmost point. The men entering the harbor on homebound ships would delight in its fragrance wafting far out to sea. Summersweet and winterberry are a stunning combination planted in close proximity, particularly in the autumn when the foliage of the summersweet is glowing in brilliant golden hues, and the winterberry, covered with masses of sparkling red berries, has as yet to lose its vivid green leaves.

Summersweet bears small florets held in racemes, and depending on the cultivar may be shaded with varying hues of pink to rose-red. The tapering spires of fragrant blossoms appear in mid to late summer. *Clethra* has a sweet and spicy, though somewhat pungent, aroma, and when the summer air is sultry and humid, the fragrance permeates the garden. Summersweet is a nectar food attractive to bees and a wide variety of butterflies, notably the Silver-spotted skipper.

Clethra are fast growers when planted in moist, rich soil enriched with compost. Our summersweet blooms profusely, despite being planted in part shade. Plantings generally hold their blossoms for a more extensive length of time when planted in part shade as opposed to full sun, though one may have comparatively fewer blossoms with the decreased light.

The blossoms of the cultivar 'Pink Spires' are white suffused with pale pink that do not fade as the flowers open. 'Rosea' (an older hybrid) is comparably colored to 'Pink Spires,' though the pink does fade. And as the name 'Ruby Spice' suggests, this summersweet has red buds, which open to rose-pink spires, and do not fade. 'Hummingbird' is a relatively smaller cultivar, attaining the height of four feet with creamy white panicles.

Philadelphus ⌣ Mock Orange

Planted along the same fence enclosing the woodland border, though sited in a sunnier spot, is a *Philadelphus* 'Natchez.' With its graceful arching branches and serrated, cordate-shaped foliage, *Philadelphus* is a splendid addition to a lightly shaded or sunny border. The common name "sweet mock orange" perfectly describes the fragrance of the sparkling white flowers. The perfume is similar to that of orange blossoms, with added notes of gardenia and honeysuckle. Citrus blossoms, in all their blended shades of scent, have to be one of nature's most evocative fragrances. As it is impossible to grow citrus trees the year round in northern climates, mock orange is a worthy substitute for the fragrance of its blossoms alone, despite the few short weeks it flowers.

This is a shrub that most assuredly should be planted close to where one can delight in its sublime perfume. Plant a *Philadelphus* near a hammock, underneath a bedroom window and alongside a *plein air* dining arrangement. Contemporary gardens rarely feature *Philadelphus*, but for a modern garden planted for fragrance, the penetrating scent of the mock orange will both provide enjoyment within the garden and the perfume wafting on the breeze will enchant passers-by.

Around the corner in a sunny spot along our fragrant path, we have growing a pair of *Philadelphus* 'Innocence.' 'Innocence' is my favorite cultivar for its single flowers, resplendent fragrance, and with the added feature of green leaves splashed with creamy white.

Philadelphus is a member of the Hydrangeaceae (Hydrangea family). They grow wild on the slopes of mountainsides, originating in countries with warm summers and cool winters. The *Philadelphus* species has an extensive range, from Europe to southwestern Asia, Mexico, and the southern and western United States.

Philadelphus coronarius are native to southern Europe. *Philadelphus* is the Greek word for "brotherly" and *coronarius* is Latin for "crown," or "wreath," as the pliable and scented branches are ideal for use in garlands. *P. coronarius* will quickly reach a height of eight to ten feet in a few years when planted in moist, well-drained soil rich in organic matter. They will tolerate partial shade, though there will be considerably fewer blossoms. *Philadelphus* bloom on the previous year's growth. To encourage sweet mock orange to flower, immediately after the shrub has finished flowering prune the branches back to the outer stems that have blossomed. Cut just above a strong outer facing bud or new shoot. This is the point from where you would expect to see new blooms the following year. Cut old wood to the ground to maintain the shape, to keep the shrub to a manageable size, and encourage new branches to grow and flower.

In early summer the Red-spotted Purple butterflies frequent our blooming *Philadelphus* 'Innocence.' The Red-spotted Purple is similar in size to the Canadian Tiger Swallowtail. The wings are a melting dark chocolate and iridescent cobalt blue swirled with hues of mineral violet, sporting a border of a paler shade of cobalt, white, and cadmium red, crescent-shaped spots. The tender young leaves of the mock orange are edible, tasting like cucumber, and are delectable tossed with a salad of mixed greens.

Beginning in the early 1880s and continuing until roughly 1920, the French nurseryman Victor Lemoine (of lilac fame) began to hybridize the genus *Philadelphus* as different species were becoming available. His first successful cultivar was a cross between the European species *P. coronarius* with the American species *P. microphyllus* resulting in *P.* 'Lemoinei.' He then introduced the pure white flowering cultivars of 'Avalanche' in 1896, 'Coquette' in 1903, and both 'Virginal' and 'Norma' in 1909. His next series of hybrids were created from *P.* 'Lemoinei' with *P. maculatus*, all with a deep rose pink flush to the center of each flower. Later still were the introductions of 'Belle Etoile' and 'Etoile Rose,' both flushed with rose pink.

Drawing from our experience with *Philadelphus*, a collection of sweet mock orange selected for their fabulous fragrance might include the following cultivars:

Philadelphus x *lemoinei* 'Innocence' ~ Six to eight feet with pure white single flowers with variegated leaves. In our garden it is the most richly scented *Philadelphus*.

Philadelphus x *lemoinei* 'Avalanche' ~ A low-growing cultivar, reaching only three to four feet with arching branches and single white flowers.

Philadelphus x *lemoniei* 'Belle Etoile' ~ The name translates to Beautiful Star, with single flowers which are blushed rose at the center. 'Belle Etoile' is slightly more compact, growing four to six feet and blooms two weeks later than *P. coronarius*.

Philadelphus x *virginalis* 'Natchez' ~ Growing six to eight feet with semi-double, two-inch flowers.

Philadelphus x *virginalis* 'Virginal' ~ Eight to ten feet with semi-double white flowers.

Philadelphus mexicanus 'Plena' ~ The scent is more reminiscent of gardenia flowers, though only hardy to zone nine. Grow it as a houseplant during the winter. Set the potted plant out of doors after all danger of frost has passed. With ivory-shaded double flowers juxtaposed against the brilliant green foliage, and blooming in the late summer to early autumn, 'Plena' is an elegant *Philadelphus* for a garden room.

Chaenomeles speciosa 'Toyo-Nishiki'

Growing in close proximity to our *Philadelphus* 'Natchez' is the ornamental flowering quince *Chaenomeles* 'Toyo-Nishiki.' Rushing out before the leaves appear and offset by the zigzagging branches, the blossoms are a stunning combination of vermilion, pink, and white in the same flower cluster, and occasionally within the same flower. 'Toyo-Nishiki' is a lovely specimen for the early spring arrangement. The flowers are borne singularly and in clusters along the length of the branches (like those of apple blossoms). The blossoms linger for an extended period of time and continue while the shrub is sending forth bronze-hued new growth.

Chaenomeles speciosa and *Chaenomeles japonica* are native to eastern Asia. Taxonomists have had a difficult time with *Chaenomeles* as *C. japonica* and *C. speciosa* hybridize easily. Highly adaptable to a variety of soil conditions, quince is safely hardy to zone 5 and grows approximately six to ten feet. Planted in full sun they will bloom profusely though they will flower adequately in partial shade as well. *Chaenomeles speciosa* have an upright, rounded habit with spiny, interlacing branches. A note of caution regarding *Chaenomeles* – the thorns are one inch in length and capable of piercing skin and clothing. Plant against a wall or an out-of-the-way place where people and pets won't be punctured by the prominent thorns.

Chaenomeles speciosa produces a bitter, though edible, two-inch, apple-like pomme fruit. The deliciously fragrant fruit is initially green ripening to yellow, and usually harvested late in the season. It is necessary for fruiting to plant more than one *Chaenomeles.* 'Texas Scarlet,' with vibrant vermilion single flowers, is a choice companion for 'Toyo-Nishiki.' The clear, red-orange tones (as opposed to a red with blue undertones) perfectly complement the varied warm pink blossoms of 'Toyo-Nishiki.' *Chaenomeles* bloom on the previous season's growth. Prune immediately after flowering for more blossoms, though if planning to harvest the fruit, leave the branches that have flowered to allow it to develop.

Flowering quince branches are one of the easiest to force to bloom indoors (see appendix). Come January and February, a single bud-laden branch of 'Toyo-Nishiki' arranged on a tabletop is a welcome harbinger of spring.

Hydrangea arborescens 'Annabelle'

Planted in the part-shade cast by our weeping cherry tree is a *Hydrangea arborescens,* the heirloom cultivar 'Annabelle,' bearing oversized floppy panicles composed of florets that initially open in a hue of light-bright summer-green. Over the next several weeks the color shifts to snowy white and as the flower heads become drier through the course of the season, transforms once again to a translucent shade of luminous green. *Hydrangea arborescens* is native to the United States, growing from southern New England to the central and southeastern states. 'Annabelle' is a versatile cultivar, adaptable to varying degrees of light and soil, though it will produce more flowers when planted in rich, moist, well-drained soil amended with organic matter.

Unlike many of the Asian big leaf hydrangea (*Hydrangea macrophylla* 'Nikko Blue' comes to mind), which bloom on last year's growth that is often damaged by winterkill, Hydrangea *arborescens* bloom on the current year's new growth. The native *Hydrangea arborescens* is reliably hardy through zone four and a more suitable choice for gardens in northern New England.

To keep the shrub trimmed to a nicely rounded form of three to five feet, and to encourage the greatest number of blooms, prune the entire shrub to the ground in late winter. By mid-spring one will observe new shoots, and come early summer, the shrub will be covered with multiple round panicles in shades of new summer green. The common name for *Hydrangea arborescens* is hills-of-snow, an apt portrait for the mounds of snowy white flower heads, refreshingly beautiful for a warm summer's day.

Rhododendron viscosum ⤳ Honeysuckle Azalea

Throughout our diminutive woodland border we have planted several native and potently fragrant honeysuckle azaleas (*Rhododendron viscosum*). The flowers are white-blushed pink and have the aromatic scent of honeysuckle and cloves. The tubes of the flowers are long, attractively off-setting the blossoms out and away from the verdant new spring growth.

Rhododendron viscosum, a deciduous azalea obtaining the height of anywhere from four to ten feet, is indigenous to North America, growing from Ontario to Florida and across the south to eastern parts of Texas and Oklahoma. The other common name for *Rhododendron viscosum* is swamp azalea, though we favor honeysuckle azalea for its more pleasant connotations. Swamp azaleas do not actually live in completely saturated soils; they are found growing in slightly elevated hummocks along a mesic, or moist, forest edge. Preferring partial shade and moist soil, honeysuckle azalea will tolerate some slight dryness, and with their high tolerance for subzero temperatures, they are a hardy candidate for the landscape.

Honeysuckle azalea blooms for an extended length of time, beginning in early summer and continuing for several weeks. The wandering fragrance of their warm-weather flowers suggests planting along a well-traversed path or near a seating area in the garden, where one can best savor their spicy-sweet scent. *Viscosum* is Latin for "gluey," an accurate description of the blossoms, which feel slightly sticky to the touch.

Franklinia alatamaha ⤳ The Franklin Tree

Tiring of a common lilac that never flowered well (dug and salvaged from an abandoned garden), we decided to grow the elegant native *Franklinia alatamaha* in its place. We did not want to lose the established perennials and bulbs growing satisfactorily at the feet of the lilac and therefore needed a small tree with a single trunk. *Franklinia alatamaha* fit the description perfectly with the added appeal of fragrant blossoms. The Franklin tree is a member of the Theaceae (Tea family) as are camellias and stewartias. The cup-shaped white flowers with clusters of bright golden yellow stamens suggest in both form and petal arrangement the flowers of the *Stewartia pseudocamellia*. The luminous pearlescent flower buds open slowly, only a few at a time, over the course of late summer and early autumn.

Oh Garden of Fresh Possibilities!

Franklinia alatamaha was discovered growing along the banks of the Alatamaha River in Georgia by the early American plant hunter John Bartram. In 1728 Bartram began a botanic garden nursery in Philadelphia. American and British landowners, as well as the Swedish botanist Linnaeus, encouraged him to collect native species of plants throughout the eastern United States. Bartram is best known for finding the Franklin tree (named after Benjamin Franklin), which subsequently became extinct in the wild and has not been seen since 1803. Fortunately it is still cultivated in gardens when people know to look for this tree of graceful beauty.

As with *Stewartia pseudocamellia*, it is better to transplant a smaller tree so as not to disturb the root system. Choose a protected site with moist and acidic, well-drained soil. Franklin trees will not stand wet feet. Stake the tree securely for its first year in the garden and mulch well after the first hard frost. The Franklin tree is slow to awake from its winter slumber. In our garden, it does not leaf out until after the summersweet and sweetbay magnolia. Plant in combination with summer blooming perennials or give the tree its own corner in the landscape. The stark look of its bare brown branches does not marry well with either the luminous hues of spring flowers or the emerging fresh spring-green foliage. The Franklin tree blooms in the Northeast later in the summer, long after most trees have finished flowering. As with all of the trees and shrubs discussed in this chapter, *Franklinia* tolerates part shade but will provide one with a greater abundance of flowers if grown in fuller amounts of sunlight.

CHAPTER FOUR

Plum Trees for Plum Street

Prunus cerasifera 'THUNDERCLOUD'

First it shows one or
  two blossoms,
Gradually we see five or
  ten flowers;
In a setting sun
  with brilliant clouds glowing
  in the distance,
How the beautiful flowers
  compete with my brush and ink.

   —SHITAO (1642–1707)

THE EVER-TRANSFORMING GARDEN inspires artistic expression. Whether it is the fugitive beauty of a cut branch from a flowering plum, a painting by Raoul Dufy, a photograph by Edward Steichen, or a poem by Emily Dickinson, the universal inspiration derived from nature is the same as planting a tree in an enclosed space and calling it a garden. Our gardens remain a place that makes the search for an enduring beauty possible.

Intimately associated with paintings and literature, there are layers of symbolism connecting the plum tree and the flowers of the plum to the Chinese cultural life. The five petals of the plum blossom represent the five gods of good luck. The plum tree, pine, and bamboo are often referred to as the "Three Friends in Winter" as they have the ability to endure cold weather and flourish under adverse conditions. When depicted together, the "Three Friends of Winter" symbolize longevity, perseverance, and integrity – the ideal virtues of the scholarly gentleman. In modern China, *Prunus* is the national flower as its five petals represent the five peoples: Han, Manchu, Mongol, Tibetan, and Mohammedan.

The "scholar garden" or "poetic garden" was designed by Daoist poets to create an atmosphere for reflection and inspire tranquil receptivity. The Chinese garden aesthetic is derived in part from the Daoist philosophy that through contemplation of the unity of creation, where nature possesses a hidden yet real order and harmony, unity will be revealed in moments of enlightenment. The Daoist believes that all forms of art are the outward and visual manifestation of The Cosmic Breath or Energy (Ch'i). Painting, poetry, calligraphy, and music along with garden design developed simultaneously and interdependently as the Chinese scholar was expected to be fluent in interpreting inspiration in all the arts. Gardening, like landscape painting, is an act of reverence as well as one of delight. Through the confluence of Daoism, Confucianism, and Buddhism, the Chinese sought to garner inspiration, self-awareness, and knowledge through nature. The well-designed garden, a place where the work of man and nature would be indistinguishable, was considered the ideal place to contemplate the natural world and divine inspiration. The Dao, or the Way, of capturing the restless spirit of nature, was more important than any specific theme or motif. This is not to imply that the private garden was used solely as a place of worship. Designed for solitude as well as family gatherings, contemplative activities, and entertaining friends, the garden was used for everyday pursuits as well as a representation of the owner's abstract thoughts. Part of the Chinese philosophy for living harmoniously derives from a profound, inherent desire to make the most of everyday existence, a longing that finds its ideal home in the garden.

The classical Chinese garden is composed of four major elements. They are water, rocks, plantings, and building structures and are arranged in a way to reflect the garden's sequential beauty, the passage of time, the contrast between morning and evening, and the successive seasons. The relationships of the four elements reflect the belief in *yin-yang*; that opposites must be in balance to create harmony.

In traditional Chinese architecture, the home and garden are oriented to create a harmonious relationship between the house and the surrounding landscape, according to the principles of *feng-shui* (which literally translates to "wind and water"), in harmony with the flow of Ch'i. As in nature, the house and garden are held in balance by *yin-yang* forces. The solar *yang* powers are represented in mountains (rocks) and the sky; and the lunar *yin* forces are represented in water and valleys. The garden is held in a harmony of contrasts,

PLANTING TREES STREET SIDE

Trees planted along a street, in particular those that are surrounded with paving materials, need special attention at the time of planting, and well into their first year.

Select a tree of a fairly good size and a sturdy nature, as a young sapling may not be solid enough to withstand the challenges of street life. Dig a hole twice as wide as the root ball and only slightly deeper. Remove any rocks and/or bits of pavement from the hole. The soil from the hole may be in very poor condition, and it will probably be necessary to correct the problem by amending the soil with compost and additional topsoil. Proceed to set the tree in its hole, watering and refilling the hole with soil, all the while keeping the top of the root ball of the tree level with the soil line. Cut away the upper layer of the burlap, allowing the burlap to stay in place around the sides of the root ball. The roots will grow through and the burlap will eventually rot.

Water deeply after planting and weekly during the tree's first growing season. Mulch with a layer of compost, three to four inches thick, spreading it from the base of the tree out to the drip-line around the tree. Mulching with compost helps keep the tree well hydrated and adds nutrients to the soil. Street planted trees need additional water during extended periods of drought. There are differing viewpoints on whether or not to stake a newly planted tree, whether planted in the garden or on a street. Although our plum trees were planted in a windy corridor, we did not stake them, the thought being that the force of the wind pushing on the trees would encourage them to root more firmly. We tilted our trees ever so slightly toward the prevailing wind to counterbalance the long-term effects of the sea breezes blowing in from the harbor.

Annually fertilize and mulch with compost, recognizing that trees planted alongside roadways and streets are more susceptible to failure as they are exposed to environmental stresses such as air pollution, and are at a greater risk for injury. With a bit of extra care, flowering street trees will thrive and prosper and offer a wealth of immeasurable benefits. Plant *Prunus* and delight in the songbirds lured by the blossoms, fruit, and sheltering boughs. Trees planted along roadways and avenues make a neighborhood look well tended, not only by improving the aesthetic appeal to the community, but also by providing shady relief from the glaring bleakness of concrete and asphalt.

with the endless *yin-yang* combinations of straight and undulating, sunlight and shadow, disclosure and concealment, delicate and gnarled. In gardens, the concept of Dao is intentionally vague, not always well defined, since definition itself would impose limits.

Representing the earthly *yin* forces reaching up toward the celestial *yang* powers, trees are an essential element in the classical Daoist garden and are also said to give the age of the garden. Flowering trees such as the plum, peach, almond, and cherry were loved for their beauty and for the unique significance associated with each tree. The plum is a symbol of strength, longevity, and the hermit. The almond and the plum together signify new life emerging in spring. While all trees possess the *yin* (feminine) powers and were considered beautiful, some are particularly loved for expressing *yin-yang* qualities. The plum is usually represented with gnarled, hoary branches called "sleeping dragons," suggesting *yang* powers to balance the delicacy of the *yin* flowers. Artists would wander by moonlight to view every stage of the "dry limbs clad in jade-white blooms."

The painting *Peach and Plum Blossom Garden* by Chou Ying (Tang Dynasty 618–906), on view at the Kyoto Museum, is an exquisite example of the significance of differing types of trees' symbolic representation. The peach and plum tree, when planted together, symbolize two brothers. The painting portrays an evening scene with the well-known romantic Chinese poet Li Bai sitting with his cousin (with whom he enjoyed a close relationship) in a garden planted with peach and plum trees. The two trees are the perfect metaphor for the close friendship Li Bai shared with his cousin.

> *He who plants a garden*
> *plants happiness.*
> — an old Chinese proverb

After having seen several old photographs of our neighborhood when it was lined with towering elm trees, our neighborhood decided to investigate the possibility of planting trees along our narrow and tree-less street. Many communities provide support for neighborhood-wide tree plantings. We were fortunate to enlist the help of our local tree warden, the Department of Public Works, and a private foundation with funds available to assist with purchasing the trees. Inspired by the name of our street, and considering their reputation for longevity and hardiness, we decided on the purpleleaf plum tree, *Prunus cerasifera* f. *purpurescens*.

Monsieur Pissard, the French head gardener to the shah of Persia (now Iran), introduced purpleleaf plums to Western cultivation. In 1878 Monsieur Pissard found a purpleleaf plum growing in Tabriz and sent propagation material to Monsieur Chatenay of France. Within a few years, *Prunus* 'Pissardii' was widely cultivated throughout Europe and North America. Many variations in flower and foliage color have developed over the course of time, some with more desirable characteristics than others.

Of the many available cultivars of purpleleaf plums, we selected *Prunus cerasifera* 'Thundercloud,' the most widely planted purpleleaf street tree in the United States. Growing roughly from twenty-six to thirty feet in an upright, vertical shape, it is an ideal choice for narrow streets. For several weeks, beginning in early April, our trees are clothed in a profusion of sweetly fragrant blossoms that are rose pink with a deeper, plum-colored eye. 'Thundercloud' has a metallic purple-crimson luster to its foliage, and the color is held all summer and into the autumn, unlike some of the purpleleaf plums that have a tendency to look dry and drab by mid-summer.

Prunus, or stone fruits, belong to the Rosaceae (Rose family). Included in this mostly deciduous group of small trees and shrubs are almonds, cherry, apricot, nectarine, peach, and plum. Indigenous worldwide to the North Temperate Zone, they are grown for their orchard fruits and decorative beauty. The flowering tree depicted in Chinese art is *Prunus mume*, which is botanically related to both the apricot and the plum tree.

Although fruit-bearing *Prunus* benefit from pruning during the trees' dormant period, from mid-winter to very early spring, we prefer to prune ornamental flowering *P. cerasifera* in early summer after the trees have flowered and leafed out. Prune weak, twiggy growth, branches crossing a more desirable branch, and unwanted vertical growth competing with the tree's main leader. The objective is to develop a light form with the underlying armature of the tree visible, which will create a dappled sun-filtered effect, rather than a dark, opaque mass. When pruning to force branches to bloom indoors during the winter, bear in mind the overall desired shape of the tree and remove branches accordingly.

Just as the Chinese poets built pavilions for viewing plum and almond trees, and lovers of the garden would move their beds out under trees to view all stages of a special flower coming into bloom, we too can enter into an inspired garden-world, one of our own design.

Plum Trees for Plum Street

Oh narcissus and plum
blossoms,
you are enjoyed together by
us,
In the wintry months, the two
of you compete for glory;
On a warm day
by a bright window,
I hold my brush,
How my quiet thoughts wander
beyond the – boundless
shores.

— SHITAO (1642–1707)[1]

END NOTE "I rack my brain all day trying to depict your beauty; heaven sent you to test a poet's wits." Thus lamented the poet-painter Shitao while attempting to paint the plum blossom. Both poems from this chapter are taken from an album of twelve small leaves (each painting leaf is 6½ in. by 4⅛ in.) of paintings, alternating between landscapes and flowers, with poetic comments accompanying each painting.

Shitao ("Stone Wave"), a scion of the Ming imperial family, became a monk and painter when his prospects of a civil career were dashed by the conquest of the Manchu in 1644 – the end of the Ming dynasty and the beginning of the Qing dynasty. After years of wandering form place to place, he "returned home" to Yangzhou and created this serenely reflective album, which is part of the permanent collection of the Metropolitan Museum of Art.

> Shitao (1642–1707). *Returning Home* (about 1695). Album of twelve paintings, ink and color on paper. The Metropolitan Museum of Art, From the P.Y. and Kinmay W. Tang Family Collection, Gift of Wen and Constance Fong, in honor of Mr. and Mrs. Douglas Dillon, 1976 (1976.280)

ENDNOTES

1. Poem translations are from the following book: *Wen C. Fong, Returning Home: Tao-chi's Album of Landscapes and Flowers*. New York: George Braziller, 1976.

CHAPTER FIVE

The Narrative of the Garden

Plant silver leaf and pine
and beckon the wind.
Plant flowering trees and red-hip dotted roses
a call to the songbirds.

Plant a haze of sweet scented lavender
and listen for bees
Plant spiral and ray blossoms
bid come to the butterflies.

Plant liquid green umbrellas of hosta and ginger,
an invitation to toads.
Plant bowers of honeysuckle
and draw forth the night pollinators.

Plant cupped-golden poppies and yellow vesselled jonquils
and drink the suns' light.
Plant shimmering white waxing lilies
to caress the moons' beams.

— LILLIAN BROOKS (1958–)

IN LINKING TOGETHER HOUSE and garden and defining the surrounding space, the pathways become the narrative of the garden, the lines of communication between the home and the garden. Walkways frame the borders into manageable shapes and organize the garden into different rooms. Paths choreograph the way you wish people to move about, under a bower, through an allée or along a beautiful vista. Imagine a curving pathway where one can only catch a partial view, awakening one's curiosity to see what lies beyond. A well considered pathway irresistibly invites one into the story of house and garden.

Throughout history garden design has reflected the cultural, religious, and landscape characteristics of different civilizations. The enclosed courtyard gardens of Persian palaces followed the rectilinear lines of the palace and its protective walls. The classical Persian garden was constructed to a geometric plan within the enclosed square or rectangle with a central fountain from which four waterways issued, one in each direction, to represent the rivers of life flowing to the four corners of the earth. Within the garden, decorative screens and doorways were used to create garden rooms. The geometrically shaped beds were planted with fruiting trees, culinary and medicinal herbs, and aromatics, all of them vitally important to human existence. As the comparatively featureless landscape was dominated by desert, the walls provided shelter from the wilderness, the trees provided food and shade from the burning sun, and water was considered precious within the garden.

The Persian word *pairidaeza* literally translates to "surrounded by walls." The Koran teaches that it is mankind's responsibility to protect and revere nature. The straight and narrow paths of the Islamic gardens lead directly into the heart of paradise. These sacred gardens were meant as a means of realizing heaven on earth. The design of the classical Persian garden as a spiritual sanctuary was intertwined with its use as a sensuous paradise delighting the senses.[1]

Similarly, tomb paintings and bas-reliefs from ancient Egypt portray formal, geometric walled gardens. The straight lines are imposed by the irrigation channels and sheltering walls, usually constructed of reeds and thorns or mud bricks. Gardens were for the nobility as well as the working scribes and artisans. The gardens, attached to temples, were presided over by Egyptian priests as places of contemplation. Ancient Egyptian tomb paintings, such as one from the time of Tuthmosis III, depict a rectangular central pond filled with fish and wild fowl, surrounded by a path with lines running parallel to the outline of the pond, and then framed with plantings of fruiting and flowering trees. Another example, from the tomb of Rekhmire ca. 1450 B.C. portrays a rectangular pool with flowering lotus (*Nymphaea* or water-lily) and a pavilion, surrounded by symmetrical plantings that included doom palms, date palms, and acacia.

These earliest paradise gardens of Persia and Egypt subsequently influenced the gardens of Greece and then Rome. The design of straight intersecting paths through symmetrical gardens was brought to Europe through the Middle East, northern Africa, and Spain during the Roman conquest of Britain and following the crusades of the Middle Ages. The European medieval monastic garden was an enclosed square or rectangle divided by two intersecting paths leading to a central fountain, representing the waters of life. The beds created by the crossing paths were planted with the flowers, Damascus rose, iris, and Madonna lily (*Lilium candidum*), which were linked symbolically with Christianity, as well as planted with culinary and medicinal herbs. The enclosed gardens were designed as pleasurable places redolent with fragrance and as peaceful sanctuaries for quiet contemplation.

The developing Italian Renaissance garden, fundamentally the medieval monastic garden in an expanded form, then influenced the formal gardens of France, Holland and England. Characterized by ordered geometric shapes to suggest the domination of man over nature, the formal gardens were designed with neatly manicured pathways that divided the garden into tidy knots, complete with foursquare and rectilinear planting beds.

There is the compelling and vast exception to the well-ordered symmetrical gardens and that is the gardens of China. Beginning several thousand years ago, the Daoist philosophers designed gardens for the nobility as well as domestic gardens, which were intended to recreate the natural world. "However small the space, the garden was never laid out as a flat expanse from which all could be viewed at once. This removal of any definite boundary made for succession, expansion, rhythm, and a sense of unlimited time and space."[2] The Daoist believes that man is not the measure of the universe; his place in the whole of Nature is to maintain the balance and harmony between *yin* and *yang*. As the mediator between heaven and earth, the garden can help maintain this harmony. Drawing from the richly varied landscape of China, the Daoist poetic gardens were designed with meandering paths following the rise and fall of the terrain. Along the winding waterways and ponds, often crossed by bridges, they symbolized the transition of communicating from one realm into another. The "moon bridge" is a half-circular wooden bridge, which when reflected in still water completes itself, forming the circle of the full moon, a symbol of perfection. The Chinese garden, combining the Daoist poetic or scholar gardens, along with absorbing symbolism – having roots in Confucianism and Buddhism – had migrated, by way of Korea, to Japan by A.D. 600

In a very different manner, the naturalistic Chinese style of gardening did not gain influence in Europe until the eighteenth century. Straight paths were replaced with circuitous paths winding through parklands and secular gardens designed for pleasure.

The narrative of the garden is continually evolving, merging and fluctuating between the informal and the formal, the natural and the architectural. The pattern of pathways, a reflection of cultural and religious influences, is often determined by the natural landscape of a civilization. We borrow from history and combine cultures, adapting and adopting from both to create our particular homes and gardens and to reflect our individual aesthetics.

When planning your garden, begin by determining the major structural elements such as terrace, arbor, loggia, pool, or garden house. Pathways provide a convenient starting point from which to organize and connect the landscape design, linking existing structures with planned elements. Practical considerations for determining the logical route to the mailbox or carrying groceries will determine the primary paths.

The choices of materials determine the garden style and should echo the architecture as well as shapes and volumes of the interior rooms. The more formal qualities of cut stone and brick are a sensible choice, used close to the home for primary paths. As you move further away from the home and into the surrounding landscape, informal materials become increasingly more suitable.

Bluestone, granite, sandstone, limestone, and brick are fine examples of materials that are ideally suited for the primary walkways, courtyards, and terraces. The surfaces of cut stone and brick are smooth and easily swept clean. A tightly constructed and well-placed stone or brick pathway helps to control water drainage, keep mud out of the home, and most importantly, provide a convenient access to and from the house. Hard loose materials such as crushed stone and seashells and materials of an aggregate type are entirely unsuitable as they can be tracked into the house and ruin floors. Cut stone and brick are easy to walk on, particularly with bare feet. When cut stone and brick are used to pave a courtyard or terrace, they provide a smooth and stable surface for furniture. Paths of cut stone, in the cool tones of bluestone, for example, recede and complement the verdant landscape. Falling blossoms from flowering trees look especially appealing scattered on the surface of smooth stone. The warm, earthy red shades of brick contrast and complement a variety of architectural styles and building colors.

Moving further into the garden, these same materials of stone and brick, as well as an extensive array of less formal materials, may be used for secondary paths to link garden spaces and rooms, and garden spaces to woodlands or out to sea. There are any numbers of patterns that can be created when any one of the materials is used singularly, and an infinitely greater variety of patterns can be created when the materials are integrated and combined.

Carpets of stone, usually fieldstone or a combination of fieldstone and other fragments of brick or stone, offer the greatest versatility for creating informal paths. The variety of shapes in fieldstone with convex, concave, and angled edges is well suited for paths that wind through the landscape, around trees and for negotiating slopes. A stone carpet is suitable for an informal terrace or courtyard transitioning into a walkway. Carpets of stone provide places for low-growing aromatics to grow around and between the stones, and herbs such as pennyroyal, chamomile, creeping mint, and lemon thyme release fragrant oils when stepped upon. Edgings of sweet alyssum or alpine strawberries are suitable for a variety of pathways – brick, cut stone, and loose materials of ground shells or stones.

The Chinese employ a great variety of paving surfaces. Stone carpets of tiles interspersed with grass may be fairly informal while elaborate mosaic pathways, one of the most beautiful elements in the overall design, depict wildlife such as butterflies, swans, phoenix, cranes, lobsters, and bats and are built with small stones and tiles set in concrete.

For over four hundred years, the Japanese have been making paths that look like carpets made of stone, called *nobedan*. The stone carpets are divided into two levels of formality. *Gy*, the most formal of the two, are pathways which combine flat, randomly shaped fieldstone or river stones contrasting against the straight edges of cut stones. The second, less formal, style is called *so*, which are path-ways created with rounded and randomly shaped stones.[3]

Stones cut or salvaged from bluestone, limestone, sandstone, and granite as well as flat boulders and beach stones are all ideal for use as stepping stones. Stepping stones wander in and out of the intimate areas of the garden and through flower borders. They blend with the landscape, are ideal for sloping hillsides, and create an informal atmosphere for entering a summer home. The act of walking over stepping stones, where one must consider each footstep, suggests sloughing off the cares of the day. Loose crunching materials such as crushed stone, seashell, and gravel as well as peastone add another layer of informality. The most natural of all pathways is the earth-trodden path, which tells the story of traveling through meadows and woodlands along timeworn trails.

Although wood is the least permanent of materials, wooden walkways and bridges are particularly suited to a variety of practical uses, as well as having their own intrinsic qualities of beauty. Wood is adaptable; it can be used in formal as well as informal designs. Wooden footbridges can elevate a path over boggy terrain, through a marsh, above a stream, or can protect a sand dune. And the natural shades of wood transition well with stone and the surrounding landscape.

The armature of paths organizes the garden to determine where strong vertical elements will be placed. Bowers, archways, and gates become integrated elements in the narrative of the garden. Flowering trees and shrubs are planted along the pathways and at intersecting rooms. An allée or loggia planted with fragrant flowering vines, wisteria (*Wisteria sinensis* and *W. frutescens*), jasmine, and honeysuckle are but a few of the array of scented vines from which to choose. Connected to the walkways, they provide comfortable privacy and shade in the most practical and delightful manner. Pathways organize the garden spaces into manageable shapes and workable planting areas. They draw people into the garden space. Beautifully designed paths lend an elegance of coherence, creating movement and flow throughout the garden. Perhaps you, as do I, find it fascinating to gaze through an entrance to a walkway, catching a glimpse through an allée of a vista beyond and imagining the story that lies ahead.

ENDNOTES

1. Julia Lawless, *The Aromatic Garden* (Great Britain: Kyle Cathrie Limited, 2001).

2. Jean C. Cooper, *Yin and Yang: The Taoist Harmony of Opposites* (Wellingborough, Northamptonshire: Aquarian Press, 1981).

3. Gordon Hayward, *Garden Paths* (Charlotte, Vermont: Camden House Publishing, 1993).

CHAPTER SIX

Through the Moon Door

Partaking of the surface quality of jade
expressing the contemplating mood of the lotus pond
in the stillness of the early dawn, in the deserted garden,
crystal dew collects in the basin . . .
One could mistake its mirror-like surface
to be a porthole into another universe.

— TU MU (A.D. 803–852)
Tang Dynasty poet

MY FONDEST MEMORIES OF CHILDHOOD are of the summers we
spent at my grandparents' cottage on Cape Cod. The shingled "Cape" style
house that my grandfather built was sited high on a bluff overlooking Cape
Cod Bay. The shutters were painted a favorite color of my grandmother's, a
fresh shade of Brittany blue, complementing the weathered gray shingles. The
front dooryard was bordered by a white picket fence planted with pale pink and
deeper pink sweet scented roses and mounds of sparkling white daisies. Off to
one side was the large screened-in porch I had watched my grandfather build.
Weather permitting, we ate breakfast and dinner on the porch. Family dinners
were a special event, with an abundance of delicious food and considerable
chatter. I recall as if it were yesterday the evening music of crickets, bobwhites,
and mourning doves mixed with the sounds of laughter and merriment. We
never tired of running back and forth through the paths of beach roses and
brambles to the top of the landing and down the long steep stairs to go for a
swim, view the sunset, catch toads, or simply delight in the exhilarating freedom of summer. Around to the back was the outside shower, from which we
looked out onto my grandmother's vegetable and flower garden with the shimmering sea beyond. The shower enclosure, also built by my grandfather, had
airy louvered walls, no roof (for star gazing), and a charming floor with all of
their grandchildren's small footprints imprinted in the cement.

In one way or another, I think we all try to re-create and recapture our happiest childhood experiences and give them back to our own families. Our decision to move out of the city and raise our children close to the sea was based in part on these dream-memories. As working artists and designers, finding an old house in a modest neighborhood allowed my husband and me the opportunity to pursue our dreams.

We built our own outdoor shower almost immediately after moving. With the ancient plumbing in the kitchen unexpectedly retiring itself for good and pending plans to renovate the bathrooms, building an outdoor shower was a handy solution.

The kitchen sink is conveniently located on the same interior wall where the exterior shower was planned. Through the back wall underneath the kitchen sink we drilled two one-inch holes for hot and cold water pipes. Several days later, our plumber fortuitously called to say he had come across an antique brass shower fixture and would we be interested? Very definitely yes!

We dug a hole four feet deep at the side close to the home, digging the hole deeper toward the side farthest away from our house and sloping downward to ensure proper drainage. The finished area dimensions were 6.5 feet in length and 4.5 feet in width. The supporting pillars are set in buckets of cement, placed at the far corners of the planned structure. The house walls support the opposite end of the shower structure. We filled the hole with bits of rubble from the yard and small stones, and then gradually smaller and smaller stones with several inches of pea stone for the top layer.

The walls are built of untreated, tightly woven trellis with the wooden edges sanded smooth. Within a few years the cedar developed a gray-hued weathered patina. The entryway to the shower is a cutout inspired by a Chinese "moon gate." We finished the floor of the enclosure with fine-textured, rounded beach rocks set in the smaller pea stones, arranged in the shape of simple ray flowers. With their even surface, they are comfortable to stand on, firm under foot, and warm up nicely from the hot water. Blue-washed river stones in petal shapes are scattered about to create additional floral patterns on the floor of the shower enclosure, and we add shells and worn sea glass found on the beach.

The Chinese word for landscape is *shan shui* meaning "mountains and water." The combination of water and stones in a Chinese garden represents the *yin-yang* dualism of mountains (represented by rocks) as the bones of the earth, while rivers and streams (*yin*) are the arteries. To represent the homes of the Immortals, mountains first became a theme for landscape design and paintings. The natural geography of the spectacular Chinese mountains, both the

Himalayan Mountains to the west and the mountains of the eastern sea, gave rise to the belief that the Immortals (*Xian*) resided on these peaks. The Immortals were enchanted beings (not quite yet gods) who could dissolve in the air and fly on the backs of cranes to their homes perched high on the mountain peaks. It is the underlying belief of the mountains as magical dwelling that is expressed through the rock piles and standing rocks in Chinese gardens. Through a sympathetic magic, rocks confer on the garden owner a kind of immortality.

Sculptural garden rocks were selected to complement each other. Large rocks accentuated smaller rocks. Rocks were juxtaposed against a white wall or placed with a complementary medley of other stones. Rocks were not only valued for their striations and graining, craggy outline, harmonizing bumps, and holes, but for the noise they made when they were struck. The three formal aspects that should be sought in a fine rock and when constructing false mountains in a garden are *tou*, *shou* and *lou*. All three terms are somewhat ambiguous. *Tou*, which literally means "go through," implies that one should be able to walk through a passageway from one place to the next (literally or figuratively) – the perforations of the rocks. *Shou*, meaning "thin," corresponds to *yin* qualities of delicate and feminine. Rocks are generally thought to have *yang* qualities. Just as old plum trees, with hoary branches and delicate blossoms, are appreciated for their *yin-yang* qualities, rocks with *shou* qualities could be thought of in the same manner. For example, rocks of mica could be extremely fragile in appearance and would confer *yin* powers. *Shou* also suggests "without visible support" and "upright in isolation." Indeed, some rocks appear to be floating like a cloud with the weightier, broader element at the top supported by the thinner part at the base. *Lou* literally means "leak" or "drip" and this connotation refers to a hole perpendicular to the surface. The desired appearance is of a series of small holes open to all sides. The implication here is that with an opening on all sides, one could see everywhere, a suggestion of wisdom.[1]

Oh Garden of Fresh Possibilities!

From its interiors rise quiet whispers. Is it the womb of winds?
— An unknown Tang Dynasty poet writing
of one particularly imposing garden rock.

Flowing and still water symbolized movement and repose, and water-worn stones reflected the interaction between the solid and the ephemeral. Along with the dragon, water is the most influential of Daoist symbols. It represents fluidity, mutability, strength in weakness, coolness of judgment, and dispassion. Whereas rocks are sometimes spoken of as "roots of clouds," water is considered the soul of the garden. The luminous, mirroring quality of water is used to heighten the beauty of the surrounding landscape and architecture.

A house would open onto a garden and the garden would come into the house. The rooms might open onto a central courtyard with flowering trees and ferns planted around a central pool or cistern. Doors were either left open, or if they did exist, were only often a means for enhancing a view into a garden or the scenery beyond. The door, which might be a perfectly shaped circle (referred to as a moon door) or perhaps shaped like a gourd, blossom, leaf, or shell, was strategically placed to enhance a special outlook and symbolized a passageway into a different reality. Windows set in the upper half of rectangular doors were carved in whimsical shapes of hexagons, circles, and fans, and often these windows were crafted with the trellis work within the frame in designs of flowers and butterflies, as well as abstract shapes such as the patterns made from cracked ice.

For our out-of-doors shower we planted scented flowering vines, which envelop the enclosure in a succession of fragrant blossoms. Blooming in very late spring to early summer is our native wisteria (*W. frutescens*). American wisteria is similar in appearance to Chinese wisteria, with slightly smaller racemes, though in habit it is not nearly as vigorously invasive as the Asian wisterias. 'Amethyst Falls' flowers in a lovely shade of pale violet-to-lilac and 'Longwood' is a deeper purple-violet than the species. *Wisteria frutescens* is a host plant for Long-tailed Skippers. Subsequently after planting 'Amethyst Falls,' we have had several sightings of the Long-tailed Skippers, with their unmistakable blue and green iridescent wing scales. They were nectaring at the *Verbena bonariensis*, near to where the *W. frutescens* is planted.

The love of flowers was and continues to be a passion among the Chinese. Trees and plants are genuinely loved as living creatures.

Enjoying flowers with tea is the best, enjoying them with conversation the second and enjoying them with wine the least. Feasts and all sorts of vulgar language are most deeply detested and resented by the spirit of the flowers. It is better to keep the mouth shut and sit still than to offend the flowers.

—from a Ming Dynasty treatise on flowers
Walters Art Museum

The idea that flowers can be offended by bad manners reflects the belief that the world we inhabit is an organism in which all phenomena inter-relate. By the same reasoning, someone who drinks tea from a peach-shaped pot will live longer (peaches symbolize longevity), and someone who dips his writing brush in a peony-shaped bowl will have good fortune, as the peony is a metaphor for success and wealth.

The next to flower is the Japanese honeysuckle, *Lonicera japonica* var. *purpurea*, which is an intensely fragrant and hardy purple leaf honeysuckle. Planted in a moist location where it receives full sun, this honeysuckle reblooms inter-mittently throughout the late summer and early fall. Scrambling through the honeysuckle vines is the prolifically blooming and heavenly scented tea-noisette rose 'Mme. Alfred Carrière.' A favorite of the favorites, 'Mme. Alfred Carrière' flowers in a shade of creamy white washed with pearl pink that makes an elegant backdrop for an array of summer blooming shrubs and perennials. The fragrance is the kind that seeks your attention with just one in bloom. By late summer the entire structure is covered with 'Sweet Autumn' clematis (*Clematis paniculata* is synonymous with *Clematis ternifolia*). The fragrance of *Clematis paniculata* is mutable and I suggest purchasing one to test while it is in bloom, as we have found several versions of *C. paniculata* to be completely odorless.

Continuing with scented plantings, growing at the feet of the flowering vines are primrose (*Primula vulgaris*), lily of-the-valley, English bluebells, *Viola* 'Etain,' marsh milkweed (*Asclepias incarnata*), and the fragrant hosta 'So Sweet,' with vivid light, bright green foliage banded with pale creamy yellow.

On the shadier side of the shower enclosure we planted the large-flowered clematis with the evocative name 'Silver Moon.' How could one resist clematis with the name 'Silver Moon' planted to encircle a moon door? The flowers are a luminous lavender mother-of-pearl color. In early summer the vine is laden with buds and blossoms. This clematis gives an occasional repeat bloom in early autumn when it is covered with swirly, spiraling seed heads. 'Silver Moon' is one of the few large-flowered clematis that will do well in a shadier location.

As the poem by Tu Mu suggests, stepping through a porthole is like entering another universe – our porthole being the moon door entryway. The experience of showering out of doors surrounded by the fragrance of the flowers, while gazing into the garden through the lattice and listening to the songbirds is completely relaxing. Over time we purchased a 1940s weathered iron garden chair, painted Chinese red and slightly faded, with a round back and seat having a cutout radial design handsomely mirroring the shape of the moon door. Separated from its bowl, the base of a salvaged three-foot birdbath makes a useful table for soap and shampoo.

On a practical note, a friend reports that her plumber spends a good part of the summer routing out sand-clogged bathroom drains, another advantage to an outside shower. With children and guests returning from the beach throughout the summer, the outdoor shower is thoroughly enjoyed and thoroughly practical. Before the temperature dips below freezing, dismantle the showerhead and store it inside, and drain the pipes. This will prevent the plumbing parts from freezing and thawing, preserving the life of the fixtures.

ENDNOTES

1. Maggie Keswick, *The Chinese Garden* (Cambridge, Massachusetts: Harvard University Press, 2003).

CHAPTER SEVEN

Scented Lilacs

Lilacs,
False blue
White
Purple,
Colour of lilac
Heart-leaves of lilac all over
    New England,
Roots of lilac under all the soil
    of New England,
Lilacs in me because I am New
    England,
Because my roots are in it,
Because my leaves are of it,
Because my flowers are for it,
Because it is my country
And I speak to it of itself
And sing of it with my own voice
Since certainly it is mine.

— from *Lilacs* by AMY LOWELL (1874–1925)

SURELY AT THE TOP OF THE LIST of shrubs to grow for creating the framework of an intimate garden, or garden room, are lilacs, in particular *Syringa vulgaris* and their French hybrids. *Syringa vulgaris* are grown for their exquisite beauty in both form and color of blossoms, although it is their fragrance flung far and throughout gardens and neighborhoods that make them so unforgettable.

Not all species of *Syringa* and cultivars of *Syringa vulgaris* are scented. The early French hybrids and hybrids of Leonid Kolesnikov have retained their fragrance. *Syringa oblata* has a similar fragrance, though is not nearly as potent. Several of the Chinese species have a spicy cinnamon scent, while many of the Asian species and their hybrids have very little, if any, fragrance. To find your personal preference, I suggest a visit to a local arboretum, or take your nose to the nursery during the extended period of time (six to eight weeks, or so) in which the different cultivars of *S. vulgaris* are in bloom.

Nearly everywhere lilacs are grown (and here I am only referring to *S. vulgaris*), they are called by some variety of the word lilac. Perhaps the word lilac stems from the Persian word *Lilak* or *Lilaf* meaning bluish. The French say *Lilas*, the Spanish say *Lila*, and the Portuguese *Lilaz*. In old English lilacs were called *Laylock, Lilack*, and *Lilock*.

Lilacs are native to and found growing among the limestone rocks on the hillsides and mountainsides throughout southeastern Europe, in the Balkans, Moldavia, Serbia, Macedonia, and Yugoslavia. Cultivated by local mountain herdsmen, they were taken from the peasant villages of central Europe to the garden courts of Istanbul. In 1563, the Flemish scholar and traveler Ogier Ghiselin, Count de Busbecq, Ambassador of Ferdinand I of Austria to the court of Suleiman the Magnificent, brought back to Vienna gifts from the sultan's garden. Attracting much attention was the lilac. Seven years later, in 1570, Ogier Ghiselin, Count de Busbecq, and then Curator of the Imperial Court Library, accompanied the Archduchess Elizabeth from Vienna to Paris where she was betrothed to King Charles IX of France. Count de Busbecq journeyed to France with a shoot of *Syringa vulgaris*, where it soon began to fill the gardens of Paris.

Two color variants sprang up in European gardens beside the wild blue-flowered lilac, a nearly white flowered variant with lighter foliage and a taller-growing variant with deeper purple flowers. Hybridizers quickly set about to create different forms and color versions from these two variants.

Victor Lemoine of the famed nursery Victor Lemoine et Fils at Nancy in Lorraine Province continued the work of hybridizing lilacs. From 1878 to 1950, Victor and his wife, their son Emile, and their grandson, Henri, created 214 lilac cultivars. The cornerstone of the Lemoine's lilac hybridizing program was a natural sport that bore two corollas, one inside the other, making it the first double. This double was subsequently named 'Azurea Plena.' Because of the Lemoine family's success in turning ordinary lilacs into fancy double-flowered lilacs in nearly every hue imaginable, they became known as the "French lilacs." Spreading throughout Europe, the French lilacs were brought to the Russian court by French travelers. Well suited to the soil and climate of Russia, they soon spread far and wide. Several decades later, the Russian hybridist Leonid Kolesnikov continued the successful work of the Lemoines with his own exquisite variants.

The French and Dutch colonists transported lilacs to North America. These cherished cuttings, wrapped in burlap and wet straw tucked into suitcases for the long journey across the Atlantic, traveled well and were soon growing throughout the colonies. By 1753 the Quaker botanist John Bartram of Philadelphia was complaining that lilacs were already too numerous. One of two of the oldest collections of lilacs in North America are at the Governor Wentworth home in Portsmouth, New Hampshire, planted by the governor in 1750. The second collection, perhaps one hundred years older, is at Mackinac Island in Michigan, where French Jesuit missionaries living in the area are thought to have planted them as early as 1650.[1]

With their traveling fragrance, versatility in the landscape, and their ability to live tens, perhaps even hundreds of years, lilacs are garden heirlooms. When selecting lilacs to grow for creating the framework of the garden, take the time to choose wisely. Some lilacs grow readily into a tree shape ('Beauty of Moscow'), while others are somewhat relatively lower growing cultivars; 'Wedgwood Blue' comes to mind, and still others, the common white lilac (*Syringa vulgaris* var. *alba*), sucker more freely. And bear in mind that different lilacs bloom over an extended period of time. If you wish to have a blue lilac blooming simultaneously with a white lilac, then it is worthwhile to determine whether a specific cultivar is an early, mid, or late season bloomer. The following is a selection of lilacs growing in our garden, arranged in their sequential progression of flowering, with considerable overlapping. They are all highly scented or we wouldn't grow them. The accompanying illustration shows the different colors in lilac blossoms of white, pink, blue, lavender, magenta, and deep purple.

～

S. x hyacinthiflora 'Maiden's Blush' (1966) Skinner ~ Single, pale rose pink; shows different colors of pink under different soil conditions. In a warmer climate and lighter soils it is a paler shade of pink, in heavier soils 'Maiden's Blush' has more lavender undertones.

'Krasavitsa Moskvy' translated to 'Beauty of Moscow.' Leonid Alexseevitch Kolesnikov (1974) ~ Double, lavender-rose tinted buds opening to white-tinted pink. Grown throughout Russia. Vigorous upright habit, useful for growing into a tree-shape. Very extended blooming period.

Syringa vulgaris var. purpurea. Common purple lilac ~ Lavender, the wild species seen growing throughout its native land. The common purple is the most widely distributed form of lilac. The lilac of old gardens.

'Wedgwood Blue' John Fiala (1981) ~ Hanging panicles of beautiful true blue florets. Lilac-pink hued buds. Somewhat lower growing.

'Madame Florent Stepman' (1908) ~ Satiny ivory white florets from rose-washed buds. Pure white when fully opened. Tall and upright growing. One of the most extensively cultivated for the florist trade.

'President Grevy' Lemoine (1886) ~ Pure blue, immense panicles of sweet starry florets.

'Marie Legraye' (1840) ~ Single, diminutive florets, radiant white, lighter green foliage.

'Monge' Lemoine (1913) ~ Vivid, intense plum wine fading to deepest rose.

'Andenken an Ludwig Spaeth' Nursery of Ludwig Spaeth (1883) ~ Single, rich purple-violet with a smaller pointed-head panicle.

~

The blooming period of the above deliciously scented lilacs overlap, providing us with armfuls of cut flowers for well over a month. The varying shades of purple, violet, white, blue, lavender, and rose harmonize splendidly. Loosely arranged in an old white ironstone pitcher placed in the center of our dining room table, their sweetly insinuating fragrance wanders throughout the rooms of our home.

Lilac Culture

Lilacs are found growing (where winters are cold enough to afford proper growth and ample blossoms) from the smallest rural village to the urban court-yard. They grow the very best in zones 3, 4, and 5, in the colder regions of zones 6 and 7, and in the warmer regions of zone 2. They will tolerate temperatures of -35 to -40F, though they may suffer some damage from wind-chill. If temper-atures dip to such extreme cold in your region, site the lilac out of the path of chilling winter winds. Lilacs will tolerate frozen ground but not frozen pockets where water does not drain properly. Requiring excellent drainage, they grow best along rocky, limestone hillsides, suggesting just how important good drainage is. When planted in a mesic site, lilacs flower adequately, although, by late summer the foliage may wilt and turn moldy.

Lilacs perform best in sandy, gravelly loam mixed with organic matter such as compost and aged manure. Keep the surrounding soil free from weeds with an annual mulch of compost. In early spring sprinkle a cup of wood ashes around the base of the lilac and work it gently into the top layer of soil. Every three years or so apply a cup of ground limestone to the soil, again gently working it into the soil so as not to injure the roots.

Lilacs require full sun to nearly full sun to set flower buds. Where optimal sunlight isn't always available, one may have some success with pushing the envelope. We are growing lilacs in several locations in half sun, and although they would be fuller in form with far more flowers, all are growing well.

The overall shape of lilacs is greatly improved with an annual pruning. Immediately after flowering is the ideal time to attend to this not unpleasant task. The job becomes less manageable as the shrub grows tall and leggy in a few short years.

After the lilac has become established and is a desirable size and shape, cut to the ground approximately one third of the oldest branches and thinnest suck-ers. This allows the bush to renew itself and for the energy of the bush to go into the remaining growth. Leaving the strongest trunks that form the armature of the shrub, prune diseased or pest-infested shoots or branches, and remove all declining stems, thin suckers, and small, twiggy branches. Some lilacs produce suckers rarely, if at all, and others sucker aggressively. Remove all spent flowers immediately after blooming, snipping very close to the tail end of the panicle so as not to remove the new growth that will provide you with next year's flowers.

If you are growing lilacs as a background shrub or as a tree, allow only two to three main stems as trunks, removing lower branches and cutting all other shoots to the ground. 'Beauty of Moscow', 'Madame Florent Stepman' and the common lilac, both var. *purpurea* and *alba*, are all well suited for growing into a tree-shape. Conversely if you do not want your lilac to become a tree, prune to a height of eight to nine feet, which keeps the blossoms at eye level.

With its versatile form and lovely heart-shaped leaves the lilac is an exceptional companion to a wide range of flowering trees and shrubs. Just as the Sargent crabapple (*Malus sargentii*) is at its flowering peak, with masses of sublimely scented white blossoms, the earliest lilacs begin their fragrant parade. In our garden, the blossoms of *Prunus*, namely peach, pear and plum, overlap with the flowering of 'Beauty of Moscow,' 'Maidens Blush,' and 'President Grevy.' They are planted in close vicinity along the garden path. The newly emerging fragrant blossoms of *Prunus* interwoven with the pervasive perfume of lilacs give The Scent of All Spring!

Lilacs are one of the loveliest shrubs to grow as a tall hedge, and they integrate magnificently into the country hedge of mixed shrubs and trees. The ineffable beauty and fragrance of lilacs are enhanced by the many varieties of suitable companion plants. The short list of plants described here is particularly appealing during the lilac's period of flowering, for their compatible scents, colors, and foliage or for creating a sequentially blooming combination of fragrances. 'Korean Spice' viburnum, nearing the end of its florescence while the lilacs are beginning theirs, blooms in pink infused white, snowball shaped flower heads, with an intensely sweet and spicy aroma, variegated Solomon Seal, *Viola* 'Etain,' mid-season jonquils and narcissus, and lily of-the-valley all bloom simultaneously with lilacs. The most sublimely scented tree peony 'Rockii,' with white petals washed with pale rose, and magenta-purple splotches at its heart center, also flowers during

'Maiden's Blush'

'Monge'

'President Grevy'

Common Purple

'Beauty of Moscow'

lilac time. Later in the season, to coincide with later-flowering lilacs, come the *Iris pallida* and *Iris germanica*, English bluebells, early species daylilies with their honey-citrus scent, 'Bridal Wreath' spirea, blue and white columbine 'Origami,' and white bleeding hearts (*Dicentra spectabilis* 'Alba'). Just as 'Therese Bugnet,' the earliest of roses to flower (with its *Rugosa* heritage) joins the scene, the lilacs are finished for the season. Lilacs, when pruned to a tree shape, allow a variety of plants to grow happily at their feet. Herbaceous peonies, although their blooming period usually does not coincide with lilacs, make an ideal garden companion. In our yard, *Paeonia lactiflora* follow lilacs almost to the day in order of sequential blooming. The dense, full mounds of foliage of the herbaceous peonies visually fill the space left by the trunk of the lilacs, as do hosta. The foliage of hosta, planted on the shady side, makes a companionable partner. Hosta will appreciate the filtered sun and both plants benefit from an annual blanket of compost. Species daylilies, Montauk daisies, and chrysanthemums are ideal companions when planted on the sunnier side of lilacs.

Spring never lasts long enough in New England, with some years leaping from bitter cold to balmy, summer-like temperatures. Despite freezing rain and late spring snow, lilacs bloom and bloom resplendently. For the extended period of time in which the spires of sweet florets are in bloom, our garden is redolent with their heavenly fragrance. The blossoms of *Syringa vulgaris*, and especially the fragrant sorts, are a nectar source for the Eastern Tiger Swallowtail. The diminutive "violet afloat," better known by its common name Spring Azure, is captivatingly beautiful floating about the pure white flowers of 'Marie Legraye.' Throughout the seasons our lilac hedge is alive with a chattering collection of songbirds. The height and the crooks of the branches are enticing to the innumerable songbirds, though it is the cadmium orange oriole alighting on the blue-hued spires of 'President Grevy' that causes the heart to skip a beat.

ENDNOTE

1. For an expanded version on the history of lilacs, reading *Lilacs the Genus Syringa* written by Fr. John L. Fiala is highly recommended. Filled with hundreds of color photographs and including chapters on the culture of lilacs, hybridizing techniques and propagation, we have turned to this book repeatedly. Fortunately it has been reprinted and is once again available through Timber Press.

CHAPTER EIGHT

Hydrangea paniculata 'Grandiflora'

Answer July—
Where is the Bee—
Where is the Blush—
Where is the Hay?

Ah, said July—
Where is the Seed—
Where is the Bud—
Where is the May—
Answer Thee— Me—

Nay— said the May—
Show me the Snow—
Show me the Bells—
Show me the Jay!

Quibbled the Jay—
Where be the Maize—
Where be the Haze—
Where be the Bur—
Here— said the Year—

— EMILY DICKINSON

SMALL TREES AND SHRUBS FORM a permanent and delightful relationship between the home and the garden. Shrubs naturally complement trees,
visually filling the space surrounding the trunks of trees, and when trees and
shrubs are grown together they create varying densities of mass with their diver-
sity in form and texture of foliage. The interplay sunlight and shadows provide
gives the light a greater brilliance as the shade becomes more deeply subtle.

On a great estate large trees form the framework of the garden design. For
those of us who live on comparatively smaller lots, or those wishing to create a
garden room, it is undesirable to have more than but a few, if any, large trees.
Small trees and shrubs form the backbone of the intimate garden. While shrubs

and small trees can be maintained in a manageable size, large trees planted next to a home rob it of sunlight and air. Small trees and shrubs grow quickly (generally speaking) and form an effective screen for privacy or hiding an unsightly view while contributing masses of fragrant and colorful blossoms and fruit. Sheltering branches, nectar-rich blossoms, and protective foliage held high welcome the pollinators.

During the initial stages of planning the garden, take walks and drive around your neighborhood and surrounding communities during different seasons to find what appeals to you. While we were in the earliest stages of planning our garden, we kept our eyes peeled for different planting ideas. Our children teasingly referred to it as "shrub patrol." The notion of planting lilacs at opposing ends of our porch came from one of these excursions. After viewing a pair of ancient lilacs planted on either end of a lovely neighborhood home, I imagined how much more delightful it would be to sit on our front porch or work in my home office with the fragrance of the lilacs carried on the breeze.

Throughout our community are growing what are commonly referred to as "classic shrubs." They are the trusty, tried and true, extremely cold tolerant and long-lived shrubs that graced the earliest garden picture and will continue to reliably enhance the most contemporary of home gardens. These flowering shrubs of great merit include lilacs, mountain laurel, rhododendron, weigela, spirea, quince, holly, beautybush, forsythia, Japanese andromeda, mock orange, and *Hydrangea paniculata* 'Grandiflora' (commonly know as Peegee, pee for paniculata and gee for grandiflora).

Hydor is the Greek word meaning water, and *aggeion* describes a vessel. *Hydrangea paniculata* is so named because the seed capsule resembles a small water pitcher; *paniculata* is "with panicles." The ease with which one can selectively prune a 'Peegee' into a tree shape highlighting its grand panicles of blossoms is what sets it apart from the more blowsy forms of hydrangea.

The inflorescence of the 'Peegee' is a large, loosely pyramidal panicle, made up of individual florets. The panicle is fully developed in size by mid-summer and lingers on the branch. The colors become ever more lovely as the summer drifts past. The florets open creamy white, gradually transform into shades of pink and green, and then turn coppery bronze, shifting colors over a period of several months. When the flowers are at the height of their loveliness with all their differing hues in evidence and the blossoms feel like gossamer organza, they are ready to be picked and dried. Our 'Peegee,' when only a few years old, began to provide us with armfuls of flowers. If left on the branches, the flower heads provide interest throughout the winter.

Hydrangea paniculata 'Grandiflora'

Hydrangea paniculata is one of the mountain hydrangeas of eastern China and Japan. It was introduced to Western gardens during the mid-1860s, where it was a popularly grown garden plant in Japan. *Hydrangea paniculata* thrive in full sun to partial shade, planted in rich, organic, well-drained soil. Our 'Peegee' is growing alongside our woodland border and benefits from the natural mulch of fallen leaves provided by our neighbor's American linden. Nature's mulch, with its warm blanket composed of many layers of light material, also offers protection from the summer sun's drying heat and is one of the many benefits of *not* raking the borders in autumn.

The arching branches heavy with flowers form a dense canopy, creating a beautiful floriferous umbrella. Lily of-the-valley, epimedium, violet, primrose, maidenhair ferns, Japanese painted ferns, and hosta are all lovely companion plants that will grow well when underplanted beneath the canopy of a 'Peegee,' when it is pruned to a tree shape. Suggestions for suitable companions for the sunnier side of the 'Peegee' are early spring flowering bulbs, lilies, and columbine.

Left unpruned, *Hydrangea paniculata* 'Grandiflora' is a massive, heavily flowering shrub. With selective pruning the 'Peegee' is easily trained into a tree shape. In early spring, before the buds begin to swell, examine the shrub to assess the overall shape. Leave intact the most desirably shaped and sturdiest one, two, or three stalks as the main trunks. Remove the lowest branches to direct the plant's energy to the top growth. Repeat this process of removing the lowest branches annually in early spring. The shrub will continue to remain attractive throughout the several years it takes for it to grow into a tree-like shape. Mature 'Peegee' hydrangeas have usually been pruned with their lowest branches at about chest high. *Hydrangea paniculata* 'Grandiflora' are quite often offered for sale with branches that have been grafted to a slender trunk. I do not have much experience with this plant, as I don't care much for its awkward appearance and prefer the pruning method.

The classic shrubs are the hardiest of shrubs seen growing in well-established landscapes. Grown together and in balanced combination with small trees, they add an unaffected grace and elegance to the garden composition. They were the beloved flowering shrubs that were tucked along with belongings and successfully transported to new frontiers. They are the plantings that have been and will continue to be treasured by future generations, for they are hardy and resilient and "earn their keep" with their lovely fragrant flowers and attractive foliage.

INFLORESCENCE

Strictly speaking, an inflorescence is the arrangement of flowers on a plant. The many forms of flower clusters or arrangements fall into several distinct categories. The stalk of a single flower or flower cluster (inflorescence) is called a peduncle (in bulbous plants, such as a lily, it is called a scape). The stalk of an individual floret in a cluster is called a pedicel. If a cluster of flowers has neither peduncle nor pedicle, it is said to be sessile, meaning that it is set directly against the main stem. Several types of inflorescence commonly used to describe flowers are noted here.

A single flower borne at the end of a stem is called a "solitary." Tulips and poppies are examples of flowers that form singularly on upright stalks.

A spike arrangement is an inflorescence where the flowers are attached to the main stalk along the sides, either sessile as in hollyhocks, or on very short pedicel as in lavender.

A raceme differs slightly from a spike in that the flower stalks are slightly longer, as exemplified by lily of-the-valley.

A panicle is a highly branched inflorescence with a loosely pyramidal form. The flower clusters are at the ends of the branched pedicel. *Hydrangea paniculata* and lilac are examples of a panicle inflorescence.

The composite head inflorescence is composed of a cluster of tightly packed disc flowers surrounded by a ring of ray flowers. Sunflowers, daisies, and asters are examples of a composite head.

The shape of an inflorescence relates directly to the behavior of the pollinating insect or animal. The ray flowers of composite heads form ideal landing pads for small insects, with multiple disc flowers to feed from. Hummingbirds favor larger flowers projecting from spikes and racemes. Other species of birds, orioles for example, are attracted to inflorescence with clusters of nectar-rich flowers and convenient branches that the birds can grasp while perching. Bats pollinate flowers at night, and the flowers they favor are clustered on isolated branches away from the plant's mass of leaves where a bat could become entangled.

CHAPTER NINE

A Note on Hollies

THE BEE

Like trains of cars on tracks of plush
I hear the level bee:
A jar across the flowers goes,
Their velvet masonry

Withstands until the sweet assault
Their chivalry consumes,
While he, victorious, tilts away
To vanquish other blooms.

His feet are shod with gauze,
His helmet is of gold;
His breast, a single onyx
With chrysoprase, inlaid.

His labor is a chant,
His idleness a tune;
Oh, for a bee's experience
Of clovers and of noon!

—EMILY DICKINSON

OUR GARDEN HAS GROWN UP and about from plantings that we consider too beautiful to live without. Flowering trees and shrubs are planted within close proximity to the house, along pathways and in sightlines to be viewed from within the house, so that we may touch, smell, and observe their beautiful transformations throughout the four seasons. Hollies are another species without which our garden would be incomplete.

Growing at my husband's childhood home in southwestern Ohio is what must be one of the most beautiful trees native to North America, *Ilex opaca*. Planted when his parents built their home in 1962, the holly tree is approximately thirty feet tall, pyramidal in shape, and is growing fairly close to the home, just outside the guest bedroom window. No matter the time of year, the tree is always a thing of beauty and even more so during the winter months. Whenever we visit, I purposefully leave open the shutters of the window that is closest to the tree. The very first thing I look for upon awakening is the holly tree. The level branches bear masses of sparkling red berries and the foliage is a brilliant, glossy viridissimus green. With a cloak of fresh, new-fallen snow, the tree becomes even more splendid, the combination of green and red shrouded with feathery white. The evergreen enveloping foliage and horizontal branches create a year-round hideaway for the songbirds.

Unfortunately *Ilex opaca* is not suitable for an intimate garden as it grows tall and spreads broadly. Fortunately we have another option, that of the hybrid hollies developed by Kathleen Meserve. Many of the species holly from North America, China, and Europe that bear red berries grow twenty feet and more. The hollies hybridized by Kathleen Meserve were spurred by her interest in creating a dwarf form of evergreen holly that was small enough to be grown as a foundation planting.

Kathleen Meserve grew up on Park Avenue in Manhattan and did not become interested in gardening until World War II, when the United States Department of Agriculture began the Victory Garden program. After the war, she moved to Long Island, to a shaded estate unsuitable for growing vegetables. Becoming acquainted with hollies at a local garden club meeting, she began to collect them, limited to species available from local nurseries. In the early 1950s, she obtained seeds from a dwarf evergreen holly native to northern Japan and Korea, *Ilex rugosa*. She crossed the English holly (*Ilex aquifolium*) with *Ilex rugosa*. Many of her crosses succeeded, and she soon had enough seeds to plant. Two years later she had seedlings from the crosses. The following winter was a disaster, with temperatures dipping to minus seventeen degrees. The only seedlings that managed to survive had *Ilex rugosa* as one of their parents.

These first successful hollies developed by Kathleen Meserve were called 'Blue Boy' and 'Blue Girl,' so named for the bluish cast to the green leaves. 'Blue Prince and Blue Princess' followed these, which were created by crossing the original hybrid back to the parent *Ilex rugosa*. 'Blue Prince' and 'Blue Princess' proved even more hardy and compact than their parents.

A Note on Hollies

The Meserve hollies are ideally suited to northern climates and will tolerate a range of light conditions. In southern climates they should be planted where they receive some afternoon shade. For the most part, they will grow to twelve feet tall and no more than twelve feet wide, although 'Dragon Lady' (*Ilex x meserveae* 'Dragon Lady') is an exception.

Our hollies host a great collection of songbirds, including mockingbirds, cardinals, downy woodpeckers, cedar waxwings, and flocks of overwintering and migrating robins. With brilliant red berries and glossy evergreen foliage, they are beautiful in the garden composition throughout the year. Come springtime, the holly bears diminutive white and nectar-rich flowers, attracting all manner of bees, especially honey bees and bumble bees.

A swarm in May
Is worth a load of hay.
A swarm in June
Is worth a silver spoon.
But a swarm in July
Isn't worth a fly.

How should a holly, or any shrub or small tree, be arranged in the small garden? Rather than dotting them about the landscape, the best rule of thumb is to plant them in connection to the lines of the home. Shrubs and small trees soften the hard line where the foundation meets the land and fills in corners around the sharp angles. A home surrounded by flowering trees and shrubs gives a sense of nestling in rather than suddenly leaping out from the landscape.

I had read that growing hollies near an entryway will bring good fortune and envisioned for our home two pyramidal-shaped evergreen hollies planted on either side of the front steps, with fragrant climbing roses supported by the porch pillars behind the hollies, framing the entryway. At a nearby garden center we spotted two 'San Jose' hollies pruned to petite pyramids in their little nursery pots. Planting this variety of holly in that particular spot was definitely a mistake – they quickly outgrew our narrow front border, becoming much too tall and rangy-looking, not the lush evergreen cone-shape I had imagined. Although we decided the front border was not wide enough for any type of evergreen foundation shrub, I am delighted to report that the roses are thriving. Climbing the porch pillars are the sweetly scented roses 'New Dawn,' with a pale seashell pink blossom, and 'Aloha,' which flowers in hues of carmine, coral, and pink.

HOLLY WREATH

1 wreath form made of branches or vines – 15″ in diameter
    approximately
100 or more sprigs of holly, each 6–7″ in length with the lower 2–3″
    of leaves removed
Green florist's wire
Pruning shears
Red berries – wild rosehips, garden-variety rosehips, holly,
    winterberry

To make a wreath form from vines of bittersweet or grapes, gather several long lengths of vines to create a circle of 15–16″ in diameter, and wrap florist's wire around the ends. Weave several more lengths around to round out the circular shape, and secure with wire.

Group 4–6 sprigs of holly together to form a bouquet. Lay this on top of either a purchased or homemade wreath form, secure and wrap wire around several times tightly. Take another 4–6 sprigs and lay these on top of the previously placed sprigs, covering their stems and wire. Wrap wire around the stems several times tightly. Continue working around the form. After the form is completely covered, use another length of wire to create a loop with which to hang the wreath. The red berries or hips may be added with the sprigs as you are circling the form, or tucked in later and secured with additional wire.

Halfway down the path, dividing the herb and cutting garden in front from the rear yard living area, on opposing sides of the walkway, are planted our two 'Dragon Ladies.' They are tall and slender, clothed in glossy cinnabar-colored fruits with shiny evergreen leaves that are terribly prickly. Their evocative name suggests two sisters elegantly adorned in brilliant green silk satin Mandarin style robes trimmed with red silk Chinese ball button and frog closures. I imagine they are guarding, or keeping separate, the private areas of the rear yard from the more public front yard. The 'Dragon Lady' has the most fastigiate outline of all the different varieties of hollies planted in our garden. This worthy specimen is a good selection for planting alongside the house or narrow pathways, when space is limited. It will grow to fifteen feet tall and up to six feet wide, though we keep ours pruned to approximately three feet wide.

Planted beneath one of the 'Dragon Ladies' and trained to climb in a spiral through its branches is the rose 'Alberic Barbier.' This is a noteworthy combination of pale buttery yellow buds opening to creamy white flowers entwined with the blue hued foliage, and is a look that is easily accomplished as 'Alberic Barbier' sends out long, long shoots of thirty feet or more.

In a shady corner around to the back is a plumply rounded pyramidal shaped 'Blue Maid' (*Ilex* x *meserveae* 'Blue Maid'). The leaves are plush blue-green, with much less prickly foliage than that of the 'Dragon Lady,' and it is covered with Chinese red berries throughout the fall and winter.

Growing in the opposite corner of the rear yard are the hardy, resilient and widely planted 'Blue Prince' and 'Blue Princess.' They have a broadly spreading habit of growth. The foliage is a glossy bluish-green and the 'Princess' is covered with vermilion berries. As common as the 'Prince' and 'Princess' are, the blue hue of their leaves creates a striking contrast planted near a 'Bridal Wreath' spirea (*Spiraea arguta*) and a 'Texas Scarlet' Japanese flowering quince (*Chaenomeles*), both with more finely textured and brighter green leaves. A single male of one Meserve hybrid holly (in our garden it is the 'Blue Prince') planted within one hundred feet or so is all that is required for the bees to pollinate the female hollies of different Meserve varieties. Hollies depend on the bees for fruit set. All hollies flower, but only female hollies produce berries.

The Meserve hollies grow and bear fruit planted in a variety of light conditions, from full sun to dappled shade. They prefer a rich, fairly moist soil and appreciate a blanket of mulch – leaves, seaweed, compost, or whatever is on hand. Annually in December we prune the evergreen hollies and these cuttings, along with rosehips from 'Climbing New Dawn,' make a festive wreath to adorn the front door during the holidays.

PART TWO

Candidates for the Borders

CHAPTER TEN

The Fragrant Path

THE GARDEN BY MOONLIGHT

A black cat among roses,
Phlox, lilac-misted under a first-quarter moon,
The sweet smells of heliotrope and night-scented stock.
The garden is very still,
It is dazed with moonlight,
Contented with perfume,
Dreaming the opium dream of its folded poppies.
Firefly lights open and vanish
High as the tip buds of the golden glow
Low as the sweet alyssum flowers at my feet.
Moon-shimmer on leaves and trellises,
Moon-spikes shafting through the snowball bush.
Only the little faces of the ladies' delight are alert and staring,
Only the cat, padding between the roses,
Shakes a branch and breaks the chequered pattern
As water is broken by the falling of a leaf.
Then you come,
And you are quiet like the garden,
And white like the alyssum flowers,
And beautiful as the silent sparks of the fireflies.
Ah, Beloved, do you see those orange lilies?
They knew my mother,
But who belonging to me will they know
When I am gone.

—AMY LOWELL

A GARDEN, A SMALL GARDEN ESPECIALLY, is made more intimate when planted with an abundance of fragrant blooms and foliage. The air impregnated with the scents of flowers and foliage imbues a memorable atmosphere in the garden, playing the subtle, and sometimes not so subtle, role of strengthening the ambiance we wish to create. Fragrance, elusive, emotionally colored, and so entirely related to experience, welcomes us as we walk through the pathways of our garden.

The idea of creating a fragrant garden is deeply rooted in ancient history. One of the earliest aromatic gardens was the Hanging Gardens of Babylon, built in the 6th century B.C. by King Nebuchadnezzar for his wife Amytes, daughter of the King of the Medes. The Greeks described these resplendent gardens, supported by stone columns with irrigated terraces. The most potently fragrant plants were grown here, and the terraces, which bloomed with lilies and roses, were favored by Queen Amytes for her walks.

The countries of the Middle East abound with an array of scented trees and plants. From historical records dating back to 2500 B.C. we know that the enclosed courtyards of the Persian palaces were planted with jasmine, fruit trees (especially oranges), hyacinth, myrtle, and jonquils. But above all other flowering plants, the rose was held in the highest esteem. The Damask rose grew in nearly every garden in Syria. The country takes its name from the word *Suri* (a delicate rose), hence *Suristan* (the land of roses).

From tomb paintings and bas-reliefs we learn of gardens and the use of plants in ancient Egypt. The verdant, fertile flood plain created by the annual rise and fall of the Nile, coupled with the Egyptians' skill in engineering and irrigation, allowed a wealth of indigenous and imported fruiting trees, vines, and flora to grow in abundance.

One of the earliest botanic collections was that of plants and seeds brought back from Syria in approximately 1450 B.C. The images of the plants were carved on the walls of the temple of Thothmes II in Karnak. The Egyptian Papyrus Ebers (written about 1552 B.C.) describes scented plants and remedies and their methods of use. The gardens, enclosed by mud walls, were planted with aromatics and medicinal herbs. Some of the plants described include frankincense, myrrh, saffron crocus, Madonna lily (*Lilium candidum*), cinnamon, and orchards of pomegranates.

The Egyptians were among the earliest peoples to show an appreciation for perfume. Incense and perfume were used extensively for religious and funeral rites. Fragrant oils were used to massage their bodies and concoctions of scented herbs were taken to sweeten the breath.

Priests performed the daily ritual of burning fragrant woods as offerings to the gods. The wood was burnt on alters in the temples. The word "perfume," from the Latin *per*, "through," and *fumun* "smoke," shows that the origin of the word lay in the burning of incense, both to 'offer up' the gratitude of the people to the gods for favors received, and to ask for their blessings in time of trouble. The Egyptians believed their prayers would reach the gods more quickly when wafted by the blue smoke that slowly ascended to heaven.[1]

The Egyptians' reverence for nature is noteworthy in their use of floral motifs in decorative ornamentation. The lotus and papyrus are by far the most prevalent, together with the daisy, palm, convolvulus, and grape vine. The 'Blue Lotus of the Nile' (*Nymphaea stellata coerulea*), a member of the water lily family, is the lotus flower depicted in ancient Egyptian decorative ornamentation. The fragrance emanating from the lotus creates an intoxicating atmosphere; they have a scent similar to hyacinths. The flowers are star-shaped and sky-blue with brilliant golden centers and stand several inches above the water. The lotus had an inexhaustible symbolism in ancient Egypt, Daoism, Buddhism, and Hinduism alike.

The lotus is significant as it was the symbol of Upper Egypt. When used in ornamentation with the papyrus it symbolized the union of Upper and Lower Egypt, whose symbol was the papyrus. A well-known example of this is the soaring twin pillars that tower over the ruins at Karnak. One capital is decorated with the lotus and the other with papyrus.

The 'Blue Lotus of the Nile' had a deeper religious significance. Because the lotus blooms each day, withdraws under the water at sunset, and reemerges the following morning, it was closely linked to the daily rhythm of the rising and setting of the sun and thus to the story of the sun god, creation, and rebirth. The blue petals represented the sky and the golden center the emerging sun. The lotus motif was used to decorate pottery, jewelry, clothing, and appears extensively in the decoration of the capitals of pillars and columns. A wide variety of designs using the lotus flower were employed, in repeating border patterns and in alternating patterns with lotus buds or bunches of grapes. The buds fit harmoniously into the curves between the flowers. During the reign of Akhenaten (New Kingdom, 18th Dynasty) the lotus designs become less stylized and more freely expressed.

The Fragrant Path

When thinking about the history of garden design in the context of our own gardens, we are free to determine our own personal preferences while drawing inspiration from what has come before. By following one's intuitive powers and adhering to nature's contours specific to an existing site, the inherent beauty of the garden can be realized. In describing our fragrant path, rather than draw for you a picture of what to grow precisely, as each individual garden setting is unique, the following are suggestions of plants for a well-orchestrated sequence of fragrant flowering plants. The underlying framework would ideally be composed of as many fragrant flowering and fruiting trees and shrubs as are reasonable, including an abundance of aromatic and healthful herbs. And the garden overflowing with scented blossoms provides you with armfuls of flowers to cut and bring indoors to scent the rooms of your home.

Located on the southeast side of our home is the primary pathway, which we walk up and down many times in the course of the day. We built the path using bricks from a pile of discarded chimney bricks. Ordinarily I would not recommend chimney bricks, as they are fired differently from paving bricks and are therefore less sturdy. We laid the brick in a herring bone pattern and luckily they have held up without cracking and splitting. The warm red tones of the brick complement the creamy yellow clapboards of the house. A tightly woven brick path is a practical choice for a primary path as it helps keep mud out of the home. Planted alongside the house walls and on the opposing side of the path, in close proximity to our neighbor's fence, are the larger plantings of *Magnolia stellata*, 'Dragon Ladies,' *Syringa*, *Philadelphus* and semi-dwarf fruiting trees, *Prunus* and *Malus*. Weaving through the background tapestry of foliage and flowers are fragrant flowering vines and rambling roses. These include the most richly scented cultivars of honeysuckle and Bourbon roses. *Viburnum carlcephalum*, butterfly bushes, meadowsweet, and New Jersey tea comprise a collection of mid-size shrubs. They, along with perennials, bulbs, and annuals – narcissus, tulips, iris, herbaceous peonies, lavender, Russian sage, lilies, and chrysanthemums – are perfect examples of fragrant plants growing at mid-level. Closer to the ground is a carpet of scented herbs, full and abundant and spilling onto the brick walkway. The length of our pathway is lined with aromatic alpine strawberries, thyme, and sweet alyssum. This most sunny area in our garden permits us to grow a variety of kitchen herbs. The foliage of the herbs releases their scents when brushed against. Including herbs in the flower borders provides an attractive and practical addition to the fragrant garden.

The fragrances are held within by the house and neighboring fence and the living perfumes of flowers and foliage are noticeable throughout the growing season. All the plants are immediately available to see, touch, and smell. The intimate aspects of the garden are revealed by the close proximity of plantings along a much-used garden path.

When selecting plants for a fragrant garden, it is not wise to assume that just because your grandmother had sublimely scented peonies growing in her garden, all peonies will be as such. This simply is not the case. Take the time to investigate nurseries and arboretums during plants' blooming period and read as much literature as possible. There is an abundance of information to be gleaned and sifted through to find the most richly scented version of a plant. When seeking a fragrant cultivar, one may find that it is usually an older variety, one that has not had scent replaced for an improbable

Alpine strawberries have the growth habit of bearing fruit while simultaneously producing flowers. Kept well hydrated, they provide a continuum of fruit from May through October. Alpine strawberries are sweetly scented when left unwashed. To remove the sand, gently shake them about in a slightly dampened tea towel. The French have a tradition of serving these tiny fruits in diminutive baskets (one basket for each guest) lined with strawberry leaves and a dollop of crème fraiche.

color, convenient size, or double blossoms by a well-meaning hybridizer. And despite our best effort to find the most richly scented version, there will be disappointments along the way, as fragrance is highly mutable. Soil conditions and climate play their role, and some plants simply don't perform as advertised.

A well-thought-out pathway looks inviting when seen from the street and the fragrance beckons the visitor to enter. The interwoven scents emanating from an array of sequentially blooming flowers and aromatic foliage create a welcoming atmosphere. Have you noticed your garden is more fragrant after a warm summer shower or on a day when the morning fog has lifted? Scented flowers are sweetest when the air is temperate and full of moisture. Plant your garden of fragrance to reflect the time of year when you will most often be in the garden to enjoy your hard work.

Fragrances of Early Spring Through Early Summer

Roman crocus (*Crocus suaveolens*)
'Cream Beauty' (*C. chrysanthus*)
Japanese andromeda (*P. japonica*)
Japanese plum (*Prunus mume*)
'Water Lily' magnolia (*M. stellata*)
Apricot (*Prunus armeniaca* 'Harglow')
Peach (*P. persica* 'Belle of Georgia')
Purpleleaf plum (*P.* 'Thundercloud')
Primrose (*Primula vulgara*)
Scented *Narcissus* and *Tulipa*
Carolina allspice (*C. floridus* 'Athens')
Spring snowflake (*Leucojum vernum*)
Mayflower (*Epigaea repens*)
Lily of-the-valley (*Convallaria majalis*)
Oyama magnolia (*M. sieboldii*)
'Korean Spice' viburnum (*V. carlesii*)
Fragrant viburnum (*V.* x *carlcephalum*)
Pear (*Pyrus communis*)

Alpine strawberry (*Fragaria vesca*)
Fothergilla (*Fothergilla gardenii*)
Viola 'Etain' (*Viola*)
Sargent's crabapple (*Malus sargentii*)
Black chokeberry (*Aronia melanocarpa*)
Lilacs (*Syringa vulgaris*)
Bluebells (*Hyacinthoides non-scripta*)
'Joseph Rocks' peony (*Paeonia rockii*)
'Honoribile' lemon iris (*I. germanica*)
Dalmatica iris (*I. pallida*)
Purple Chinese wisteria (*W. sinensis*)
White wisteria (*W. sinensis* v. *alba*)
'Vossii' laburnum (*L.* x *watereri*)
American wisteria (*W. frutescens*)
Dames violet (*Hesperis matronalis*)
Sweet woodruff (*Galium odoratum*)
Hemerocallis dumortieri
Jacob's ladder (*P. caeruleum*)
Peony (*Paeonia lactifolia*)
Madonna lily (*Lilium candidum*)
Star daylily (*Hemerocallis minor*)
Honeysuckle azalea (*R. viscosum*)

Sweetbay magnolia (*M. virginiana*)
'Betty Corning' (*Clematis viticella*)
Lemon lily (*H. lilioasphodelus*)
Meadowsweet (*Spiraea latifolia*)
Mock orange (*Philadelphus*)
Virginia sweetspire (*Itea virginica*)
'Belgica' honeysuckle (*Lonicera*)

Summer Scents

Fragrant Roses (*Rosa*)
Astilbe (*Astilbe*)
Sweet alyssum (*Lobularia maritima*)
Purpleleaf honeysuckle (*Lonicera japonica* 'Purpurea')
Japanese stewartia (*S. pseudocamellia*)
Nasturtium (*Tropaeolum majus*)
Sweet pea (*Lathyrus odoratus*)
Japanese honeysuckle (*L.* 'Halliana')
Regal lily (*Lilium regale*)
'Hyperion' daylily (*H.* 'Hyperion')

Russian sage (*Perovskiax. superba*)
Night blooming daylily (*H. citrina*)
New Jersey tea (*Ceanothus americanus*)
Thunberg's daylily (*H. thunbergii*)
Mimosa tree (*Albizia julibrissin*)
Butterfly bush (*Buddleia davidii*)
Butterflyweed (*Asclepius incarnata*)
'Graham Thomas' honeysuckle (*Lonicera*)
'Bountiful Valley' (*Hemerocallis*)
Datura 'Belle Blanche' (*Datura*)
'Serotina' honeysuckle (*Lonicera*)
'Goldflame' honeysuckle (*L. heckrotii*)
Oriental lily 'Casa Blanca' (*Lilium*)
'David' phlox (*P. paniculata*)
Flowering tobacco (*N.* 'Grandiflora')
Night phlox (*Zaluzianskya capensis*)
Hemerocallis altissima
Japanese lily (*Lilium speciosum*)
Gold-Band lily (*L. auratum*)
Summersweet (*Clethra alnifolia* 'Rosea')

Scent is the oxidation of essential oils of flowers and leaves. The most intensely scented flowers, lily-of-the-valley, orange blossoms, gardenia, *Stephanotis floribunda*, and tuberose, for example, have thick, velvet-like petals that retain their fragrance by preventing the essential oils from evaporating.

The greater the amount of essential oil produced, the lesser degree of pigmentation in a flower. The oil is the result of the transformation of chlorophyll into tannoid compounds (or pigments), which is in inverse ratio to the amount of pigment in a flower. Plants with blue, orange, and red flowers have a high degree of pigmentation and *usually* generate little or no scent. Pure white flowers release the strongest perfume, followed by creamy white, pale pink, pale yellow, yellow, purple-pink and purple. As color pigment is hybridized and intensified in flowers, fragrance is usually lost or compromised.

Late Summer through Autumn Fragrances

'So Sweet' hosta (*Hosta*)
Peacock orchid (*Acidanthera murielae*)
'Honey Bells' hosta (*Hosta*)
'Fragrant Bouquet' hosta (*Hosta*)
Angel's trumpet (*Brugmansia*)
Sedum (*Hylotelephium spectabile*)
Resurrection lily (*Lycoris squamigera*)
'Aphrodite' hosta (*Hosta*)
'Sugar and Cream' hosta (*Hosta*)
August lily (*Hosta plantaginea*)
Moonflower (*Ipomoea alba*)
Golden Hops (*H. lupulus* 'Aureus')
Tuberose (*Polianthes tuberosa*) '
'Sweet Autumn' clematis
   (*C. paniculata*)
Tea (*Camellia sinensis*)
'Emperor of China' (*Chrysanthemum*)
Montauk daisy (*C. nipponicum*)
Korean daisy (*C.* 'Single Apricot
   Korean')
Sheffield daisy (*C. rubellum*)
Ben Franklin tree (*Franklinia
   alatamaha*)
Saffron crocus (*Crocus sativus*)

Winter Fragrance

Wintersweet (*Chimonanthus praecox*)
Winter honeysuckle (*Lonicera
   frangrantissima*)
'Pink Dawn' viburnum (*Viburnum
   bodnantense*)
'Pallida' witch hazel (*H. mollis*)
'Arnolds Promise' (*H. mollis*)

Fragrant Herbs

Feverfew (*C. parthenium*)
Lavender (*Lavendula augustifolia*)
Thyme (*Thymus*)
Santolina (*Santolina virens*)
Anise Hyssop (*Agastache foeniculum*)
Lemon Verbena (*Aloysia triphylla*)
Rosemary (*Rosmarinus officinalis*)
Pennyroyal (*Mentha pulegium*)
Sweet alyssum (*Alyssum maritimum*)
Scented-leaf geranium (*Pelargonium*)
Chocolate mint (*Mentha* x *piperita*)
Tarragon (*Artemisia dracunculus*)

There are few modern gardens planted purely for fragrance. Maybe this is because there is now a tremendous variety of appealing plant material, offered by growers to eager gardeners ready to purchase what is visually enticing, by color and by size. Perhaps it is so because in the past fragrant plantings served the function of disguising unpleasant odors from outhouses and farmyards, and we no longer have to address these concerns. But the pendulum has begun to swing (albeit slowly) toward planting a garden designed for fragrance. Scent, along with rhythm, scale, harmony in color, and form, should ideally be an equal component in garden design.

Plant scented flowering shrubs under windows and close to and around the porch. Plant fragrant vines to climb up the walls near window sashes that will be open in the summertime. Plant scented white flowering plants near to where you might brush against them while dining *al fresco* or to embower a favorite garden spot designed for rest and rejuvenation.

"True vespertine flowers are those that withhold their sweetness from day and give it freely at night."[2] Imagine the dreamlike enchantment of the fragrant path through the night garden. The vibrantly colored flowers have vanished. All that you will see are the white and palest shades of pink, yellow, and lavender flowers reflecting the moonlight. Perhaps you will have the breathtaking experience of an encounter with a Lunar moth. *S. vulgaris* 'Beauty of Moscow,' Madonna lily, *Philadelphus*, Japanese honeysuckle, *Lilium regale*, *Nicotianna alata*, Oriental lily, tuberose, night phlox, peacock orchid, *Stephanotis floribunda*, gardenia, *Jasminum sambac*, Angel's trumpet, and moonflowers are but a few of the white flowers with exotic night-scents for an entrancing sleeping garden.

A thing of beauty is a joy for ever:
Its loveliness increases; it will never
Pass into nothingness; but still will keep
A bower quiet for us, and a sleep
Full of sweet dreams, and health, and quiet breathing.
　　　　—JOHN KEATS (1795–1821)

ENDNOTES
1. Roy Genders, *Scented Flora of the World* (London, England: Robert Hale Limited, 1977).
2. Louise Beebe Wilder, *The Fragrant Garden* (New York: The Macmillan Co., 1932).

CHAPTER ELEVEN

The Narrative of the Garden
~ Part Two ~

Oh East Wind blow, blow strong
Mucked-matted leaves and mud-brown ice be gone.

West Wind sing soft music breezes
New notes of fresh scents
Black earth alive revealed
Green emerald shoots and robin bird-song.

South Wind I am beckoning
Open my garden with warm embracing breezes.

Sunlight through rain-spangled branches
Tipped-verdant tree-tops
Long lengths of limbs
Clad in fat buds of beauty promised.

Did you brush against my shoulder?
Welcome! South Wind.

Fiddlehead spirals unfurl
Golden chalices drink warm rays of sunlight
Hot Red-riding hood tulips of Turkistan
With marked undulations of delineated foliage.

Winds of the South and Winds of the West
Stretch-long days of summer keep memorable with

Oh Garden of Fresh Possibilities!

White wreaths of jasmine and azure skies of
Heavenly blue morning glories.
Honeysuckle bower and sweet pink-orange-red screen of roses.
Night hawk in search of perfume exhaled.

Farewell, South Wind
Leave us with your late summer splendor.

Cinnamon-speckled *Lilium* of the wood—
Chinese Emperors rose-quilled chrysanthemum.
Refresh! *Verbena* for traveling amber panes with black inlaid to probe.
Vaporous evanescing moonflowers vanish.

— LILLIAN BROOKS (1958–)

THE NARRATIVE OF THE GARDEN is expressed by the relationship created between the home and the surrounding landscape. It speaks through walkways and the vertical elements of design. The relationship of the house walls to an enclosing fence, pergola, allée, pavilion, or summer house gives the garden a sense of scale and proportion, as do small trees, shrubs, and vines. They add grace of form, nestling the home into the landscape, while dynamic rhythms are created to accentuate focal points and delineate boundaries. Planted in a harmonious arrangement, in concert with the pathways, fragrant flowering trees, shrubs, and vines tell the narrative of the home and garden.

For the small garden or for creating a garden room, flowering vines expand the size of the garden, especially when ground space is limited. Vines emphasize a view, enhance a seating area, or may be utilized to disguise an eyesore. Many annual vines grow quickly from seed and can be planted with a slower-growing perennial while you wait for the permanent vine to takes its place in the landscape. Honeysuckle, a relatively quick-growing vine, nonetheless takes several years to become established. For a year or two, try growing a sweetly scented annual sweet pea alongside the honeysuckle.

Whenever there is a choice within a species, plant a fragrant vine rather than a non-scented cultivar. Chinese wisteria (both *W. sinensis purpurea* and *alba*) are highly scented, whereas Japanese wisteria (*W. floribunda*) is only mildly so. The classic companions of Chinese wisteria and golden chain tree, trained to grow through a pergola, create a sequential progression of fragrance, for as the Chinese wisteria is finished flowering, the golden chain tree begins its display.

Laburnum vossii is the most highly scented of the golden chain tree, with long racemes of freesia-scented flowers (similar in appearance to that of wisteria, pea, and lupine, all of which belong to the Leguminosae). Of course there are exceptions to only using fragrant vines in the landscape – the hummingbird magnet, our native trumpet vine – and who could resist growing a garden, without planting morning glories for a season. Trumpet creeper is one of the most effective vines for attracting hummingbirds – the cerise-colored morning glory (*Ipomoea purpurea*) comes in a close second. The delicate starry scarlet flowers of the cardinal climber (*Ipomoea* x *multifida*), another member of the Convolvulaceae, also provide a welcome beacon for the hummingbirds.

When creating a room within a garden, or for accenting or disguising an enclosing fence or wall, plant screens of fragrance. Create a mixed hedge or screen with a tapestry of sequentially flowering shrubs and vines. *Viburnum x carlcephalum, Syringa vulgaris, Wisteria sinensis, Philadelphus, Lonicera japonica repens* 'Purpurea,' *Magnolia virginiana, Buddleia davidii, Clethra alnifolia, Lonicera fragrantissima,* and *Hamamelis mollis* are listed in order of florescence from early spring through late winter and will provide you with four seasons of fragrance to enhance your garden rooms. To screen or embower a favorite seating area, particularly one that is down wind of a prevailing breeze, consider planting scented flowering vines and shrubs that will bloom when you are most often in the garden.

Lonicera

Honeysuckle takes pride of place in the garden planted for fragrance. Bear in mind, not all species and cultivars of honeysuckle produce scented flowers. There are over one hundred species of the genus *Lonicera*, of either climbing or erect shrubs. Honeysuckle is indigenous to North America, Asia, and Europe and is found growing throughout the world. An extended season of fragrance can be achieved by planting *Lonicera*, with scents that will envelope the garden throughout the day and evening. Of the cultivars that are easily obtained in the market, one might plant *Lonicera periclymenum* 'Belgica' to begin the season, next to bloom is *L. japonica repens* 'Purpurea,' which then overlaps with *L. japonica* 'Halliana.' *Lonicera periclymenum* 'Graham Thomas' blooms freely throughout the summer as does *Lonicera heckrottii* x 'Gold Flame' (white and buttery yellow blushed pink blossoms). The last climbing honeysuckle to come into flower in our garden is *Lonicera periclymenum* 'Serotina.' The buds of 'Serotina' are crimson rose; opening to creamy yellow flowers and this honeysuckle also bears clusters of brilliant red glassine berries that appeal to the songbirds.

Combining honeysuckle with companionable scented vines and shrubs will create myriad fragrant effects. The earlier blooming 'Belgica' and eglantine rose, with apple scented foliage, bloom simultaneously, as does *L. japonica* 'Purpurea' with *Philadelphus* 'Innocence.' While the ivory-blushed-pink 'Eden' rose is entwined with the lightly perfumed blue bells of *Clematis viticella* 'Betty Corning,' *Lonicera japonica* has wended its way along the fence and joined the symphony of scents.

During Elizabethan times honeysuckle, also named woodbine, was frequently used to cover arbors. Providing protection from strong sunlight and inclement weather, garden walkways and paths were covered with arches made of intertwining climbing plants. An arbor would usually be cut into the allée or walkway, with seats made of stone or wood and a table provided. The arbor was a place to enjoy the scents of the flowers and herbs. The word "arbor: was derived form the word *herber*, a place where fragrant plants grew.

For a modern garden planted for inhabitants with hectic schedules, consider designing a honeysuckle-clad arbor along a well-utilized pathway. Although we may have limited leisure time available, at the very least, fragrant flowering vines can be enjoyed while coming and going through the course of our day.

Honeysuckle grows and flowers profusely provided it is planted in full sun, though it will tolerate and flower lightly when planted in part shade. Not at all particular regarding soil conditions, it blooms lavishly when regularly spoiled with fish emulsion and compost.

Lonicera japonica is a vigorous grower and extremely invasive in warmer regions of the United States, zones seven through ten. The purple leaf cultivar 'Purpurea,' a hybrid of the naturally occurring variant *repens*, is comparatively less invasive. The buds are magenta and open in shades of white and yellow with rose undertones, and are almost as richly fragrant as *L. japonica*.

Summer blooming honeysuckle has a welcoming, "hey, notice me" fragrance. For months, our garden is sweetly redolent with sequentially flowering species. Planted under window sashes, with the windows open during the summer, the fragrance wafts through the garden into the interior rooms of our home.

"A man who makes a garden should have a heart for plants that have the gift of sweetness as well as beauty of form and color."

—William Robinson ~ *The English Flower Garden*

"Moonlight of the Groves"

Jasmine is among the loveliest of plants used to cover vertical structures – walls, arbors, porches, pergolas, bowers, and what you will. To my knowledge, and sadly so, none of the fragrant *Jasminum* are reliably hardy north of zone seven, and therefore must be potted up to spend the winter indoors.

Jasminum sambac, a woody evergreen shrub with vining tendencies, flowers freely throughout the year, covered with small (⅜″), white, single or double flowers that fade to pink as they age. The perfume is similar to lilacs and orange blossoms, an exhilarating combination of scents that insinuates itself throughout garden and home.

Jasminum sambac is the flower that the Hindus gave the poetic name of "Moonlight of the Groves." An ingredient often utilized to make perfume and flavor tea, *J. sambac* is also called *bela* when used to make garlands by women to wear in their hair during Hindu worship ceremonies.

Although originally native to India, *J. sambac* grows throughout southern China. Confucius wrote that scented flowers were strewn about on all festive occasions. Houseboats and temples alike were hung with fragrant blossoms of peach, magnolia, jonquil, and jasmine. Gardens were devoted solely to the cultivation of jasmine to make fragrant oils and perfumes, to scent wines and teas, and to adorn the wrists and hair for women to wear in the evening. Each morning the unopened buds would be collected before dawn and brought to market for the city flower sellers to string into garlands and bracelets. Enhancing the tea experience by adding aromatics began during the Song Dynasty (A.D. 960–1279). A single, newly opened blossom of *J. sambac* is all that is needed to perfume and flavor a pot of tea.

Jasminum sambac is hardy, with the protection of a warm blanket of mulch, through zone seven; grown in cooler regions, it needs to be brought inside for the winter and grown in a pot. During the warmer months, our *J. sambac* thrives with frequent watering; we douse the entire plant with the garden hose several times a week. For pot culture, water less frequently during the winter. Requiring well-draining soil, and provided with a weekly dose of an organic fertilizer such as a fish emulsion during the warmer months, "Moonlight of the Groves" will reward you with an abundance of exotically scented blossoms throughout the year. We prune ours hard, twice a year, to about six feet, not allowing it grow larger as it would become too unwieldy to bring indoors during the cooler months. Place the plant outside in a sunny to partly sunny location in late spring when the evening temperatures are consistently 50 degrees or higher. Prune leggy, dry growth and wrap healthy tendrils around the supporting framework. Prune again in mid-fall, before temperatures dip lower than 45 degrees, and bring indoors to set by a warm sunny window. We grow several *J. sambac* 'Maid of Orleans,' one is planted on the east side of our home near the outdoor shower enclosure where it benefits from the high humidity and we benefit from its intoxicating fragrance. A second 'Maid of Orleans' is grown on our patio adjacent to the back door leading to the kitchen. We can handily pick a few blossoms to scent a pot of tea, and the fabulous fragrance greets us coming and going, day and evening.

Stephanotis floribunda

With contrasting white waxen clusters of tubular flowers juxtaposed against glossy virdissimus leaves, *Stephanotis floribunda* is to my mind one of the most beautiful flowers in the world. Also referred to as bridal wreath and Madagascar jasmine, though not at all related to *Jasminum sambac* or *Jasminum officinale*, (members of the Oleaceae), *Stephanotis floribunda* has an intoxicating scent – a swirl of orange blossom, oriental lily, and jasmine. The flowers are long lasting and for that reason, along with their romantic perfume, they are often used in bridal bouquets. Stephanotis is derived form the Greek word *stephanos*, a crown or wreath.

In warmer climates *Stephanotis floribunda* can be grown out of doors, but in our climate it is a plant with which we have to content ourselves with growing in pots to bring indoors to winter over. *S. floribunda* demands light, well-aerated, and well-draining soil. The surest way to harm it is to give it too much attention by overwatering or planting in a heavy, moist soil. A friend in northern Florida grows an *S. floribunda* out of doors all year long, along the north side of her home. Hers performs best when she completely ignores it. Stephanotis, grown in a warm climate, is ideal for screening a small garden and when in bloom, creates a wall of fragrance. As the day draws to a close, the intoxicating fragrance becomes more pronounced.

During the summer our *S. floribunda* is given a place of prominence on the east side of our home, where it receives morning sun and afternoon shade. The long tendrils travel through the trellis provided for the honeysuckle. When the autumn evening temperatures begin to hover around 40 degrees, we move it indoors for the winter. Water minimally during the winter months and fertilize regularly. Stephanotis resent root disturbances and flower more prolifically when slightly pot-bound.

Passiflora incarnata

Passionflower is a genus of climbing plants primarily native to South America. *Passiflora incarnata* is the hardiest and one of the few native to North America, often seen growing throughout the southeastern United States. In our climate, *P. incarnata* dies back to the ground during the winter. When protected with mulch, it recovers and emerges in the late spring. The common name "maypop" refers to the plant's exuberant habit of escaping its confines and its ability to "pop" up unexpectedly, usually in May, but some years as late as mid-June. *P. incarnata* may be difficult to establish; plant in spring to give the roots time to settle in before the cooler months arrive. We have had greater success with wintering over young plants and treating them as houseplants for the first several years, then planting them out in the garden. Once established, maypop grows quickly in one season, flowering in July and continuing through September, simultaneously bearing fruit. The intricate, purple-mauve flowers possess an odd fragrance, a combination of sweet roses with a nose-tickling pungency. It appeals to butterflies in the Haliconia family, and the leaves are a larval food for the Zebra Longwing and Gulf Fritillary caterpillars.

Maypop will grow well and flower in full sun to part shade in well-drained, fertile soil. The fruit of the maypop is pale yellow-green and matures to the size and ovoid shape of a hen's egg. When it is fully ripe, the skin will wrinkle slightly. The gelatinous pulp is similar in flavor to that of a guava, and the fruit is usually eaten out of hand. *Passiflora incarnata* is a flowering and fruit-bearing vine valuable in the landscape for its ability to cover a structure with non-damaging tendrils in one growing season. Our maypop is planted with a 'Serotina' honeysuckle. The shades of purple and lilac-mauve of the passionflower complement the rose-hued buds and creamy yellow flowers of the honeysuckle, the vining tendrils twisting and spiraling round one another.

Campsis x tagliabuana 'Madame Galen'

Trumpet creeper is a vine with which no garden should be without. If you plant hummingbird vine, ruby-throated hummingbirds will come. Trumpet vine is covered with nectar-rich tubular blossoms throughout the summer. No matter when the ruby-throated hummingbirds are traveling through your garden, they will notice trumpet vine. Hummingbirds are unable to distinguish blue from green and therefore are usually attracted to flowers

that bloom in shades of yellow to red. For the most part, the flower blossoms with hues of scarlet to gold attract by color, not fragrance. The beaks of the hummingbirds are adapted to the tubular flowers that they visit. *Campsis radicans* is native to the southeastern and Gulf Coast region of North America, with red flowers borne all summer. 'Flava' is a hybrid with lovely yellow trumpets; one of the most beautiful of all is 'Madame Galen,' a nineteenth-century hybrid, with apricot orange to salmon red flowers. *Campsis grandiflora chinese*, native to China, was hybridized with *C. radicans* to create the very showy and floriferous 'Madame Galen.'

'Madame Galen' is less invasive than the native *C. radicans*, although the gardener should be cautioned when planting any trumpet creeper near the house. This extremely vigorous vine climbs by attaching itself tightly with aerial rootlets. The supporting structure should be indestructable, pillars or a pergola constructed of iron, similar to the support necessary for wisteria. The vine reaches a certain height and then the branches grow horizontally away from the structure, searching for light and creating a potentially top-heavy plant.

Campsis radicans is not particular in regard to soil and light conditions. It will grow in sun and partial shade, although the blossoms last longer with afternoon shade. Trumpet creeper grows in hot, dry conditions along roadsides, in thickets and woods. Pruning in early spring will not affect flowering as it blooms on new growth.

Ipomoea alba

The eagerly anticipated moonflower began to bloom in our garden on the first day of September. I had read in the *Essential Earthman*, by the eminent Henry Mitchell, that to succeed in our shorter growing season, moonflowers need gallons of water and generous doses of fertilizer. The labor of watering nearly every day, with fish fertilizer added weekly, has paid us back a thousand fold. A single glorious vine, with its glamorous and bold emerald-green, heart-shaped leaves, has threaded its way through the porch slats and the maze of climbing roses. Each evening at twilight, half a dozen or more pure white blossoms, with ribs of pale luminous green, unfurl from half-open ruffled white forms. By mid-morning of the following day, the evanescent blossoms have collapsed. The flower forms are sheer papery things, and if you touch them or cut one to bring indoors, they are quickly ruined. The ineffable fragrance is sweetly dense like a lily, airy and fresh simultaneously. Its transient beauty and color remind me of the brief life of the Lunar moth.

"You can tell in the afternoon which buds will open that night. In the South, where I used to live, it was the custom to keep an eye on the moon vine, and when sixty or so buds showed they would open that night, to ask people over to watch them. Unfortunately, people in the country talk so much that I cannot recall seeing the buds open very often. They tremble and vibrate when they open. Usually someone would say "the flowers are out," and everyone would run over to admire them, then back to jabbering. Equally festive is the night-blooming cereus. In our neighborhood there lived an old cereus in a tub. It was ninety-seven years old, the last time I saw it, and produced 120 flowers open at once. When it bloomed (and you can tell by afternoon which buds will open) its proud owner would phone round the neighbors and there would be punch or champagne (rather dangerous in hot weather) and cucumber sandwiches for refined persons, and ham and potato salad for mere mortals.

These parties, once such a feature of the American summer, were always spontaneous, since you only had a few hours to plan them and invite people. It was always astonishing to see how many people could come at the last minute."

— Henry Mitchell ~ *The Essential Earthman*

CHAPTER TWELVE

Oh Garden of Fresh Possibilities!

FLOATING BRIDGES

Oh what tremendous multitudes,
invisible and ever-changing,
come to this garden
and linger forever!

Every step we take on Earth
takes us to a new world.
Every single footstep
lands on a floating bridge

I know there is no such thing
as a straight road.
Only a vast labyrinth
of intricate crossroads.

Our steps incessantly
create as we go
immense spirals
of unfolding pathways.

Oh garden of fresh
possibilities! Oh garden
of all I am not
but could and should have been!

— FEDERICO GARCIA LORCA *Spanish* (1899–1936)

ONE OF THE FIRST TASKS WE UNDERTOOK when we moved to our new
old house was improving the sunny front dooryard. It seemed we had waited so
long to own a home of our own and make a garden of our own that, although any
infinite number of jobs of far greater importance waited to be tackled, the

warmer weather and scents of early summer were beckoning. The idea of spending all our waking hours indoors – sanding, scraping and painting – seemed unimaginably tiresome when presented with the opportunity of working outside in the glorious sun-washed days of a Cape Ann summer day.

On either side of the center stairs leading to the front porch are two borders that run the width of the house, measuring roughly ten feet deep and fifteen feet wide. With a southwesterly exposure, they are a choice location to site sun-loving flowering plants. The front borders are enclosed by a sturdy granite wall, which had been reinforced with cement cinderblocks. We thought we were going to have to demolish the blocks with a sledgehammer, but the mortar was so old and crumbly that the cement blocks fell apart in our hands. We had a good laugh and felt grateful for one uncomplicated task. Obliterating our view were two enormous and overgrown evergreen shrubs with trunks as thick as a mature apple tree. They weren't quite as easy to remove as the cinderblocks, but with some help from a friend we managed to cut them down and dig out and dispose of the dense root mass.

New homeowners are best served by waiting at least one complete growing cycle before making any major commitments to a garden design. By doing so, one can determine their particular light conditions as well as to see what is already planted. Especially in a small garden, the gardener has to consider every bit of available light and use it wisely. It isn't prudent to plant even a small tree in the one area where sun loving shrubs, perennials, and annuals will grow. And be reminded that trees and shrubs start small and quickly grow larger. Take time to discover the nuances of light and shade on the property. Go to the windows and look from the inside out, planning the garden as a continuum of the home. Imagine the outdoor sightlines as you would an interior. Determine what you would like to see from the inside looking out into the garden. Perhaps from the bedroom window you would like to view a pair of pink and white flowering dogwoods. Ask yourself what you would like to see from the dining room. Shrubs and trees with fragrant white blossoms, when planted in close proximity to the dining room windows, will be enjoyed during the dinner hour in the evening light. To frame the window sashes, while windows are open during the summer months, plant a scented rose; both 'Madame Alfred Carrière' and 'Aloha' bloom throughout the season.

Oh the possibilities! We tilled the tired, compacted soil and dug in large quantities of compost. We were not anywhere near ready to make a commitment for our front borders, nor did we want to spend the summer looking at two tidy patches of bare earth. An old New England conviction holds that flowers planted by the sea are more vivid. I decided to content my soul with a kaleido-scope of flowering annuals. We sowed seeds of Mexican sunflowers (*Tithonia*), *Verbena bonariensis*, and cosmos (*C. bipinnatus*) in the back of the border; zinnias (*Z. elegans*), Shirley poppies (*Papaver rhoeas*), and California poppies (*Eschscholzia californica*) were selected for the mid-ground; and nasturtiums were planted to cascade over the granite wall.

More often than not gardens are designed to feature flowers in the rear yard. Particularly if you dwell in a well-trafficked neighborhood, plant the front bor-ders with a combination of flowering shrubs, vines, perennials, and annuals. You will give your neighbors a beauty treat planting flowers on the paths leading to the front door and in the dooryard, rather than the formulaic and predictable, boring solution of evergreen foundation shrubs.

Many annuals will benefit from an early start in the greenhouse. However, the annuals we planted for our first summer are easy to grow when sown directly in their permanent home, and some, like annual poppies, develop a taproot and resent transplanting. With twice daily watering the new seedlings began to emerge. The Mexican sunflowers, zinnias, and cosmos grew straight and tall, and eventually some needed to be supported with stakes. The *Verbena bonariensis* grew to four feet but never dominated the border. The airy branching structure of the plant, with one-inch clusters of bobbing purple flowerets, wends its way comfortably through its neighbors. The nasturtiums filled out, forming neat, compact plants, before spilling over and down the stonewalls.

Corn poppies (*Papaver rhoeas*), especially the mixed single Shirley poppies, are one of my favorite flowers to paint, and elicit endless expressions of appre-ciation from neighbors and visitors. The flowers appear to float in the air atop delicate wiry stems. Sparse, light, bright green foliage emerges lower on the stems, away from the blossoms. Your eyes are drawn to the translucent beauty of the tissue-thin petals. Blooming in a profusion of analogous shades of vermil-ion to cadmium red to rose-red and china pink, and some with tone on tone stri-ations in the petals – if I had to choose a favorite amongst the favorites, it would be the silky, white-flowered Shirley, with a pencil-thin line of carmine outlining its ruffled petal margins.

This sounds like a cacophony, but because of the transparent, watercolor-like quality of the petals, they meld together in a breathlessly beautiful fashion. Planting Shirley poppies en masse affords the best opportunity to appreciate sensational color combinations.

Shirley poppies were developed in the 1880s by the Reverend William Wilks, the vicar of Shirley in Surrey. Reverend Wilks "noticed in a waste corner of my garden abutting of the field a patch of the common wild field poppy, one solitary flower of which had a very narrow edge of white." From this one plant his work at hybridization resulted in the broad mix of colors in single and double flower forms, along with picotee bicolor blossoms.

The common wild field poppy (*Papaver rhoeas*) is the scarlet red corn poppy, growing in drifts blanketing the open fields throughout Europe. The field poppies are single, silky-red blossoms with black blotches at their hearts. *Papaver rhoeas* thrive in cultivated, disturbed soil, hence their common name corn poppies. During World War I they became known as 'Red Flanders' and the 'Legion of Honor' poppy, for they grew prolifically amongst the crosses on the burial fields of Flanders. The poem "In Flanders Fields the poppies blow, between the crosses row on row . . . " is too sad to repeat in its entirety, in a chapter devoted to fresh possibilities. The poem was written during the midst of the First World War after "Seventeen days of Hades!" by Lieutenant Colonel John McCrae, M.D., and describes his time on the battlefield tending wounded soldiers. We still wear red poppies in our lapel for Remembrance Day and Veteran's Day, to remind us of soldiers who have perished in battle.

Shirleys grow quickly and bloom prolifically in a single season. The pepper-pot-like seed capsules form while the plant is continuing to bloom. Therefore, it is possible for a second generation to bloom from the initial sowing, during the same season. *Papaver rhoeas* prefer neutral to alkaline soil and will not thrive in compacted or heavy soil. Work the soil deeply and lightly press the seeds in; do not cover the seed with soil. With sowings spaced several weeks apart, throughout the spring and early summer, the blooming period will be extended. The seeds may be sown again in the fall, after the first frost, for earliest summer blooms. To enjoy the blossoms indoors, immediately after picking a newly opened flower, hold the end of the stem to a flame for five seconds or until the cut end is singed brown. This way the flower will last for several days in water, otherwise it will quickly droop and wilt.

A glowing shade of golden orange with satiny petals and finely cut blue-green, fern-like foliage, California poppies (*Eschscholzia californica*) flower on slender stems, and planted in drifts where they catch the summer winds, the effect is that of golden waves. California poppies brighten and accentuate a variety of flowers in contrasting and complementary colors when planted in borders, and for the same reason, they are useful for cut flower arrangements. Add them to a bouquet of blue, white, and yellow flowers; set them with flowers of differing shades of rose, pink, and magenta; or just imagine that warm shade of golden-orange with some pretty white flowers, a bouquet of feverfew or

Ox-eye daisies. Both *Eschscholzia californica* 'Mikado,' a brilliant red-orange, and 'Linen,' with creamy white flowers, are similar in shape and form but not quite as prolific as the golden-hued California poppies. From the one small packet of seeds planted during the first season in our new home, the California poppies have reseeded themselves each summer, providing a continual reminder of our first summer of fresh possibilities.

Garden nasturtium (*Tropaeolum majus*) is a tender herb native to South America. *Tropaeolum* is derived from the Greek *tropaion* (a trophy). It was an ancient Greek custom for the helmets and shields of a defeated army to be fixed to the trunk of a tree. Linnaeus was reminded of this when he saw the plant growing on a post, for the leaves represented the shields and the flowers the helmets.[1] The flowers, leaves, and buds are all edible and are sometimes referred to as Indian-cress. The leaves have a distinctive peppery flavor, the flowers not as much so, and both are delicious added to a salad of mixed greens.

A handful of nasturtiums looks charming in a bud vase. 'Creamsicle' resembles the exact pale orange shade of an ice-pop Creamsicle, while 'Alaska' flowers in brilliant hues of gold, orange, and red, with green and white variegated leaves. The flowers of the 'Empress of India' are a rich vermilion contrasting against bluish-green foliage. The 'Empress of India' is the nasturtium painted by the nineteenth-century genre artist George Cochran Lambdin in his *In the Greenhouse* on display at the Denver Art Museum.

Nasturtiums prefer average soil conditions. If the soil is too rich, one will have a plant that produces mostly foliage and only a few flowers. Occasional doses of fish fertilizer and deadheading periodically throughout the summer encourage the nasturtiums to bloom until the first frost.

Cosmos, zinnias, and Mexican sunflowers belong to the Compositae and are native to Mexico. *Tithonia* can grow to a height of twelve feet in six months from seed, though six to eight feet is the more usual height attained in a northeastern coastal garden. The ray flowers are brilliant cadmium red-orange with vivid yellow disk florets in the center of the composite flower head. Zinnias flower in an array of single and double shapes, luminous watercolor shades and jewel tones – in nearly every color of the rain-

COMPOSITAE

Flowers such as tulips form singly on upright stalks. Flowers that occur in clusters are called inflorescences. There are different types of inflorescence, for example, panicle, raceme, umbel, spike, and composite head. The Composite family is so named because their flower heads are composed of many flowers, usually two different types. For example, what appear to be the petals of a Mexican sunflower is actually a ring of ray flowers. The bright yellow, tiny flowers clustered together in the center of the Mexican sunflower are called the disk flowers or florets. Both kinds of flowers may have seed-producing ovaries and pollen-producing stamens; more frequently the ray flowers are sterile and only serve as an attractant (or road map) to pollinators.

bow (save blue) and including the pale willowy green 'Envy.' An old-fashioned expression for zinnia is "youth-on-age," for during the plant's florescence, as it is sending forth new flowers, older flowers on the same plant retain their fresh appearance while others have gone to seed.

With their fern-like foliage and ray flowers ranging in shades of white, seashell pink, rosy pink, and cerise, cosmos are easily mixed throughout the back of the border. The varying shades of pink and white of the mixed singles make a simple and charming arrangement when strewn informally together. Zinnias and Mexican sunflowers also make ideal cut flowers, as both will last a week or more in fresh water. The flowers of *Tithonia* are borne on hollow peduncles, or stems. When using the blossoms in an arrangement, very carefully cut the stems with a sharp knife. The fragile stem will bend and collapse if damaged.

Zinnias, cosmos, *Verbena bonariensis*, and Mexican sunflowers grow tall. Hybridizers have introduced dwarf varieties; for example, zinnias have their 'Profusion' series, 'Sonata' cosmos come in an array of colors, and there is a *Tithonia* named 'Fiesta Del Sol' that only grows to two feet tall. No doubt the more compact cultivars have their place in gardens planted by busy people.

The taller heirloom annuals require the extra but necessary precaution of supporting the plants with stakes, not really a very taxing chore. Perhaps you may encounter a butterfly or two while maintaining the taller plants. Butterflies flock to nectar-rich cosmos, zinnias, and Mexican sunflowers, with their ray flowers conveniently arranged for a butterfly landing pad. However, the flowering plant that is the single most successful attractant, surpassing all perennials and flowering shrubs (with the possible exception of buddleia), is *Verbena bonariensis*. Bobbing and waving atop slender stems, clusters of purple florets beckon to the butterflies. From the moment the blossoms begin to open, *Verbena bonariensis* is covered with bevies of butterflies. Nearly every one that visits makes a beeline for the *V. bonariensis*. On a single branching plant we have observed dozens, of several different species, simultaneously sipping nectar. Blooming continuously until the first hard frost, *V. bonariensis* also provides welcome fuel for the migrating Monarchs at the end of the season, when fewer nectar plants are available. The only possible objection to *Verbena bonariensis* is that they are prolific plants, reseeding vigorously throughout the borders. I do not consider this a particularly objectionable trait. Where the little volunteers are unwanted I simply pull them out. Allow the plants that have reseeded in the back of the border to grow to maturity. Smaller seedlings that have germinated where they are not welcome may be carefully dug up and transplanted to more suitable spots.

For a small garden, where available space is at a premium, *Verbena bonariensis* enhances the vertical layers with its airy appearance. The foliage of cosmos, dill, love-in-a-mist and Queen Anne's lace also have this same diaphanous, see-through quality, providing either butterfly nectar or larval host food, and are perfect for summer bouquets.

Basic Annual Culture

When even minimal conditions for growth are met, annuals are easy to grow and relatively carefree. With adequate sunlight (a half day or more) and water, occasional fertilizing and deadheading, they will bloom unstintingly throughout the growing season. Periodically amending the soil by digging in organic matter like compost, cut-up seaweed, or chicken manure will improve their vigor and extend their flowering. Although many are directly sown in spots where they will bloom, some annuals, such as morning glories and moonflowers, bloom earlier in the season, and more reliably, when started indoors.

One of the easiest methods is to plant the seeds in discarded eggshells. Gently break off the top of the eggshell leaving about two-thirds of the shell intact. Rinse the eggshells in water and dry the outside carefully (or they will stick to the carton). Cut off the top of the carton and store the eggshells in the carton until ready to plant. The eggshell will hold a tablespoon or two of soil. Plant several seeds per eggshell; set the eggshell back in the carton and place under warm lights or a sunny windowsill. Keep the soil evenly moist and cover with a clear plastic bag secured with an elastic band to create a miniature greenhouse environment. As soon as the new seedlings begin to emerge, remove the plastic bag. After the seedlings have developed their second set of true leaves, snip (do not pull out) the weakest seedlings, allowing one plant per eggshell.

After all danger of frost has passed, plant the seedlings, in their eggshells, outdoors in prepared beds that have been enriched with organic matter. The eggshells do not impede root development, quickly decay, and add trace nutrients to the soil. Water thoroughly with fish fertilizer added to the water. Continue to provide supplemental water until the young plants are well established. Annuals, for the most part, are heavy feeders. Continue to fertilize periodically throughout the growing season and water thoroughly when experiencing extended periods of drought.

With the small extra effort of deadheading, annuals will bloom continuously throughout the season and provide one with vases of flowers to fill for months on end.

Happy Accidents!

Alpine strawberry (*Fragaria vesca*)
*Anise hyssop (*Hyssopus officinalis*)
California poppy (*Eschscholzia californica*)
*Calendula, pot-marigold (*Calendula officinalis*)
Chives (*Allium schoenoprasum*)
Cosmos (*Cosmos bipinnatus*)
Feverfew (*Chrysanthemum parthenium*)
Forget-me-not (*Myosotis*)
Foxglove (*Digitalis purpurea*)
Hollyhock (*Alcea rosea, A. rugosa*)
Johnny-jump-up (*Viola*)
Larkspur (*Consolida ambigua*)

Oh Garden of Fresh Possibilities!

Love-in-a-mist (*Nigella damascena*)
Morning glory (*Ipomoea purpurea* 'Crimson Rambler')
Nasturtium (*Tropaeolum majus*)
New England aster (*Aster novae-angliae*)
New York Aster (*Aster novi-belgii*)
Oenothera 'Pink Petticoats' (*Oenothera speciosa*)
Oxeye daisy (*Chrysanthemum leucanthemum*)
Queen Anne's lace (*Daucus carota*)
Shirley poppy (*Papaver rhoeas*)
Simply-love hibiscus (*Hibiscus trionum* 'Flower-of-the-Hour')
Jewelweed (*Impatiens capensis*)
Sweet alyssum (*Lobularia maritima*)
Verbena bonariensis
Viola cornuta 'Bowles Black'
Zinnia (*Zinnia elegans*)

Happy accidents refer to annuals and perennials that have a tendency to reseed. To encourage reseeding in a particular spot, cut spent flowers stalks with ripened seed capsules (generally, fully ripe seed capsules split open). Gently shake the seeds in places where you wish new plants to grow the following year. Be warned that some, like calendula and anise hyssop, are prolific to the point of invasiveness. Anise hyssop can eat your garden!

During the first summer in our garden of new beginnings, a cheery volunteer, the cerise-colored morning glory (*Ipomoea purpurea* 'Crimson Rambler') began to grow. Perhaps by turning and tilling the soil it reestablished itself from a long-forgotten garden or possibly a passing bird dropped a seed. Every summer the morning glory takes a corner of the garden, growing vigorously alongside the porch, weaving its way through the railing and climbing up the pillars. Without the least bit of assistance, this hummingbird magnet of a morning glory grows gloriously. The remnants on our property – of the 'Crimson Rambler,' lemon-scented yellow bearded iris (*Iris germanica* 'Honoribile') and the diminutive black-purple velvet violas – along with the ancient pear trees, connect the former garden of the previous owners to our new garden of fresh possibilities.

ENDNOTES
1. *Dictionary of Plant Names* (Portland, Oregon: Timber Press, Inc., 1994).

CHAPTER THIRTEEN

Fragrant Herbaceous Peonies

A cloud is her dress
  a flower her face
Spring wind through the threshold
  stirs deep peony-dew
If unable to meet on a jade mountain peak
  we'll face at Jasper Terrace beneath the moon

—LI BAI (701–762) *Tang Dynasty Poet*

RECALLING MY MOM'S FONDNESS FOR PEONIES, and the memorable fragrance of her peony borders awash with blossoms of captivating hues, I find myself perusing nurseries and catalogues searching for varieties with irresistible colors and scent. I have a vivid memory of her in the garden with me trailing after while she picked a bouquet of white, rose pink, and red peonies, and then becoming wrapped in her joy as the fat buds were transformed into big blowsy blossoms. Some years later, while living and attending school in Boston, a favorite pastime was to become lost in the maze of Asian rooms at the Museum of Fine Arts. Then as now, the galleries were rich with images of peonies in paintings, ceramics, and textiles.

The poetic Chinese name for the herbaceous peony (*Paeonia lactiflora*) is *shao yao*, meaning "most beautiful" or "charming and beautiful." A peony in full bloom is a symbol of happiness, elegance, wealth, and good fortune. To give a gift of *shao yao* is to offer a gift of friendship.

In flower-bird painting, one of the three main disciplines of Chinese painting, the inherent beauty of the flower is expressed along with the flower's cultural significance. Healing properties might be associated with a certain plant and magic was inextricably linked to the Chinese attitude toward plants and trees. An exceptional blossom or the time of a plants florescence were interpreted as either auspicious of an omen or foretelling disaster. Plants and trees were personified and beatitude conferred to all living things.

[103]

Ten Flower Friends

Lustrous Friend ~ Peony　　　　*Meditative Friend ~ Gardenia*
Sacred Friend ~ Lotus blossom　　*Hermetic Friend ~ Cassia blossom*
Distinguished Friend ~ Crabapple blossom　*Poetic Friend ~ Kerria*
Excellent Friend ~ Chrysanthemum　*Elegant Friend ~ Jasmine*
Pure Friend ~ Plum blossom　　　*Exceptional Friend ~ Daphne*

— From Song Dynasty notes on common themes in paintings and ceramics

There are countless Chinese folk tales and legends related to the herbaceous peony and the tree peony (*Paeonia moutan*). One well-known legend has it that the Empress Wu Zeitan ordered the hundreds of flowers in her palace garden to bloom during one particular night. Every flower obeyed save for the unyielding peony, which chose to follow the natural order. The peony was subsequently banished from the capital and sent to Luoyang. After that, the peony was loved for its "firm and upright" characteristics. The city of Luoyang in Henan Province is host to the modern day annual peony festival. "The peony of Luoyang is the most beautiful under heaven," as the saying goes, and since the Tang Dynasty no city has been able to rival Luoyang in cultivating peonies.

The literal interpretation of *shao yao* is "medicine made from peony"; *shao* refers to the peony plant and *yao* means "medicine." The peony is mentioned in earliest texts as a flavoring for food. The roots of *Paeonia lactiflora* are a medicinal herb used primarily for conditions relating to reproduction, hypertension, chest pain, muscle cramping, and spasms. The root of the *P. lactiflora* is collected in the late summer and early fall, washed well, with the rhizome and rootlets removed and the rough epidermis scraped off. After par-boiling, the root is dried in the sun. The root has a bitter and acrid flavor.

The genus *Paeonia* is named for Paean, the ancient Greek god of healing. Paean, a student of Asclepius, the god of medicine and healing, was instructed by Leto (Apollo's mother and the goddess of fertility) to obtain a magical root growing on Mount Olympus. The root was believed to soothe the pain of women in childbirth. In a jealous rage, Asclepius threatened to kill Paean. Saving him from the wrath of Asclepius, Zeus turned Paean into a peony plant.

Paeonia moutan, *P. lactiflora*, and *P. mlokosewitschii* are the three species that bear scented flowers. *Paeonia lactiflora*, formerly known as *P. albiflora* and *P. chinensis*, is by far the most influential species for fragrance, and is the ancestor of thousands of garden peonies, notably the cultivars with scented blossoms.

P. lactiflora grows from Siberia and Mongolia to northern China and parts of Tibet in steppe grassland and scrub.

Herbaceous Peony Culture

Despite the fact that peonies are available from local nurseries and catalogues for spring planting, one would be ill-advised to purchase a new plant, or divide an established peony, at any time of year other than late summer or early fall. The Chinese traditionally plant herbaceous peonies on the 15th day of the seventh lunar month – mid-August – and tree peonies on the 15th day of the eighth lunar month – mid-September.

When purchasing a peony, request a division with a strong set of growth points or eyes (the magenta-colored swellings growing along the tuberous roots). A clump with only three eyes is barely adequate; four to five are preferable. Spring is absolutely the worst time of year to disturb the root system of the plant, and spring-planted and/or undersized peonies may take years to bloom.

I suggest visiting friends' gardens, peony gardens, and nurseries during the blooming period of peonies, from May to June, resisting the temptation to purchase impulsively. Make a note of what you like, and don't forget to smell the different varieties. Look at books, catalogues, and photos, and plan where to plant and what arrangement of color would be best suited to your garden. Order the plants for fall delivery. The very best nurseries that specialize in peonies prefer to (and some will only) ship the plants in late August and early autumn.

Well-planted peonies will survive in a garden after years and years of neglect. They are a good indicator plant if one acquires an older property and some sleuthing will discover where a garden previously existed. Herbaceous peonies are very long lived; plant them properly from the outset.

Peonies will tolerate neither cramped quarters nor wet feet. Select a site where the plant will receive excellent air circulation. Dig a hole roughly 24″ across and 18″ deep. Fill the hole with water. If the water does not drain fairly quickly, successful culture is questionable. Add to the hole a shovelful of organic matter (preferably compost) and mix with the soil dug from the hole. The process of setting the plant requires alternately adding and filling the soil and testing the depth of the plant. When in doubt, lay a stick across the opening of the hole to better judge the soil line. The very tiptops of the pink eyes must be planted between one to two inches below the soil line. Firm and water the soil around the buds while filling the hole; otherwise the soil will settle and pull the plant down. Peonies will not flower if the tip of the eye is buried more than two inches below the soil line. Water thoroughly. Adding fish emulsion to the water will encourage the development of feeder roots.

Peonies have a reputation for being fussy, which is emphatically not true. Peonies thrive in a garden planted for more leisure and less work. They will grow in full sun to partial shade in average garden soil, and they will reward the gardener with even greater vigor and more blossoms if they are given a top dressing of compost in the fall. To prevent diseases and pests from overwintering, cut off the stalks of the foliage two inches above the base, after the first hard frost, and discard the leaf litter.

Inevitably you will find the peonies become hosts to ants harmlessly scurrying about. In exchange for sweet nectar the ants are guarding the peonies from bud-eating pests.

The peonies listed below were selected for their form and notable fragrance. Sometimes growers will describe a plant as fragrant, 'Shirley Temple,' for example. I find her only moderately so, however scent is mutable and the strength of the fragrance may vary according to soil conditions. The list is arranged by degree of color intensity, in shades of the palest ivory white to rose pink to deepest crimson.

'Kelway's Glorious' ~ 1909, perfectly formed glistening white flowers with a warm cream center. Hybrid tea rose scent, freely flowering.

'Duchesse de Nemours' ~ 1856, petite flowers, ivory white with yellow shading toward the center, richly fragrant and free flowering, very extended period of florescence. The buds open several at a time, rather than rushing out all at once.

'Festiva Maxima' ~ 1851, creamy white, double, with an occasional inner petal edged in crimson, and a fresh sweet scent.

'Edith Cavell' ~ 1916, creamy-yellow blooms, richly scented.

'Shirley Temple' ~ origin unknown, blush fading to white, light fragrance.

Fragrant Herbaceous Peonies

'Madame Calot' ~ 1856, pale pink-tinted blooms and heavily scented.

'Sarah Bernhardt' ~ 1906, seashell and apple-blossom pink, sweet fragrance, free flowering.

'Roselette' ~ 1950, warm blush-pink crinkly petals framing yellow stamens, single form, the earliest peony to bloom in our garden, with a mild lemon-rose scent. Flowers look their best planted in light shade, as they fade in the hot sun.

'Edulis Superba' ~ 1824, old rose pink, good fragrance, free flowering.

'Attar of Roses' ~ 1951, semi-double, vibrant pink, rose fragrance.

'Bouchella' ~ deep rose pink, fragrant.

'Irwin Altman' ~ 1940, clear light red, wonderfully fragrant.

'Mt. St. Helens' ~ 1981, deep quinachrodine magenta and fragrant.

'Philippe Rivoire' ~ 1911, crimson-black with a tea-rose perfume.

Peonies are the beauty queens of the early summer garden. The foliage is lush and attractive from early spring through early fall. Whether one is dreaming of borders bursting, vases overflowing or a single blossom floating in a shallow bowl, their sensuous fragrance permeates the rooms of the home and garden.

An established herbaceous peony is easily divided in late summer and early fall. Gently dig around the perimeter and unearth the entire clump. Wash the roots and rhizomes. Divide the roots into generous sections with four to five eyes. By dividing a peony and passing it along to friend one is following in the Chinese tradition of giving a gift of *shao yao*.

Oh Garden of Fresh Possibilities!

Duchesse de Nemours

Festiva Maxima

Sarah Bernhardt

Edulis Superba

Attar of Roses

Bouchella

Irwin Altman

Mt. St. Helens

CHAPTER FOURTEEN

Roses for the Intimate Garden

ONE PERFECT ROSE

A single flower he sent me, since we met.
All tenderly his messenger he chose;
Deep-hearted, pure, with scented dew
    still wet—
One perfect rose.

I knew the language of the floweret;
"My fragile leaves," it said, "his heart enclose."
Love long has taken for his amulet
One perfect rose.

Why is it no one ever sent me yet
One perfect limousine, do you suppose?
Ah no, it's always just my luck to get
One perfect rose.

           —DOROTHY PARKER (1893–1967)

FOR THOSE WHO ARE NEW TO GARDENING, and for more experienced gardeners, deciding which roses to grow and how to care for them can be daunting. There are thousands of heirloom roses from which to choose, along with an ever-growing number of new hybrids. Pest management is an issue, along with diseases to avoid. Different types of roses require different methods of pruning. Roses demand steady maintenance for their good looks and good health. Yet, despite these challenges, anyone can become a successful rosarian armed with knowledge, patience, and perseverance.

From the earliest stages of planning our garden, decisions were made simpler by using one specific criterion from which I have not deviated. First and foremost, a rose should be fragrant, *very* fragrant, intoxicatingly so. None of those scentless whatevers in my garden, no thank you! What is the point of growing a rose lacking fragrance? How utterly disappointing to put one's nose to a rose and come away with not a hint of perfume!

After first taking into consideration a rose's fragrance, the next priority is to determine if the form of the flower and the overall shape and size of the plant are appropriate for their planned location. Large flowered climbing roses and ramblers ('New Dawn' and 'Aloha,' for example) planted in the background of the mixed border become part the framework of the overall garden design. When mid-sized Bourbon and Alba roses such as 'Louise Odier' and 'Konigin von Danemark' are interplanted with fragrant perennials and small shrubs, their fragrances mingle, creating vibrant associations. Imagine the June garden redolent with honeysuckle, mock orange, and lavender fused with the scent of the rose! Roses that are the most highly scented are generally in the white to pale pink to mid-pink hues (there are exceptions – 'Fragrant Cloud,' for example); therefore, within the borders, the flowering plants surrounding the roses are in complementary shades of the blue to purple color family, white, clear orange, apricot, lemon, and creamy yellows.

Particularly lovely for a small garden are the single flower form of species roses, *Rosa virginiana*, 'Sweet Briar' rose (*Rosa eglanteria*), and rugosa roses. One might assume that beach roses (*R. rugosa*) are native to America, as they have naturalized and are seen growing prolifically along seacoasts. *Rosa rugosa* was introduced from China to New England in 1845. Rugosa orchards thrived in coastal communities. The edible fruits are too seedy for modern palettes accustomed to seedless varieties. "Sea tomatoes" are rich in Vitamin C and the seeds contain Vitamin E. Hybrids with rugosa parentage, 'Sir Thomas Lipton' and 'Thérèse Bugnet,' for example, make beautiful specimens in the border all year round with their gracefully arching stems. Both are extremely hardy with a repeat blooming habit, sweetly fragrant, and 'Thérèse Bugnet' has deep red-rose canes for winter beauty.

Inspired by the voluptuous look of the old roses rendered by eighteenth- and nineteenth-century artists (painters such as Jan van Huysum, Redouté, and Henri Fantin-Latour come to mind), during the early stages of planning our garden we decided to focus on growing a selection of old roses, the damask, rambler, Alba, and Bourbon roses, as well as the more recent introductions from France, the Romantica series. We sought roses that are repeat bloomers, although I sacrificed this criterion if the rose was sublimely fragrant or had some very interesting characteristic as in 'Albéric Barbier,' a once-blooming rambler with canes scrambling tens of feet and the ability to grow through the branches of trees. And occasionally one just sees and smells a rose growing in a friend's garden, falls passionately in love, and simply must have it.

The following is a list of roses presently growing in our garden along with roses we have tried to grow. The list is composed primarily of successes with failures noted. Grown on their own roots, the roses listed below are hardy through at least zone five, with the exceptions of 'Madame Alfred Carrière' and 'Albéric Barbier.' 'Madame Alfred Carrière' is hardy through zone six (possibly hardier although I have not tested her below zone six), and 'Albéric Barbier' is only reliably hardy through zone seven.

'Virginia Rose' ~ *Rosa virginiana* ~ Species rose native to eastern North America. Pale pink single flowers, deliciously fragrant, blooms throughout the summer. Fruit are a food plant for songbirds; leaves are a host plant for butterflies and moths. Five to six feet.

'Sweet Briar Rose' ~ 1551 ~ *Rosa eglanteria* ~ Medium pink single flowers, arching canes. The foliage is richly fragrant of green apples! Plant near a pathway where you may brush against the foliage to release its delightful perfume. Once-blooming. Five to six feet.

'Amelia' ~ 1823 ~ Alba ~ Graceful, arching canes with beautiful, clear pink shaded to paler pink flowers and pronounced yellow stamens. Sublimely fragrant rose. Once blooming. Six feet.

'Konigin von Danemark' (Queen of Denmark) ~ 1826 ~ Alba ~ Divine fragrance, fully quartered, rose pink perfection. Once-blooming. Six feet.

'Louise Odier ~ 1851 ~ Bourbon ~ Delicate china pink, camellia-style flowers, enchanting and intensely fragrant. Blooms lavishly throughout the season, from early June to November, with a brief rest after the first flush of June flowers. Grows four to five feet.

'Souvenir du Docteur Jamian' ~ 1853 ~ French Hybrid Perpetual ~ Rich, velvety cerise color, wonderfully fragrant. Some repeat blooms. Grown in our garden as a small, seven-foot climber.

'Zéphirine Drouhin' ~ 1868 ~ Bourbon ~ Clear hot pink. Thornless. The sensuous Bourbon fragrance is there, only not as intense relative to some others noted here. Repeat blooms. Twelve feet.

'Madame Alfred Carrière' ~ 1879 ~ Tea-Noisette ~ Ivory white petals washed with pearl pink. Heavenly tea rose scent. Part-shade tolerant. Blooms continually. Twelve- to sixteen-foot climber.

'Madame Isaac Pereire' ~ 1881 ~ Bourbon ~ Deep raspberry-magenta. Considered to be one of the most fragrant roses. Six to seven feet. Note: We no longer grow Madame Isaac Pereire as its buds usually turned into brown, blobby globs that rarely fully opened due to damp sea air.

'Souvenir de Victor Landeau' ~ 1890 ~ Bourbon ~ Deep rose pink, richly fragrant and consistently in bloom through October and into November. Pairs beautifully with Louise Odier. Four to five feet.

'Albéric Barbier' ~ 1900 ~ Rambler ~ Pale yellow buds opening to small double, creamy white flowers. Dark green foliage, easily grown into trees. Only moderately fragrant. Once-blooming. Twenty feet or more.

'Sir Thomas Lipton' ~ 1900 ~ Rugosa Hybrid ~ Diminutive, recurring semi-double white blossoms with that unmistakable rugosa fragrance. Part-shade tolerant, hardy and vigorous. Seven feet.

'Darlow's Enigma' ~ Early 1900s ~ Hybrid Musk ~ Clusters of one-inch, single, pure white blossoms that open flat with golden centers. Sweet, far-traveling scent. Shade tolerant. Constantly blooming well into the fall, producing hips while blooming. Eight to twelve foot rambler.

'Variegata di Bologna' ~ 1909 ~ Bourbon ~ Creamy pale pink with rose-red striations. Suffused with the heady Bourbon fragrance. The foliage becomes tattered-looking later in the season. Slight repeat bloom, although it initially flowers for an extended period of time, four to six weeks in all. Tall growing, best supported against a pillar.

'Souvenir de Saint Anne's' ~ 1916 ~ Bourbon ~ Ivory flushed with warm pink and cream single to semi-double blossoms. Sensuous Bourbon fragrance. Compact growing, ideal for the garden room. Continually blooming. Two feet. Note: 'Souvenir de St. Anne' is a sport of 'Souvenir de la Malmaison' (1843), with the similar lovely colorway. The unopened buds and blooms of 'Malmaison' have the tendency to be ruined in damp air, whereas 'St. Anne's' do not.

'New Dawn' ~ 1930 ~ Rambler ~ Blooms in shades of pale seashell pink. Sweet, fruity fragrance. Very vigorous. Anyone can grow it, blooms all summer. Large flowered climber to fifteen feet.

'Aloha' ~ 1949 ~ Climbing Hybrid Tea ~ Opening from cerise buds, carmine petals with light coral on the reverse, Constantly in bloom, insinuating and delicious scent. Parent of many of the David Austin roses. Ten feet, pillar type.

'Thérèse Bugnet' ~ 1950 ~ Rugosa Hybrid ~ Masses of rose to lilac-pink-hued ruffled flowers. The flowers look like that of a damask rose. Richly fragrant. Magenta canes for winter interest. The earliest rose to flower in our garden, then intermittently during the summer. Six feet.

'White Dawn' ~ 1959 ~ Rambler ~ Creamy white seedling of New Dawn. Mild, sweet fragrance, blooms all summer. Not bothered by pests or diseases. Twelve to fifteen feet.

'Fragrant Cloud' ~ 1967 ~ Hybrid Tea ~ Vivid, vibrating vermilion. Fabulous spicy-sweet scent. Continuously blooming. Pairs well with Frederick Mistral. Four to five feet.

'Angel Face,' Climbing ~ 1981 ~ Climbing Floribunda ~ Semi-double ruffley blooms in a silvered lavender-rose color. Large flowered climber blooms continuously all summer, with rich green foliage. Citrus to damask rose scent. Twelve feet.

'Eden,' Climbing ~ 1992 ~ Romantica Series ~ The look of 'Souvenir de la Malmaison,' with creamy ivory petals blushed pink at the outer margins. Although

'Eden' is comparatively less fragrant, the blossoms are not as disfigured by damp weather as 'Malmaison.' Ideal climber for a small garden. Eight to ten feet.

'Frederick Mistral' ~ 1993 ~ Romantica Series ~ Clear, fresh pink, perfectly formed flowers. Spicy and sweet, intensely fragrant. Ever blooming through October. Four to five feet.

'Polka' ~ 1997 ~ Romantica Series ~ Apricot shaded blossoms with a spicy scent. Fair repeat bloom. Eight to ten feet.

Rosa bourboniana

The Bourbons comprise one of the most extravagantly scented class of roses, along with having a wide range of growth habit in form and height. From the shrubby and compact 'Souvenir de la Malmaison,' growing to about two feet, to the thornless climbing 'Zephirine Drouhin,' there is a suitable Bourbon rose available to fill nearly every conceivable desired effect in the landscape.

Named for the island of Reunion, formerly called Isle de Bourbon, *R. bourboniana* is a natural crossing of the China rose (repeat blooming) with the

Autumn Damask rose. Reunion belongs to the archipelago of Mascareignes in the Indian Ocean and lies east of Madagascar. Originally discovered by the Portuguese, then colonized by the French in the seventeenth-century, Reunion had a diverse population of settlers from around Africa, Asia, and southern Europe. The Bourbon rose was discovered growing wild in Reunion in approximately 1817.

Hybridized Bourbon roses flower in hues of white to china pink to cerise and purple. The flowers are quartered at the center and filled with overlapping petals. With their tolerance for cold temperatures, sublime fragrance, and freedom of flowering ('Louise Odier' remains in bloom from June until the first frost), Bourbons are amongst the most distinctive of all roses. Bourbon roses require minimal pruning. In early March, and again after the first flush of flowers, remove weak and twiggy growth and apply a three- to four-inch layer of compost to the drip-line to help control black spot.

Rose Culture

Roses need excellent air circulation and plenty of sunshine; a minimum of six hours daily is ideal. In our garden, where shade prevails, we are constantly experimenting with trying to coax roses to bloom where they are planted in less than perfect light conditions. Several roses have a much greater tolerance for a partially shaded site, 'Madame Alfred Carrière' and 'Darlow's Enigma,' for example, although roses will always give more flowers when planted where they receive more sunlight.

Large flowered climbing roses are preferably grown in the back of a mixed flower border, intermingled with shrubs, herbaceous perennials, annuals, and herbs. To invoke a sense of summer splendor, plant a fragrant rambling rose and honeysuckle against a fence or pillar, surround the climbers with mock orange, Oriental and species lilies, peacock orchids, and lavender. Herbaceous peonies, with their neat and attractive foliage, make an ideal companion to grow at the feet of a pillar rose. This is a more appealing arrangement for the small garden, rather than the typically seen formal-looking rose garden planted singularly with roses lined up neat as sentinels. And practically speaking, roses are bothered by fewer pest and diseases when planted in a mixed border, as opposed to a monoculture arrangement.

Early on in my life as a new gardener, with my enthusiasm to give whatever we were planting its best new beginning, I was constantly adding unnecessary and fussy amendments to the soil. I am somewhat reluctant to repeat this story as the reader may think one would need to repeat this every time a rose is planted, which is not true.

While walking in the woods near our old home, I came upon the remnants of an abandoned garden. Growing willy-nilly here and there amongst jumbles of briars were divinely scented roses redolent of an old rose garden. The ruffled rose-pink blossoms, with open centers of golden yellow stamens, flowered along the length of the tall, arching canes. Each June thereafter I would look for this fabulously fragrant rose. A single cut flower would envelop a room with its heady scent. As we were readying ourselves to move to our new home, I was afraid I would never again either see or smell my beautiful mystery rose.

The day before we moved, I set off into the woods with shovel and gloves to collect several of the canes. The canes were far more deeply rooted than anticipated, but I forged ahead. After one last vigorous tug and landing hard on a painfully prickly bramble, I finally had a cane with an acceptable chunk of roots!

We kept the roots moist, and as soon as possible planted the cane alongside the porch of our new home. Lollygagging along for weeks, the lifeless-looking cane looked pitiful. Terribly disappointed and thinking it was a lost cause, we decided to plant near it a 'Rosie O'Grady' clematis. With its silky and ornamental seed heads, I had fallen for this *Clematis macropetala* weaving through a trellis at a friend's antique shop. We left the rose cane in the ground and dug a large hole next to it, approximately twenty-four inches wide and eighteen inches deep (as you should for clematis, peonies, and long-lived perennials). To the hole we added the following amendments, mixed with dirt dug from the hole: several shovelfuls of compost, peat, and well-rotted manure, a handful each of 5-10-10 fertilizer, lime, and super phosphate, all mixed well.

Later that summer our mystery rose sprouted new shoots and the canes grew six feet. The following June our rambling rose was covered with sublimely fragrant blossoms. Presently it is simply growing fantastically; vigorous, floriferous with several canes attaining the unbelievable feat of climbing beyond our second story bedroom window. The canes seem a bit longer each time I look, clearly headed toward the third floor. The success of the rose has more to do with the obvious vigor of the cultivar than the clematis formula. There are far more reliable, and less strenuous, methods of rescuing and propagating old roses.

HOW TO PROPAGATE A ROSE

The ideal time to root (propagate) a rose cutting is late summer to mid-fall. Choose cuttings from the parent plant that are roughly ¼″ to ⅜″ in diameter, approximately 6–8″ in length, and are still green. Gently snip off the foliage and any spent flowers. Cut at an angle just above a bud at the top and straight across below a bottom bud. Dip the cutting in water, then in hormone powder. Shake the excess powder back into the container. Plant the cutting several inches in depth in a six-inch-deep pot prepared with a soilless mixture of half peat and half sand. Firm the soil and water thoroughly with water enriched with Neptune's Harvest fish fertilizer. Fish emulsion is recommended for virtually every plant, and particularly new plantings, as it aids in the development of feeder roots. Cover the pot with a clear plastic bag secured in place with an elastic band. Place the potted cuttings on a sunny windowsill. Check periodically and water, very gently, when the soil is dry to the touch.

When the cutting has taken root, one will see new growth within a few weeks. Remove the plastic bag as soon as the new growth is visible. Continue to grow the plant in a sunny and not too drafty spot throughout the winter. Allow the soil to dry slightly between watering. By late May or early June one will have two choices: to replant in a larger pot and continue to grow for another year, or to plant the rooted cutting directly out in the garden. The cutting is very fragile at this stage and prone to quickly drying out. Water frequently during the first growing season. Place a protective barrier around the tender cutting to bring your attention to its place in the garden. The rose is so small initially, you will need to protect it from stray balls, thoughtless cats, and your own clumsiness.

When planting a bare-root rose, dig a large hole and add a shovelful or two of compost mixed well with the existing soil. With soil dug from the hole, create a cone shape in the center of the hole. Place the rose plant in the center of the hole and spread the roots downward around the cone. Pack the soil firmly around the roots to prevent pockets of air. To help maintain adequate moisture for trees, shrubs, large perennials, and in particular roses, use additional soil to create a ridge two to three inches high around the diameter of the stalk. During the early stages of growth the moat helps to collect and contain water. Eventually the burr will wash away and by then the rose will be well established. Water the newly planted rose with fish fertilizer mixed to the specifications on the container. Cover with several inches of compost to retain moisture and provide additional nutrients. Roses appreciate plenty of water, and no more so than in their first growing season. Water several times weekly, at least an inch or more. A well-watered and fertilized rose is vigorous and less prone to disease. When watering roses, direct the hose to the base of the plant, to avoid wetting the foliage as much as possible.

The typical rose plant from your garden center is grafted – a cutting of a desired rose that has been adhered to a rootstock of a generally hardier species. Grafted rose plants need special care in planting because the union of the graft is susceptible to damage by extremely cold weather. Plant the grafted union several inches above the soil line. Otherwise, if the union is covered with soil, the new growth will be that of the rootstock, rather than the desired rose.

Fortunately, many varieties of heirloom roses grown on their own roots are available for purchase. Own-root roses are simply this: a cutting from any cultivar that has been rooted – that is, grown on its own set of roots. The benefits of planting roses grown in this manner are significant. Own-root roses are less prone to disease and are more vigorous. I am more convinced than ever of the advantages of growing these non-grafted varieties after observing the extensive damage caused by the extremely frigid winters of recent memory. All our roses grown on their own roots have survived the brutally cold winters with flying colors. The one own-root rose that suffered winter kill and died to the ground recovered dramatically and grew four feet in a single growing season. This is quite a different story from the sad tale of cherished roses lost by fellow gardeners. Our grandmothers grew roses from rooted cuttings, and European nurseries typically offer own-root roses.

The vast majority of roses have the potential to be plagued by several per-

vasive problems – black spot, aphids, and Japanese beetles. Old roses growing in coastal regions are especially susceptible to black spot, a soil and airborn fungus that generally begins at the base of the plant. Left unchecked, it will eventually cover the entire plant, creating ugly black areas on the foliage, causing the leaves to turn yellow and drop off. This virus does not damage the plant, but it looks unsightly. Clean up and discard (into the trash, not the compost pile) all leaves that are infected. The problem is only perpetuated if the diseased leaves are allowed to remain on the ground and begin to decompose.

To help prevent and control black spot spread a generous amount (four inches deep) of compost from the base of the rose extending to the drip-line, in early spring. Unlike aphids, I do not find black spot irritating. If you do, then I suggest spraying susceptible varieties, every three to four days, with the following recipe from the Brooklyn Botanical Gardens: Mix one tablespoon of baking soda with one gallon of water. Add to this a few drops of insecticidal soap.

Aphids are soft-bodied, gnat-sized insects in a range of colors, bright green, reddish brown, orange, yellow, and black. They form colonies on the tender new growth tips of roses, and even worse, will suck all the moisture out of every flower bud. Vigilance is key. Simple and organic methods for controlling aphids include spraying the infested area vigorously with a garden hose set on a jet stream directed onto the infested new growth (preferably in the very early morning to allow the foliage to dry) and then repeating this routine for a total of three days; snipping the infested tips and discarding them into the trash; or introducing beneficial insects such as ladybugs and praying mantises. Ladybugs and praying mantises will stay if there is a continual supply of food. If spraying with a garden hose proves to be ineffective, or you do not want to wet the foliage for three days during a particularly damp season, try a mixture of one tablespoon (begin with a tablespoon or two, gradually increasing the dose as needed) of Dr. Bonner's peppermint soap to one gallon of water. Spray liberally; this will suffocate the pesky creatures.

For the past several years we have done nothing at the onset of an aphid invasion. The welcome green lacewings have decided to call our garden home. The larvae of the green lacewing efficiently eradicate the aphids as confirmed by the tiny white aphid carcasses dotted about tender new growth and buds. Their nickname, aphid lion, gives an indication of the role the lacewings play in the rhythm of the garden.

Japanese beetles are beautiful insects, with hard-bodied, iridescent shells, and if they weren't so terribly destructive, they might actually be considered appealing. The damage caused by Japanese beetles is easy to identify. They start at the top and work their way down, leaving skeletonized foliage and mangled flowers. Removing Japanese beetles by hand is your best method of control. The presence of one beetle on a rose bush attracts more beetles. Their shiny light-refracting shell is a beacon. With daily monitoring, far fewer beetles are attracted to the plant compared to those on which the beetles are allowed to remain. Some gardeners have on hand a pail or jar of soapy water and shake the beetles loose into the container. This method is most effective done early in the morning, when the air temperature is cool and the beetles are sluggish. Frankly, I don't bother carrying a bucket around the garden in which to drown the pests. With only a tinge of regret, I derive a certain satisfaction in squishing them.

Pruning is necessary to maintain the overall desired shape of the rose plant, to increase its number of blossoms, and to keep pests and diseases at bay. While becoming established, climbers and ramblers should not be pruned, to encourage vertical growth. When it does become necessary to prune a rose plant, cut off to the base old, dark brown woody canes that are no longer flowering. Canes crossing over other canes can be removed for a neater appearance. Weak and twiggy growth and blackened tips from winter damage should also be removed.

There are essentially two ways in which roses bloom and therefore two different methods of pruning, each suited for the different type of growth.

1) Roses that bloom once a year (Alba, for example) should be pruned just after the plant is finished blooming for the season.

2) Roses that bloom repeatedly throughout the summer (this includes Rugosa hybrids, Romanticas, and Bourbons) should be pruned just after the first flush of flowering. Repeat bloomers also benefit from diligent deadheading and an occasional neatening during their extended period of florescence, by removing tattered foliage and twiggy growth.

When unsure how far to cut back a cane, prune by degrees. Look for sturdy green wood and remove dry, brown woody material. Cut just above an outward facing bud, angling the cut to slant away from the center of the plant.

I find a large rose bush pruned to a fountain shape to be visually appealing and practical in the mixed border, allowing smaller plants to grow around the base. Let the canes grow tall and, for the most part, they will naturally arch over. Remove the oldest, nonflowering canes, pruning to the ground, to encourage new shoots to develop. Cultivars with which it is possible to achieve this effect are Rugosa hybrids, 'Therese Bugnet' and 'Sir Thomas Lipton,' and Bourbon roses, 'Louise Odier' and 'Souvenir de Victor Landeau.'

The ripe fruit of the different rose species extends our interest into the fall.

Oh Garden of Fresh Possibilities!

There are the voluptuously plump hips of the rugosas, and, just as prolifically as 'New Dawn' flowers, it arrives dressed for autumn spangled in shiny fat fruits. Sweetbriar rose (*R. eglanteria*) adorns the garden picture with glossy orange, ovoid fruit, and 'Darlow's Enigma' bears masses of wild blueberry-sized hips, nourishing and much appreciated by the songbirds. Leave the spent flowers on the once-blooming roses to encourage the development of the hips. Avoid dead-heading the last of the season's flowers on the repeat blooming roses for the same reason.

For all of the challenges they present, the gifts of fragrance and the beauty of their blossoms make it seem as though roses are hardly any bother. Like children, they require nurturing and tender care. And like children, their beauty returns your care with joy and spirit renewed.

> *A sepal, a petal, and a thorn*
> *Upon a common summer's morn—*
> *A flash of Dew—A Bee or two—*
> *A Breeze—*
> *A caper in the trees—*
> *And I'm a Rose!*

—EMILY DICKINSON

CHAPTER FIFTEEN

Flowers of the Air

TWO VOYAGERS

Two butterflies went out at noon
And waltzed above a stream,
Then stepped straight through the firmament
And rested on a beam;

And then together bore away
Upon a shining sea,—
Though never yet, in any port,
Their coming mentioned be.

If spoken by the distant bird,
If met in ether sea
By frigate or by merchantman,
Report was not to me.

— EMILY DICKINSON

LIKE DREAMY FLOATING FLOWERS, BUTTERFLIES entering our gardens invite one to pause and take note. We gaze up to see where our sojourner is headed, what has tempted the intrepid traveler, and how we can make their venture to our garden worthwhile. Butterflies bring to our garden the dimensions of transient movement and beauty evanescing.

Planted with an intermingling of colorful and scented flowers, a butterfly garden is a joy to create and a delight to view. Lepidoptera flock to the garden planted with native and ornamental flowering trees, shrubs, vines, and drifts of perennials and annuals. The nectar-rich flowers preferred by butterflies, skippers, and moths are often fragrant and make the best cut flowers for an informal summer bouquet. Plant a tapestry of flowers to create an inviting habitat and mingle the attractants with garden stalwarts such as roses, poppies, and Oriental lilies that are generally of no interest to butterflies.

Butterflies prefer to nectar at flowers planted in the sunny and sheltered locations of the garden, although in our garden they are lured to the dappled shady backyard, where shade-tolerant nectar-rich flowers and larval food are provided. Planted there are species violets, 'Empress of India' nasturtiums, Queen Anne's lace, butterfly bushes, New England asters, *Verbena bonariensis*, white clover, summersweet, bee-balm, turtlehead, sweetbay magnolia, honeysuckle, Dutchman's pipevine, blueberry bushes, New Jersey tea, and spicebush.

Included in the appendix is a list of large and small trees, shrubs, perennials, and annuals favored by butterflies specific to our region. The "Favorite Flowers for Butterflies" list is arranged to extend the butterfly season as long as possible by planting a broad selection of nectar plants that flower from early spring through the autumn months. I don't mean to confuse my reader by suggesting that the individual flowers listed in "favorite flowers" will bloom from spring to autumn; the list is arranged sequentially and with much overlapping. Designing with a combination of indigenous and nonnative species provides sustenance throughout the butterfly season. In our coastal New England garden, round and about the first of April is when the earliest butterflies begin to appear. By November's end, we are nearing the close of butterfly days with a lingering farewell from Sulphurs, Painted Ladies, straggling Monarchs, and Red Admirals.

Nectar plants attract transient butterflies. To encourage butterflies to remain and colonize one's garden, native larval host plants must be planted as well. Whether one observes a butterfly in the neighborhood or turns to a guidebook for recommendations of butterflies specific to your region, by planting the correct food plants for the caterpillars, the butterfly is drawn to the garden and its population increased. The idea is to *attract* the butterflies and *sustain* their caterpillars. Although caterpillars feed on the plant's foliage, the damage is usually minimal and temporary.

Chemical pesticides used to control unwanted insects are extremely harmful and often deadly to Lepidoptera, bees, toads, and songbirds. Chemical pesticides have no place in a garden designed to invite pollinators. The damage done by the vast majority of pesky insects is kept to a minimum through the use of organic deterrents and by encouraging and supporting beneficial insects.

Butterfly eggs and caterpillars come in a variety of colors and shapes. Lepidoptera guidebooks that include illustrations of eggs and caterpillars are particularly handy for identifying the larvae unique to each butterfly. The Great Spangled Fritillary is an excellent example of the importance of learning about the life cycle of Lepidoptera that frequent our gardens. The female Great Spangled Fritillary lays her eggs in late summer at the base of species violet plants. The tiny caterpillars, black with black-tipped orange spines, hatch soon after and hibernate in and around the violet plants. They are nocturnal and difficult to see. In early spring, the waking caterpillars feed on the leaves of the violets. Coinciding with the summer solstice, the male Great Spangled Fritillary completes the cycle and emerges as an adult, the female, several weeks later. Consequently, one wouldn't want to tidy up leaves around or under violet plants until the middle of July. Butterfly eggs we have observed in our garden look like miniature luminous pearls, and domes, no larger than the head of a straight pin. The eggs are often arrayed singly or in clusters on the undersides of leaves. Prior to taking pruning sheers in hand, carefully investigate host plants for eggs, caterpillars, chrysalis, and hibernating adults.

When feeding from flower to flower, butterflies prefer clusters and drifts of the same species. It takes time for a perennial garden to become established. Eventually healthy perennials fill out and form good-sized clumps. There is an old saying about perennials that goes something like this: The first year they sleep, the second year they creep and the third year they leap. You will have a wide range of species visiting your garden from early spring to autumn planting a combination of annuals and perennials, both larval host plants and nectar-rich flowers.

Butterflies prefer flowers planted in warm, sunny, and sheltered areas protected from wind. Lepidoptera wings do not work very well until the air temperature has warmed. They are the most active from mid-morning through mid-afternoon, although we observe Monarchs nectaring at dawn and Summer Azures at dusk. Flowers in the Composite family (think of New England asters, ox-eye daisies, pearly everlasting, and Mexican sunflowers) offer butterflies their ray flowers as a landing pad while they are drinking nectar from the disk florets. Butterflies taste with their proboscis (drinking tube) and *feet*, called tarsi. If, after landing, they determine the flower tastes good, they unroll their proboscis and probe each floret for a drink of nectar. Butterflies like to light into puddles after a soaking rain or thorough watering. They will drink the water in the mud puddles. Because butterflies cannot eat solid food, the soil they ingest from the puddles provides salt and needed trace nutrients.

Butterflies and moths are attracted to flowers by sight and scent. The most strongly scented flowers are usually those that are fertilized by Lepidoptera. For the most part, flowers pollinated by night flying moths are found growing in their native habitat in either calm, humid, tropical conditions, low lying woodlands, or wooded valleys sheltered from cold winds. Many of the evanescent blossoms with nocturnal perfumes only open for an evening and change color after fertilization, a signal to the Lepidoptera to look elsewhere for nectar. Japanese honeysuckle (*Lonicera japonica*) initially blooms in pure white, quickly fading after pollinization to buttery golden yellow.

Flowers, where the nectar is secreted at the base of long tubes, are heavily scented to attract long-tongued Lepidoptera, which are drawn by scent, rather than sight. Survival of plant and insect are interrelated. Where blossom color and flower scents are given by nature for the plant's pollinization, they are of equal importance for the survival of the fertilizers.

The butterfly is known as "flower of the air" not only because of its beauty, but also because of its fragrance. Scent varies in different species of butterflies, some smell like flowers of the Leguminosae (Legume family) some like jasmine, but usually they carry the fragrance of honey. Some Lepidoptera only pollinate blossoms emitting a scent similar to that carried by themselves, confining fertilization mostly to honey-scented flowers such as buddleia and honeysuckle. The scent glands of butterflies, from where the oil is secreted, are at the base of the hair-like scales that are folded along the inner edge of the wings

Nectar flowers and water are not the only source of sustenance for butterflies. Some probe the moisture from rotting fruit and dung. During an *al fresco* Sunday brunch we were captivated with a visit from the Camberwell Beauty (Mourning Cloak), alighting on the dining table and fearlessly joining our party. He sipped the blackberry-peach compote warming in the sun and then flew above us to investigate the ripening pears. Striking in its wing patterning, the Camberwell Beauty is a silky chocolate brown, with creamy ivory beading dotted with brilliant lapis lazuli blue outlining the wing margins. The following week we spotted a second Camberwell Beauty flitting about the wild flowers along the shoreline. Although the adult Camberwell Beauty will visit meadow flowers, it prefers the more mundane pleasures of rotting fruit and dung.

During a mid-spring excursion to a local meadow we observed Cabbage Whites, the European import. Considered a pest by some, I still look forward to its arrival each spring as it is among the earliest butterflies to appear. There were countless sightings of Painted Ladies, commonly known as the Thistle butterfly for the caterpillars' food preference. The Painted Lady is the most widely distributed butterfly the world over. Approaching the sweetly scented flowering apple trees we were dazzled by the sight of a dozen or more celestial blue Spring Azures fluttering about. Coined "a violet afloat" by the early American naturalist Samuel H. Scudder, the Spring Azure is another of the early spring arrivals. The tiny, pink caterpillar is often seen nestled in the center of the flower bracts of native dogwood (*Cornus florida*) and nasturtium flowers.

The combination of the delicately colored white blossoms blushed pink with the gossamer blue of the Spring Azures was inspiringly beautiful. I cut a branch and took it home to work on a painting and began to imagine how I could fit an apple tree, or two, into our very small garden. Though I had been heartsick about losing a treasured flowering almond tree, a victim of successive, brutally cold winters, we now had the opportunity to replace it with a mini-dwarf apple tree. The apple and crab apple trees in our neighborhood are less affected by harsh winter conditions when compared to other members of Rosaceae, flowering almonds and roses, for example.

An apple tree grafted to a mini-dwarf rootstock grows four to six feet, compared with a dwarf rootstock, which produces a tree that grows eight to fourteen feet. The mini-dwarf apple trees are high yielding and compact, making them ideally suited for the small garden. Once the mini-dwarf tree begins to bear heavily, it will stop growing. As hard as it may be to follow this suggestion, it is best for the future health and vigor of a newly planted whip to remove any fruit growing for the first two years. Mini-dwarf apple trees should be permanently staked. They require well-draining, fertile, and slightly acidic soil.

That is how it is in our garden, where one inspiration leads to the next. Although it is worthwhile for the gardener to form a well-designed framework and palette from which to work, one needs room for the serendipity of nature's misfortunes and fortunate opportunities. We planted two mini-dwarf apple trees, each centered on either side of the entryway stairs in the front borders (the part of our garden which receives the greatest amount of sunlight), where flowering almonds had once lived. We selected a variety of Fuji apple, 'Beni Shogun,' as the Fuji is one of our favorite eating-out-of-hand apples. 'Beni Shogun' grows in regions with cool summers and ripens a month earlier than the parent Fuji. Planted on the opposing side is the self-fertilizing 'Queen Cox,' a clone of the better-known 'Cox Orange Pippin.' With its enticing catalogue description of disease-resistant qualities, aroma and lovely coloration, the 'Queen Cox' sounded too good to live without, perhaps too good to be true. We are looking forward to a cloud of "violets afloat" visiting our mini-dwarf apple trees.

⌒

You may wish to grow, as do we, specific plants to attract specific butterflies. The following is a list of butterflies and several skippers that we have observed frequenting our borders along with the nectar and host plants provided to invite these spellbinding creatures into the garden. The names in boldface denote larval host plants.

Swallowtails ~ Generally large and colorful with "tails" on the hind wings.

Spicebush Swallowtail ~ **Spicebush, sweetbay magnolia**, azalea, anise hyssop, mimosa tree, honeysuckle, zinnia, coneflower, milkweed, lantana, butterfly bush, summersweet, Joe-pye weed.

Pipevine Swallowtail ~ **Dutchman's pipe vine**, azalea, lilac, honeysuckle, zinnia, butterfly bush, *Verbena bonariensis*.

Eastern Tiger Swallowtail ~ **Black cherry, sweetbay magnolia**, blackberry, lilac, mimosa tree, honeysuckle, hollyhock, phlox, *Verbena bonariensis*, milkweed, bee-balm, butterfly bush, Joe-pye weed, ironweed.

Canadian Tiger Swallowtail ~ **Black cherry**, blackberry, lilac, honeysuckle, multi-flora rose, azalea, mountain laurel, common milkweed.

Eastern Black Swallowtail ~ **Queen Anne's lace**,

parsley, **dill**, **fennel**, lilac, phlox, clover, *Verbena bonariensis*, milkweed, butterfly bush.

Giant Swallowtail ~ Japanese honeysuckle, bougainvillea, milkweed.

Zebra Swallowtail ~ **Pawpaw**, blueberry, blackberry, lilac, milkweed.

Whites and Sulphurs ~ Family Peridae are mid-sized white, yellow, and orange.

Orange Sulphur ~ **Lupine, white clover**, mint, mimosa tree, pincushion, phlox, coneflower, zinnia, milkweed, goldenrod, New England aster.

Pink-fringed Sulphur ~ **Lowbush blueberry**, **highbush blueberry**, yarrow, anise hyssop, clover, coneflower, butterfly bush, New England aster.

Cabbage White ~ **Nasturtium**, lavender, yarrow, *Verbena bonariensis*, anise hyssop, mints, zinnia, New England asters.

Clouded Sulphur ~ **White clover**, New England asters, goldenrod, Joe-pye weed.

Cloudless Sulphur ~ Bougainvillea, hibiscus, lantana, wild morning glory.

Gossamer-wings ~ Classified together as they share an iridescence to their wings.

Spring Azure ~ **Dogwood, lowbush blueberry, arrowwood viburnum, New Jersey tea, meadowsweet, lupine**, holly, mountain laurel, forget-me-not, apple, lilac, chives, lavender, thyme, mint, milkweed.

Eastern Tailed Blue ~ **White clover**, mint, oregano, thyme, chives, yarrow, zinnia, butterfly bush, wild strawberry, milkweed, lowbush blueberry.

Frosted Elfin ~ **Lupine, blueberry**.

Henry's Elfin ~ **Redbud (*Cercis canadensis*), Hollly (*Ilex opaca*), blueberry**.

Brushfoots ~ "Brushfoot," from the shortened forelegs that are covered with long fur-like scales.

Monarch ~ **Milkweed (*Asclepius incarnata*, *A. syriaca*, *A. verticillata*)**, New England aster, New York aster, seaside goldenrod, *V. bonariensis*, butterfly bush, phlox, Mexican sunflower, lantana, zinnia, Mexican marigold, Joe-pye weed, coneflower, ironweed, gaillardia, cosmos.

Viceroy ~ **Plum, apple**, *V. bonariensis*, phlox, catmint, milkweed, butterfly bush, Joe-pye weed, New England aster.

Red Admiral ~ **Hops**, New Jersey tea, lilac, red clover, phlox, catmint, zinnia, pincushion, milkweed, coneflower, *Verbena bonariensis*, butterfly bush, leadplant, anise hyssop, summersweet, New England aster, New York aster, Korean daisy.

Painted Lady ~ **Clover, hollyhock, New England aster, ox-eye daisy, pearly everlasting**, zinnia, cosmos, ironweed, Joe-pye weed, butterfly bush, anise hyssop, phlox, yarrow, *V. bonariensis*, lupine, pincushion, Mexican sunflower, leadplant, bee balm, Korean daisy.

American Lady ~ **Pearly everlasting**, New England aster, New York aster, milkweed, goldenrod.

Red-spotted Purple ~ 'Korean Spice' viburnum, mock orange, Joe-pye weed, milkweed.

Great Spangled Fritillary ~ **Many species of *Viola***, ox-eye daisy, cosmos, coneflower, zinnia, *V. bonariensis*, milkweed, butterfly bush, New England aster, ironweed.

Pearly Crescentspot ~ **New England aster**, clover, mint, zinnia, milkweed, black-eyed Susan.

Baltimore Checkerspot ~ **Turtlehead** (*Chelone glabra*), viburnum, wild rose, black-eyed Susan, milkweed.

Wood Nymph ~ *V. bonariensis*, milkweed, butterfly bush, Joe-pye weed, New England aster.

Camberwell Beauty ~ New Jersey tea, butterfly bush.

Question Mark ~ Butterfly bush, *V. bonariensis*.

Eastern Comma ~ Hops, milkweed, summersweet.

⌣

Butterflies, moths, and skippers are members of the insect order Lepidoptera; the name is derived from Greek *lepidos* for "scales" and *ptera* for "wings." Their scaled wings distinguish them as a group from all other insects. Unrivalled in the living world, their wings are adorned with myriad patterns and solid colors in the full spectrum of the rainbow, as well as pure iridescent hues of blue, green, and violet.

The foundation of the Lepidoptera wing consists of a colorless, translucent membrane supported by a framework of tubular veins, radiating from the base of the wing to the outer margin. They are covered with thousands of overlapping scales, arranged very much like overlapping shingles on a roof. Like miniature canoe paddles, the scales are attached to the wings by their "handles." So small that they feel like and are a similar size to the silky granules of face powder, their purpose is multi-fold. Scales protect and act as an aid to the aerodynamics of the entire wing structure, help regulate Lepidoptera temperature, and are the cells from which color and patterns originate. This color and patterning are used for sexual signaling and as a means of eluding birds and other would-be predators.

There are two fundamental mechanisms by which color is produced on the wings of Lepidoptera. Ordinary color is due to organic pigments present that absorb certain wavelengths and reflect others. Extraordinary iridescence on butterfly wings is caused by the interference of light waves due to multiple reflections within the physical structure of the individual scales. Iridescent scales are composed of many microscopic thin layers; each scale has its own color, from pigment present and from the diffraction of light on the surface (the surface of iridescent scales are intricately corrugated and grooved). The iridescent effect is created much like a prism and is called structural coloration. When viewed under a microscope, the iridescent scales of some species of butterflies have a similar appearance to that of the tiered layers of a pine tree. Sometimes structural color and pigmented color occur simultaneously and a secondary color is created in the usual way color is added. For example, when blue iridescent color is produced from the structure of a scale that also contains yellow pigment, the resulting color is iridescent green.

When Lepidoptera with iridescent scales fly, the upper surface of their wings continually change from brilliant hues to the underlying relatively duller scales on the underside of the wings, as the angle of light striking the wing changes. The ability of the Lepidoptera to rapidly change colors and patterns is one of their defense mechanisms against predators. Along with their undulating pattern of flight and the figure-eight movement of their wings, the effect is of ethereal flashes of light disappearing and reappearing.

We are enthralled with the ever-increasing bevy of butterflies visiting our flower borders. Working and enjoying our garden during the sun-warmed days of summer we are richly rewarded with the magnificence of butterflies, skippers, and day-flying moths exhibiting endlessly fascinating behaviors. Captivating are the Monarchs dancing their aerial courtship dance above the milkweed and nectaring at the florets of butterfly bushes, verbenas and composite flowers. On occasion, we catch a glimpse of a Wood Nymph basking in the sun-soaked boards of the weathered picket fence, a Pearly Crescentspot fancying a nasturtium leaf, or a Snowberry Clearwing moth hovering at the tubular florets of the verbenas. There are the daily sightings of the fabulously colored Painted Ladies juxtaposed against the deep marine blues and purples of the butterfly bushes. Tidying up withered leaves around the hollyhock patch, I am startled by the elusive Tiger Swallowtail fluttering away from my rustling about its habitat. I have experienced the enchantment of the friendly Red Admiral alighting on my shoulder and a Question Mark resting on my hand while taking its photo.

Ephemeral floating flowers capture our hearts and imaginations. Creating and maintaining a butterfly garden will delight you and your family. Not only is designing and caring for a butterfly garden gratifying in the sense of enjoying the bounty and beauty of one's garden, it is also a worthwhile endeavor. Due to encroaching development and overcollecting, many native species of wild flowers that are butterfly nectar and larval food plants are endangered. When we create in our own backyards a habitat designed for adult Lepidoptera and their caterpillars, we give back, one garden at a time, the gifts of grace and beauty we receive from Mother Nature.

Butterfly gardening with a child is an invaluable way to pass along knowledge gleaned and to connect children with the natural world. Teaching children that butterflies need our help through creating a butterfly garden is an opportunity not to be missed. Along the way they will develop their powers of observation, an awareness of the interconnected world that we human beings share with plants and wildlife, and become imbued with the spirit of responsibility we all share in maintaining our planet's biodiversity.

CHAPTER SIXTEEN

A Summer of Fragrant Yellow Daylilies

Nature rarer uses yellow
 Than another hue;
Saves she all that for sunsets,—
 Prodigal of blue,

Spending scarlet like a woman,
 Yellow she affords
Only scantly and selectly,
 Like a lover's words.

— EMILY DICKINSON

THERE ARE DOZENS OF WAYS TO ACQUIRE PLANTS. Several in our garden were recovered from digging about the decaying stone foundation and garden of a former estate – hardy evergreen ivy with fine-textured leaves and prolific lily of-the-valley. Thankfully, I helped myself when I did, for later that same year the property was purchased and subsequently leveled with a bulldozer.

I like the idea of a "friendship garden," a garden that grows up and about when planted with gifts of passalongs and cuttings from friends and neighbors, where you regularly share plants with friends and they in turn share plants with you. We tend to think of and to describe these gift plants as the "irises from Aunt Amy" and the "violets that came from your great, great grandmother's garden by-way-of your great grandmother by-way-of your great aunt."

For our first summer in our new home, my sister-in-law sent from her old farmhouse garden located in southern Ohio, a large box overflowing with fans of tawny daylilies (*Hemerocallis fulva*) and bearded iris rhizomes (*Iris pallida* subsp. 'Dalmatica'). When I inquired as to what do the bearded iris look like, she off-handedly said, "some blue ones." What a cherished gift they became, and continue to keep giving, as we are in turn are able to share with friends bits of the rhizomes. The 'Dalmatica' iris of southern Europe is indestructible, the color a clear sky-blue, and the fragrance! The scent reminds me of sweet sun-ripening Concord grapes.

Species daylilies are one of the easiest plants to pass along. With the exception of the hottest of summer days, they can be successfully divided at nearly any time of year. The ease with which the species are divided is not necessarily true for the hybrids. The species and earliest hybridized daylilies could not be more dissimilar to their modern counterparts. Contemporary daylilies feature ruffled and picotee margins, halos, unusual color combinations, and ever-larger blossoms, deformed, to my eye, by their very gaudiness. In contrast, species *Hemerocallis* have a classic lily bell shape, some like delicate pendulous bells, and some open facing the light reflecting a golden chalice. The well-tailored, narrow petals have a no-nonsense appearance and the foliage properly proportioned, more grass-like, rather than dense forming clumps. Although species daylilies come in a comparatively more limited palette, the colors are fresh and clear, ranging in hues of singing lemon-lime to warm marigold to vivid orange.

One of our most cherished species daylily, the lemon lily (*Hemerocallis lilioasphodelus*), came from a vale where they had naturalized. I had gone for a walk early one summer morning and chanced upon a scene, startling in its unexpected beauty. Growing in golden waves were chalice-shaped lilies bending on arching scapes, rising above swaying, slender leaves caught by the wind. Surprising too was their dreamy fragrance of honeysuckle and citrus blossoms.

The exquisite grace in form and sublime fragrance of the lemon lily inspired a search for daylilies that have a similar scent and shape. The following is a list of daylilies chosen to create a patch of cheery yellow that will bloom in succession throughout the summer, while meeting the all-important criterion of having a delicious scent. The species *H. lilioasphodelus, H. minor, H. citrina, H. thunbergii,* and *H. altissima* are classified in the Citrina Group[1] and share the common traits of marvelous fragrance. They bloom in a clear singing yellow, without a hint of tawny tones. With the exception of *H. dumortieri,* this list does not contain additional notations on fragrance, although I would like my reader to understand that if you grow only one of the species listed here, you will be seduced, based on fragrance alone! Included are several hybrids, worthy of inclusion, as they are also richly fragrant and will extend the season as long as possible.

Hemerocallis dumortieri ~ One of the earliest daylilies to flower, begins to bloom in May in eastern Massachusetts. The copper-hued buds open to warm marigold-yellow, star-shaped flowers; the backs of the tepals are washed with reddish brown striations. The golden-orange-hued flowers have a scent to match its color; the fragrance has a decided note of orange, rather than lemon, combined with the sweet scent of honeysuckle. The plants are compact, with narrow, arching leaves. *H. dumortieri* is native to Manchuria, eastern Russia, Korea and Japan.

Hemerocallis minor ~ The common names for *H. minor* are grass-leaved daylily and star daylily. Another early bloomer, with the flowering times of *H. dumortieri*, *H. lilioasphodelus*, and *H. minor* overlapping. The flowers are cadmium yellow and bell-shaped. The blossoms of both *H. dumortieri* and *H. minor* are more diminutive, relative to the other species here listed, approximately one-half to two-thirds the size of the blossoms of *H. citrina*. *H. minor* is native to northern China, Mongolia, eastern Siberia, and Korea

Hemerocallis lilioasphodelus ~ (Formerly *H. flava*) Referred to as lemon lily or custard lily in our grandparents' day. The compact plants with grass-like foliage blend easily in the mixed border. The flowers are clear, bright lemon yellow and chalice shape. *H. lilioasphodelus* is indigenous to northeastern China, Korea, and eastern Siberia.

Hemerocallis 'Hyperion' ~ Hybridized in the mid 1920s, the jazzy and sweetly fragrant 'Hyperion' has remained a perennial favorite and justifiably so. In hybridizing it has retained its fragrance (a feature all too often ignored), is a beautiful shade of canary yellow, forms sturdy clumps and, like species daylilies, is relatively disease and pest free.

Hemerocallis citrina ~ *H. citrina* sends out long three- to four-foot scapes with seemingly endless, slender-petal, citron-yellow flowers. *Hemerocallis citrina* has vespertine flowers that open before sunset and close by mid-morning. *H. citrina* is native to northeastern China.

Hemerocallis 'Bountiful Valley' ~ 'Bountiful Valley' extends the season of fragrant yellow daylilies and lives up to it name of 'Bountiful,' sending forth copious blooms for well over a month. Large and lemon-colored trumpet-shaped flowers with lime-hued throats.

Hemerocallis thunbergii ~ Thunberg's daylily. *H. thunbergii,* 'Hyperion,' and *H. citrina* are all mid- to later-summer bloomers with flowering times that overlap. *H. thunbergii* is a brilliant lemon yellow with two- to three-foot scapes. *H. thunbergii* is native to Japan and northern China.

Hemerocallis altissima ~ Of all the species daylilies, *H. altissima* is the tallest, with scapes reaching the height of five to eight feet. *Altissima* blooms later in the season from mid-July to September. The refined, trumpet-shaped flowers are clear bright yellow. *H. altissima* is indigenous to southwest China, growing in the purple mountains near Nanking.

Surrounding our sweetbay magnolia (*M. virginiana*), with creamy white flowers, we grow yellow daylilies planted in combination with flowering perennials and bulbs in shades of white and shades of blue to purple. The cool tones of blue and purple attractively offset the sunny, warm yellow of the species daylilies. Winding through the lattice at the back of the flower border, surrounding the windows, is a Japanese honeysuckle (*Lonicera japonica* "Halliana') and an *Ampelopsis brevipedunculata* 'Elegans' with variegated white and green foliage and porcelain blue berries. The unobtrusive foliage of the species daylilies is easily woven into the tapestry of a mixed border. If you find the plants increasing in width, simply divide and pass along to a friend. The following are suggestions of reliably beautiful flowers with white, blue, and purple hued blossoms to complement species daylilies during their extended florescence.

Companion Plants for Yellow Daylilies

WHITE FLOWERS

> Bleeding hearts (*Dicentra spectabilis* 'Alba')
> Sweet white violet (*Viola blanda*)
> Lily of-the-valley (*Convallaria majalis*)
> Summer snowflakes (*Leucojum aestivum*)

'Snow Queen' iris (*Iris sibirica*)
Ox-eye daisy (*Leucanthemum vulgare*)
Japanese honeysuckle (*Lonicera japonica* 'Halliana')
Feverfew (*Chrysanthemum parthenium*)
Chinese bellflower (*Platycodon grandiflorus* 'Fuji White')
Coneflower (*Echinacea* 'White Swan')
Oriental lily (*Lilium siberica*)
'White Profusion' butterfly bush (*Buddleia davidii*)
Peacock orchid (*Acidanthera murielae*)
Japanese anemone 'Honorine Jobert' (*Anemone japonica*)
Turtlehead (*Chelone glabra*)
Pearly everlasting (*Anaphalis margaritacea*)
Boltonia (*Boltonia asteroides*)

FLOWERS IN SHADES OF BLUE AND PURPLE

Periwinkle (*Vinca minor*)
Forget-me-not (*Myosotis*)
English bluebells (*Hyacinthoides non-scripta*)
Dalmatica' iris (*Iris pallida* subsp. 'Dalmatica')
Himalayan blue poppy (*Meconopsis betonicifolia*)
Spiderwort (*Tradescantia virginiana*)
'Earl Grey' larkspur (*Delphinium ajacis* 'Earl Grey')
Brazilian verbena (*Verbena bonariensis*)
'Endless Summer' hydrangea (*H. macrophylla* 'Endless Summer')
Belladonna delphinium (*Delphinium* x *belladonna*)
Blue pincushion flower (*Scabiosa columbaria* 'Butterfly Blue')
Butterfly bush 'Nanho Blue,' 'Nanho Purple,' (*Buddleia davidii*)
Chinese bellflower, balloon flower (*Platycodon grandiflorus*)
Maypop (*Passiflora incarnata*)
Joe-pye weed (*Eupatorium purpureum*)
Leadplant (*Amphora canescens*)
New York aster (*Aster novi-beglii*)

The Chinese bellflower, or balloon flower, is one of my favorite companions to the yellow species daylilies. Poufy, pillow-shaped buds gradually inflate before bursting into pentagonal stars, in hues of blue, white, and seashell pink.

Blue balloon flowers are especially appealing planted with the lemon yellows of the citrina group. This stalwart bloomer begins to flower with 'Hyperion,' continuing through the florescence of *H. citrina*, 'Bountiful Valley,' and ending about the same time as Thunberg's daylily.

The Chinese bellflower is indigenous to China, eastern Siberia, and Japan. The dried roots are ground and administered as an antiinflammatory to treat coughs and colds. *Platycodon grandiflorus* grows to approximately two feet, with the lovely five-pointed, saucer-shaped flowers opening, several at a time, along the length of the stalks. The plants take several years to become established. Chinese bellflowers tolerate a variety of less than ideal conditions, though they will thrive in fertile, well-draining soil, annually dressed with mulch, and a steady diet of fish fertilizer. Their florescence will be considerably longer when planted in dappled shade. The plants are slow to emerge in the spring and the crowns of new growth, lying just under the surface of the soil, are easily damaged. Leave several inches of the old stalks in place over the winter to mark the plant's location. Chinese bellflowers are fairly easy to propagate. When several inches of the new shoots are visible, usually by early summer, gently dig around the gnarled roots and find the point where the stem joins the root mass. With a sharp knife, carefully cut off a chunk with several stems and an inch or so of attached roots. Plant immediately. The newly propagated plant should be kept constantly moist until new growth is apparent. Water and fertilize regularly, with particular diligence paid during the first year.

A Brief History of Species Daylilies

Truly wild and indigenous species daylilies are found throughout Asia, from Manchuria and Siberia, as far south as Northern India and to the Caucasus in the west, and including Korea and Japan. In its natural habitat it is found growing in swamps, the meadows near the seashore, the edges of forests, and mountainsides up to ten thousand feet. From the roughly twenty known Hemerocallis species come the tens of thousands of hybridized daylilies that have been developed over the past century.

Hemerocallis lilioasphodelus and *Hemerocallis fulva* were the earliest daylilies to be cultivated in Europe. The lemon lily was described by Pena and Lobel (*Historia*) in 1570 under the name *Aspho-delus luteus liliflorus*. Six years later Lobel published a woodcut illustration of the lemon daylily. At the same time he described a clone of *Hemerocallis fulva* (*H. fulva* 'Europa') as *Liriosphodelus phoeniceus*.[2] Linnaeus assigned these two daylilies their generic names in his first edition of *Species Plantarum* in 1753. His name for the tawny daylily was *Lilio-Asphodelus* var. *fulvus* and the lemon daylily he called *Lilio-Asphodelus* var. *flavus*. Both species were the earliest daylilies to be introduced to America by way of Europe during the colonial era.

There is some confusion on the taxonomy of the species within the genus for various reasons. *Hemerocallis* species have a natural ability to cross, creating fertile hybrids. Within a single species there may be variety in size of flowers and foliage, color, and flowering time.

Daylilies for Dinner

Daylilies have been cultivated for their medicinal properties and Asian cuisine for over 2,500 years. Written records and depictions in paintings and textiles date back as far as the time of Confucius. The roots have a folk history in the treatment of cancer. All parts of the plant are edible including the flower blossoms, leaves, and roots. Throughout Eurasia, daylilies are prepared and eaten in a variety of ways.

Although *Hemerocallis* is Greek for "beauty for a day," the flowers of species daylilies begin to open in the late afternoon and early evening. The newly opened blossoms are delicious when eaten raw. They have a mild lemon-like and nutty flavor and crunchy texture, and become sweeter toward the base of the tepals due to the nectar glands. Harvest fresh blossoms of *H. citrina* late in the afternoon to provide a festive receptacle to serve fruit, sorbet, or ice cream for the evening meal. Another typical use of the flowers comes from China. Newly withered blossoms are harvested and dried and used as a thickener and flavoring for soups. *Hemerocallis citrina* is the daylily most commonly used in Chinese cuisine.

Daylily buds sautéed in olive oil taste like the most tender and sweetest of freshly picked green beans. They are a good source of vitamins A and C, with some protein content as well. A simple recipe from an English friend is to dip the plump buds in batter, deep fry and serve with tomato chutney. The young leaves of the daylily are tender, similar in flavor to scallions. They gradually become tougher and harder to chew as the season progresses.

Species Daylily Culture

Species daylilies are *very* easy to grow. They will live for years and years in tended as well as neglected gardens. Although species daylilies will succeed in almost any soil, they will flower prolifically in soils that are rich, moist, well draining, and not compacted. *Hemerocallis* species will grow in dappled to full sun, and their range of color, height, and different florescence through the season make them suitable and sensible for almost any site in the garden landscape. They will grow and flower more freely in a sunny location, though the individual flowers will linger longer when planted in light shade.

Hemerocallis species are an ideal groundcover; they spread readily though not invasively. Eventually one may notice the plant is sending forth fewer and fewer flowers, a signal that it's time to divide the daylilies. The first step is to water the clump thoroughly. Allow the water to seep in and wait an hour or two for the roots to relax. Dig around the perimeter of the plant with a pitchfork, and gently lift out the entire clump. Water again to remove soil from the root mass. The roots are generally tightly entangled and hard to pull apart. Use a sharp, clean knife to cut the clump into smaller parts, allowing a set of roots for each viable section. Trim the plants to roughly half their original height. Do not remove more than half of the foliage as it is necessary for the plant to process light and air to develop strong roots for the following year's flowers. If you are not planting immediately or plan to pass along the daylilies to a friend, wrap the divisions loosely in dampened newspaper and cover the roots with moist soil.

To replant the daylilies, loosen the soil to a depth of a foot or so. Add a few shovelfuls of compost and soil, mixed well, to the hole. Form a mound in the center of the hole and place the division atop the mound with the crown and the roots below the soil line, and with the green growth above. The crown is the white part at the base of the plant between the roots and the green growth. Refill the hole, packing the soil firmly around the roots to avoid pockets of air. Water well with fish fertilizer added. The newly planted division will require occasional supplemental watering while it is becoming established in its new setting, particularly during a dry spell. Periodically we throw compost over the daylilies in the late fall or early spring and every now and then, during the growing season, water with fish fertilizer.

At the end of the season, after the foliage has withered and died back, clean up and remove the remaining leaf debris to eliminate hiding places for insects. Daylilies have a slight tendency to be bothered by snails and slugs. Do as we do for any plant that is assailed by those pesky creatures: sprinkle crumbled eggshells around the circumference of the plant to form a barrier. We have had neither slug nor snail damage since we began applying eggshells to potentially problematic plants (including, and in particular, hosta). The best time of year to discourage snails and slugs from making a home in one's garden is in the early spring, at the first sign of tender new growth. Nevertheless, species daylilies will recover easily from slug or snail attack.

Several growing seasons ago, an elderly couple was strolling past our home when they stopped to admire our front borders. Covered in dirt from head to toe, I nonetheless was glad to show off our garden. She mentioned her grand-mother had a patch of lemon lilies. The fragrance from "Aunt Amy's blue bearded iris" was also reminiscent of her grandmother's garden. I gave her a clump of lemon lilies and several rhizomes from the bearded iris and they soon departed. A few weeks passed when I was pleasantly surprised with a gift on my doorstep, of rose-colored lily of-the-valley pips and a cluster of unusual double-flowered, violet-colored myrtle. I hope my gifts to the thoughtful flower-lovers have become well established in their garden, as their treasured gifts have made a home for themselves in ours.

ENDNOTES

1. Linda Sue Barnes, "The Daylily Species" in *The Daylily: A Guide for Gardeners,* ed. John Peat and Ted Petit (Portland, Oregon: Timber Press, Inc., 2004).

2. A. B. Stout, *Daylilies* (Sagaponack, New York: Sagapress, Inc., 1986).

CHAPTER SEVENTEEN

Terrace Plantings

Across time and cultures words such as a *piazza, veranda, loggia, porch, lanai, terrace, patio,* and *courtyard* have been used to describe structures human beings have built to extend their indoor environment to outdoor living rooms. From earliest recorded history, the Persian and Chinese courtyards served their inhabitants as ways of experiencing the outdoors on a day-to-day basis, within the safety of walls. The modern day counterpart of a patio or a terrace allows for gracious living while creating a transition between the interior rooms of a home and the garden. A cohesive flow is formed when one plans an overall design that creates a transition between the indoor environment and outdoor rooms.

Planning a terrace creates an opportunity for the gardener to easily express his or her individual aesthetic. Along with a satisfactory underlying structure of hardscape (a carpet of brick or stone) combined with vertical elements – a trellis to create screening or a pergola, for example – the terrace provides a blank canvas to create a garden room. Plantings in pots are relatively impermanent. If you're dissatisfied with a particular plant or group of plants, you can move the pots about and perfect the arrangement. When temporarily not looking its best, after a flush of flowering or in recovery from a pest infestation, a terrace plant can be relegated to the background or tucked in a corner to rejuvenate.

The terrace, framed with climbing fragrant vines and planted with an array of small trees, shrubs, herbs, flowering annuals, and perennials, is an invitation to step into a welcoming environ. As part of the architectural backdrop, train deciduous trees and shrubs to grow into a standard shape. The fruit tree grafted to dwarf rootstock, rose, golden chain, and wisteria are examples of trees, shrubs, and vines ideally suited to this method of pruning. Festoon an outdoor hearth with fragrant vines, and then position a pair of standard trees on either side, surrounded by pots with cascading flowers and foliage, all of which soften the edges of hardscape and make for a relaxed composition. Fashion pots planted with aromatic evergreen foliage and pair with seasonal fragrant flowers, to create interest the year round. Group edible herbs with scented leaves together or arrange them with Oriental lilies and peacock orchids. Picture swimming in a pool surrounded by pots of bougainvillea, camellia, and hibiscus with their blossoms in a range of beautiful hues. Conversely, imagine swimming languidly in that same pool, after a long hectic day when it is the "blue hour" and, while the light is fading, the air becomes impregnated with the night scents of the white- and the pale-hued flowers – orange jasmine, angel's trumpet, and gardenia.

Gardeners in warmer climates can readily fill their terrace with tender fragrant citrus flowers, fig trees, and *Brugmansia*. Gardeners in northern regions can do the same by bringing the plants indoors to winter over. Growing scented flowering vines in pots, for example Madagascar jasmine, poet's jasmine and 'Moonlight of the Grove,' has the added benefit of providing fragrance for your home throughout the long winter months.

Brugmansia 'Charles Grimaldi'

There are nearly an infinite number of plants with an outdoor-indoor life suitable for pots and for terrace planting. *Brugmansia* 'Charles Grimaldi' immediately comes to mind, not only for its remarkably large pendulous and trumpet-shaped blossoms, but also for its permeating lily-like night fragrance. 'Charles Grimaldi' is an old favorite pass along, and understandably so, for it is one of the most fragrant *Brugmansia*. The blossoms open in a warm hue of buttery yellow that fade to a gentle shade of apricot. *Brugmansia suaveolens* 'Jamaica Yellow' is a pure lemon yellow cultivar, also richly scented, and 'Cypress Gardens' is somewhat smaller, making it an ideal selection for pot culture. The fragrant, creamy white flowers fade to palest hues of coral pink.

The angel trumpet is native to southeastern Brazil and performs best in a rich and well-draining soil, with plenty of water and supplemental nutrients provided throughout the growing season. In early spring, bring the plant into a warm sunny room to break dormancy. After all danger of frost has passed, place *Brugmansia* outside for the season. Fertilize and add a fresh topcoat of compost. *Brugmansia* bloom on the current season's growth; pruning the stems in early spring will not affect the plant's florescence. By removing lower growing branches, *Brugmansia* is easily pruned to a standard, with a single tree trunk. Angel trumpet has the potential to grow quickly – several feet in one season. Grown in full sun to very light shade, the plant is laden with flowers by midsum-

mer, and continues to bloom until the first frost. After the first frost, remove withered and decaying leaves, place in an unheated basement, and water infrequently and only when the soil feels nearly bone dry.

Camellia sinensis

The elegant tea plant, *Camellia sinensis*, from which beverage tea is harvested, makes an ideal shrub for a sunny or mildly shaded terrace, when maintained to a moderate size of several feet, and is easily wintered over indoors. 'Tea Breeze,' a readily available cultivar, is a graceful plant with evergreen and glossy elliptical foliage. The nodding, cupped-shaped, pure white flowers appear in autumn and are sweetly scented. 'Blushing Maiden' is similar to 'Tea Breeze,' with white flowers blushed pink.

Camellia sinensis grows on the hillsides of the tropical regions of China, India, Ceylon, Malaya, and Indonesia, and in its native habitat, the tea plant thrives in humid climates. This tells us that it requires both plenty of moisture and a well-draining site. Camellias prefer sheltered locations, out of the path of cold winds, planted in rich, loamy, acidic soil. A top dressing of compost helps retain moisture. During the winter months place the tea plant on a tray of pebbles kept moist. In hot, dry weather, as well as in warm, dry homes, it is necessary to periodically spray or mist the foliage.

Second to water, tea is the most widely consumed liquid on earth, its medicinal benefits numerous and well known. Tea leaves contain compounds such as vitamins, minerals, purines, alkaloids, and polyphenols (catechins and flavonoids). The polyphenols have antibacterial and antioxidizing activities produced in an inverse ratio to the darkness of the tea. The longer tea is allowed to ferment (oxidize), the darker it becomes. For example, black tea, which is fermented during processing, has lower levels of plyphenols than green or white tea. Fermentation decreases the rejuvenating and healing properties of tea. Tender young tea leaves are harvested and then allowed to oxidize, then dried to various degrees to produce different types of tea. Green tea is made from freshly picked leaves that are quickly wilted, steamed, and then dried immediately. Black tea is produced from tea leaves that are wilted and crushed in rollers (which hastens the fermenting stage), then allowed to oxidize for several hours before drying.

White tea is thought to be the healthiest of all three types of tea. Outside of China, the production of white tea has been shrouded in obscurity for centuries. Because of its ancient history and evolving processing techniques, there is some confusion surrounding their production. Contrary to popular belief, white teas are not steamed. The tender fleshy buds, first set of leaves, and second set of leaves are harvested from specific varieties, allowed to wither slowly, hand selected, and carefully baked dry. As early as the Tang Dynasty (A.D. 618–907), a form of compressed tea, referred to as white tea, was produced. During the Tang Dynasty the preparation and drinking of tea were quite different from how it is enjoyed today. Tea leaves were compressed into cakes and prepared by boiling pieces of the cakes in earthenware kettles. The white tea of Tang was harvested in early spring when the new leaves resembling silver needles were abundant. These "first flushes" of white tea were used to make the compressed cakes of tea.

The production and preparation of all tea changed during the Song Dynasty (A.D. 960–1279). To preserve the delicate flavor favored by court society, it was produced in different loose leaf styles, as well as in a new powdered form. The tea leaves were harvested, quickly steamed to preserve their color and character, and then dried and ground into a fine powder. The powdered tea was whisked into wide ceramic bowls; the tea liquor was esteemed for both its deep emerald or light iridescent appearance, and its healthful and rejuvenating properties.

The Song style of tea preparation, where participants partook of powdered tea in ceramic bowls in a ceremonial aesthetic, was known as the Song tea ceremony. Japanese monks traveling through China brought the Song tea ceremony back to Japan, where it evolved into the Japanese tea ceremony we know today.

For one's own culinary purposes, it is possible to harvest tea leaves after the tea plant has become well established in three to four years. Experiment with different recipes of drying, fermenting, and baking to simulate the three types of teas to determine your personal preference.

Ficus carica 'Lattarula'

And every man 'neath his vine and fig tree
Shall live in peace and unafraid,
And into plowshares beat their swords,
Nations shall learn war no more.

—ISRAELI FOLK TUNE (Sung as a round)

Native to the Mediterranean, the vast majority of cultivars of *Ficus carica* are only hardy in zones eight through ten. Fig trees are highly adaptable and grow successfully in containers. They can winter over, in either a dormant state left in an unheated basement or, growing in a warm, sunny window. The permeating fragrance of the distinctive, deeply lobed leaves is unmistakable, and the spicy aroma becomes even more noticeable as one comes nearer to the tree. 'Lattarula' bears yellow-green fruit with delicious strawberry-amber-colored flesh. Nicknamed the 'Italian golden honey fig,' 'Lattarula' is synonymous with 'White Marseille,' 'Lemon Fig,' and 'Blanche.' The fruit, delectably sweet plucked from the tree and eaten out of hand, can also be recommended for making preserves and drying. The rounded shape of the yellow fruit gives rise to the regional name 'Lemon Fig.' 'Lattarula' is a good choice for gardeners in the northern regions with relatively short, cooler summers.

Figs develop singly along the length of branches above the point where leaves have been shed and in the leaf axils of the current year's growth. Depending on the length of the growing season and the cultivar, the tree can bear one or two crops a year. The first, or "breba" crop, is produced on the previous season's growth.

The fruit of all *Ficus* are the syconium, an enlarged, fleshy, hollow receptacle (or peduncle) that bears closely massed tiny flowers on its *inner* wall. The true fruits are tiny drupelets that develop from their flowers. When we eat a fig, we are eating the container that holds the tiny fruits. In their native land, specialized fig wasps pollinate the flowers by climbing into a tiny hole at the end of the receptacle, opposite the stem end. Cultivars grown in North America are self-pollinating; only one tree is necessary to harvest fruit.

Growing in the ground, the roots of a fig tree are far reaching, which make it extremely drought tolerant. Pot-grown figs require supplemental water, especially during extended periods of dry weather during the summer months. To cultivate a fig tree in a pot and have it bear fruit, it is necessary to water, feed, and prune it regularly.

In early to mid-spring, bring the fig into a warm, sunny room. The tree may have already broken dormancy. Prune stems and branches judiciously. Leave some of the past season's growth as these branches will bear the first or "breba" crop.

Every few years the roots of the fig tree will require a modest root pruning. Slide a sharp knife around the outer perimeter and remove the tree from its container. Tease out the roots and trim away approximately one-third of the root mass. Figs require excellent drainage. A soil suitable for cactus and citrus, along with some compost added makes a nutrient-rich and well-draining combination. Add fresh soil to the pot, firming around the roots to prevent pockets of air. Water and fertilize regularly with an organic fish fertilizer.

After all danger of frost has passed, cart the plant out to the warm, sunny terrace. Fig trees require full sun for the fruit to ripen, and even with the proper amount of sunlight, they still ripen slowly in a north coast garden. To hasten ripening by keeping the warmth emitted from the syconium contained, try dabbing the tiny hole, opposite the stem end, with a drop of olive oil. After the first frost, bring the tree into an unheated basement and snip off any remaining leaves. Allow the tree to go dormant and water only occasionally when the soil is very dry.

Citrus

We would grow citrus plants, whether they bore fruit or not, for the lilting sweet scents of the blossoms alone. Whether entering a room in which a citrus is in bloom or approaching the plant on the terrace, one cannot help appreciatig their exquisite fragrance.

During the Baroque period, orange and citrus fruits became equated with the golden apples from the mythical Garden of Hesperides. In 1664 Louis XIV of France commissioned the architect LeVall to build the first orangerie at Versailles. It was the Sun King's love for gardens, and in particular his admiration for the "Seville" orange, which brought both citrus plants and the conservatory into prominence. The orangerie protected exotic and tender plants during the winter, and when the plants were moved out of doors during the warmer months, the orangerie was transformed into a setting for courtly events and celebrations.

Oh Garden of Fresh Possibilities!

The genus *Citrus* is indigenous to southeast Asia, occurring from northern India to China and south through Malaya, the Philippines, and the East Indies. The earliest records of its cultivation date back to about 500 B.C. The four original wild species from which all domesticated fruits are thought to have been hybridized are *Citrus medica*, *Citrus aurantifolia*, *Citrus grandis*, and *Citrus reticulata*.

The calamondin orange (*Citrus mitis*), with heavenly scented, pure white flowers, is among the easiest to grow. Although the fruit is too acidic to eat out of hand, it is fine for cooking, seasoning poultry prior to roasting, or combining with honey to make a piquant glaze. The key lime (*Citrus aurantifolia*), has an insinuating sweet and fresh fragrance and is used for preserves, garnishes, and juice. Oil of citral is extracted from *Citrus aurantifolia* for use in perfumes. Highly valued in Japan and China for use in Buddhist ceremonies, the Buddha's Hand (*Citrus medica*) is a thorny shrub with fragrant fruits that resemble a human hand. The flowers are comparatively large (3–4 inches across), white shaded purple, and intoxicatingly fragrant.

One of the most beautiful and widely available citrus for pot culture is the Meyer lemon (*Citrus limon* x *Citrus sinensis*), also known as the Chinese lemon. It grows to a manageable size, less than two feet, and in a standard shape with a nicely rounded-head form. Not a true lemon, but a hybrid cross of *C. sinensis*, an orange, and *C. limon*, its fruit is sweeter than that of a pure lemon cultivar. But it is for the flowers that I grow the Meyer lemon. The blossoms are thick and velvety, creamy white tinted rose. Blooming in notes of honeysuckle and jonquil-like fragrances, the tree flowers prodigally.

Citrus thrive in a well-draining soil similar to what is an ideal medium for cactus. They must be grown in clay pots to insure good air circulation. The surest way to kill a citrus is by overwatering. Wait until the soil is thoroughly dried between watering. Place your finger a full three inches into the soil and water only when it feels dry at your finger tips, and then water deeply until a bit of water comes out the bottom of the drainage hole. With regular feedings of fish fertilizer throughout the summer and an all-purpose fertilizer during the winter months (when we find the odor of fish fertilizer to be repugnant indoors), citrus plants grow strong and healthy and are less likely to succumb to insect infestations.

Citrus plants are fairly indestructible, although they will quickly let you know when they're unhappy. A few leaves will yellow and fall off, and if the problem is not resolved immediately, the entire plant will defoliate. This is typically due to overwatering and/or a soil mixture that does not allow for excellent drainage. Do not be discouraged, even if the entire plant becomes leafless. Water less frequently and try repotting the plant in a more suitable growing medium. Usually, they can be revived and the survivor will be healthier.

When grown indoors, citrus are occasionally bothered by spider mites and scale. Spider mites are easy to detect because they make a visible white web. Scale is a more challenging problem to diagnose as the light brown, pinhead sized and hard-bodied pest is difficult to see. They remain well hidden, where they attach themselves to the stems and along the ribs on the underside of the leaves. Scales produce a sticky substance that coats the leaves. For both pests,

The purpose of fragrant oils on the foliage of plants is for protection against animals, insects, and strong rays of sunlight. The plants with the most highly aromatic foliage grow in hot, arid climates. Plants protect themselves from the sun's potentially desiccating rays by releasing an oily vapor from their leaves. Many plants carry their protective powers a step further and produce foliage covered with downy hairs, similar to the thick, velvet-like leaves of the pelargonium (scented-leaf geraniums). Pelargonium is indigenous to the southern regions of the African continent, where they grow in an arid climate.

Insects rarely attack plants with scented foliage. Interspersing plants with fragrant leaves – marigolds, lavender, and thyme, for example – amongst insect-prone plants such as lilies and roses helps keep the surrounding plants free from pest infestations. Lavender is repulsive to mosquitoes and therefore worth considering for a sunny terrace. Plants with fragrant foliage, an adaptive alternative to the formation of thorns, also repel animals, for with only a few exceptions, plants with aromatic leaves rarely also have thorns.

spray with a solution of diluted rubbing alcohol (three parts water to one part rubbing alcohol) to keep them in check.

Considered a harbinger of prosperity and good fortune, citrus have been grown in Chinese gardens and courtyards for thousands of years. We can take a lesson from how seasonal changes are reflected in a Chinese garden. Different areas of the garden are used in rotation for social events, depending on the prominence of a particular tree or shrub in flower, and flowering plants growing in pots are brought into the current living areas. After blooming, they are moved to a less visible location, and the focus shifts to flowers that are coming into florescence.

The possibilities of plant possibilities for the patio or terrace are limitless. *Murraya paniculata* (orange jasmine) and hardy Chinese species gardenia are wonderfully scented, imbuing your outdoor living area with exotic scents. The climbing fragrant Bourbon rose 'Zephirine Drouhin,' grows well in a pot and, because it is thornless, creates an ideal background plant for the lived-in patio. Vigorous herbs with scented foliage, chocolate mint comes to mind, are well suited for pots since their roots are contained and the plants won't overrun the garden. For roses and herbs, when it simply isn't practical to bring the entire terrace plant collection into the home for the winter, bury them, pot and all, in the soil, in a sheltered area in the garden, and cover with a thick layer of mulch. Tuck herbs with scented leaves into the cracks and crannies around the terrace. Once established, creeping thyme and pennyroyal are hardy herbs that can withstand foot traffic. Nasturtiums make delightful container plants. Plant directly in the pot where they will spend the summer. The fat seeds germinate readily, and they flower continually throughout the summer, when regularly fertilized and deadheaded. Both flowers and foliage are lovely in a salad. The worse pest that afflicts them is colonies of black aphids, easily removed with a forceful zap of the garden hose. 'Empress of India' is a variety attractive to both hummingbirds and butterflies, and the braver sorts will come investigating within arm's reach!

CHAPTER EIGHTEEN

Late Summer Splendor
in the Garden

BULBS

I have planted lilies, but will they grow well with me?
Will they like the glitter of this north-looking hillside?
Will they like the rude winds, the stir, the quick-changes?
Would they not have shadowy stillness and peace?

Lilium chalcedonicum, calla aethiopica,
Lilium auratum, candidum, the martagon,
lilium speciosum, pardalinum, umbellatum,
Amaryllis, convalleria, nerine.

All these lovely lilies. I wish they would grow well with me,
No other flowers have the texture of the lilies,
The heart-piercing fragrance, the newly alighted angel's
Lineal poise, purity, and peace—

(We wait their pleasure. Yet if they grow not
Need only take patience a little while longer;
For these are the flowers we look to find blooming
In the meadows and lanes that lie beyond Jordan—
All kinds of lilies in the lanes that lead gently,
Very gently, by degrees, in the shade of green trees,
To the foothills and fields of Paradise.)

— MARY URSULA BETHEL *New Zealand* 1874–1945

LOOKING OUT FROM THE VIEW OF OUR SUNNY PATIO onto the little
garden, I am not too bothered by the untidy appearance of the paths, a touch too
abundant and lush with summers' foliage. Thoughts of fall chores are relegated
to the far recesses of my mind. I envision the old cement patio giving way to a

lovely brick terrace with a fine shade-providing arbor, though we are not ready just yet to embark on this project. Soon enough there will be bulbs to plant and plants to move about for improved design. For this moment, in this summer afternoon's spangled sunlight, I delight in the splendor in the garden of the season's glorious outpourings of flowers and fragrances.

Lilium speciosum

There is a flower that blooms in our late summer garden whose arrival I eagerly anticipate. Its graceful beauty seems to temper the melancholy one feels as the days grow shorter and the inevitable winter draws near. With daylight hours waning, evening temperatures rapidly cooling, and the realization that time spent in the garden will soon end, the splendid Japanese species lily (*Lilium speciosum* var. album) begins to gently unfurl its pure white tepals. With undulating, ruffled margins, the tepals twist and recurve nearly to the back. Their perfume is similar, though less heady than the hybrid Oriental lilies, and closer to that of the sweetest and purest "heart-piercing" lily fragrance.

L. speciosum blooms over an extended period of time, several weeks in all. *Lilium speciosum* var. rubrum is also a brilliant beauty with rose-splashed tepals sprinkled with madder spots converging to a bright, light green star at the center.

Rubrum has a similar fragrance, though not quite as potent, as the white variation. Both album and rubrum are easy to grow, relative to the challenges posed by some species lilies that have a deserved reputation for temperamental behavior. *L. speciosum* prefers the sheltered semi-shade of the woodland edge. Japanese species lilies are available in catalogues for spring and fall planting, but you will have greater success with *Lilium speciosum* by waiting until the late spring, well after the ground has dried and warmed a bit. While becoming established, the Japanese lily cares little for the wet, soggy conditions often caused by endless freezing spring rains. It prefers rich, humusy, slightly acidic, and well-draining soil. The plant takes several seasons to become established, in which time a single stalk may be covered with twenty blossoms. Arrange *L. speciosum* in the woodland border with trees and plants that also thrive in an acidic soil – dogwoods, *Stewartia pseudocamellia*, *Magnolia virginiana*, lily of-the-valley, fragrant hosta, rhododendron, and hydrangeas of all sorts.

This past growing season the dreaded red lily beetle attacked our lilies. I had heard innumerable reports from fellow gardeners of this nasty import with its voracious appetite for lily foliage and wasn't too surprised when evidence of

them began appearing on several choice Oriental lilies. The larvae decimate the leaves of the plants by chewing notice-able round holes. About ⅜-inch in length, the beetles are bright cadmium red with thin black legs. Because they have no known predators in North America and because of their extended egg-laying season, from spring through summer, they are difficult to control. As soon as you see signs of the beetle (be on the lookout as early as the first of April), monitor the plants daily. Squash any beetles that are visible. They are quick, and you have to be quicker. Next check the *undersides* of the leaves for the following three signs: glistening, miniscule reddish orangish eggs (usually, arrayed in a tiny line), their vile black, gloppy excrement, under which is concealed a growing larger larvae, and hiding adult beetles. Destroy the leaves that are hosting the larvae. The only way to maintain attractive lilies throughout the season is by constant vigilance, handpicking the beetles and their larvae in all stages.

With forethought it is possible to create a continuous arrangement of sultry, exotically scented species and Oriental hybrid lilies blooming from mid-summer through early autumn. *Lilium regale* (another introduction collected from north-ern Sichuan by E. H. Wilson) is a white trumpet lily with a wash of lavender-pink striations on the back of the tepals and cadmium yellow throat, is purportedly less vulnerable to the lily beetle. We planted several this year, and thus far the tender new foliage appears to be safe from that red devil. The splen-did summer blooming lily, *Lilium auratum platyphyllum* (golden-rayed lily), flow-ers several weeks prior to *L. speciosum*. Another Japanese wildflower (as is the 1832 introduction *Lilium speciosum*), the golden-rayed lily was introduced to America in 1862. The large, trumpet-shaped flowers are white with striped gold bands radiating from the center and speckled with cinnamon-colored dots. The voluptuous fragrant flowers are borne on four-foot stalks. They require a cool sheltered location with filtered sunlight, similar growing conditions to that of *Lilium speciosum*. This is the 'Gold-band' lily so beautifully painted in John Singer Sargent's "Carnation, Lily, Lily, Rose" on view in the permanent collection of the Tate Gallery, London.

The blossoms of the 'Gold-band' lily perfectly illustrate one of the many ways plants have evolved to attract insects and animals to deliver pollen from the flower's anther to its stigma. The bands of color converging to the center (called nectar guides) visually draw in the pollinator. The dots, in contrasting colors and slightly raised, radiating out along the center of the tepals, are additional road maps guiding the pollinator to the drops of nectar at the base of the nectar glands.

The most romantic and most eagerly awaited of vines, the moonflower (*Ipomoea alba*), begins blooming in the first days of September. The 'Blue Star' morning glory (*Ipomoea purpurea*) has grown up the side of the house that faces southeast, weaving its way through our heirloom mystery rose, several stories in all, both vine and clambering rose benefiting from steady doses of fish fertilizer. 'Blue Star' flowers in light timbre of luminous aquamarine, with ribs of a deeper blue, nearly a French blue, emanating from a pale cadmium yellow throat. The annual vines of moonflowers and morning glories are members of the Convolvulaceae, and in northern temperate climates they do not come into their own until late summer, when they provide a profusion of evanescing trumpet-shaped blossoms.

The *Hydrangea paniculata* 'Grandiflora' always looks splendid from July through early winter. By late summer the 'Peegee' is at its most luxuriant, with creamy white panicles shifting from shades of transparent pale green to coppery pink. Surrounding the hydrangea is lily of-the-valley, with its late summer dress of perfectly round, vermilion-colored seed capsules. Glinting in the sunlight like miniature, brilliant red glassine marbles, we catch a glimpse of 'Serotina' honeysuckle berries. They must be exceptionally tasty to the songbirds as the fruit is never on the vine for long.

Late Summer Splendor in the Garden

The fragrant varieties of hosta do not bloom until later in the summer – perhaps it is nature's way of saving the best for last. This is the season for hosta with aptly descriptive names such as 'So Sweet,' 'Sugar and Cream,' and 'Fragrant Bouquet.' For those who have never smelled a fragrant hosta, or were unaware that a hosta *could* be fragrant, the scent is similar to the scent of honeysuckle. The species hosta 'August Lily' (*Hosta plantaginea*) has my undying affection for its divinely scented, pure white flowers. 'August Lily' blooms through the dog days of August and into September, perfectly coinciding with the sultry air of late summer, which only intensifies their potent perfume. *H. plantaginea* makes a compact and reasonably scaled mounding plant, unlike some hybrids such as 'Honeybells.' Although 'Honeybells' bears scented flowers, our plant doubled in size every year, eventually suffocating all its neighbors. If one is looking for a foundation-sized shrub for a shady location, 'Honeybells' fits the bill. We eventually dug out the root mass and gave it (with fair warning) to a friend with a much larger garden.

'August Lily' lights up the shady border with vivid apple green, deeply ribbed, undulating foliage, and is always crisp and fresh looking, despite a nibble here or there from slugs or snails. The double form of *H. plantaginea*, 'Aphrodite,' which we went to great lengths to purchase from a grower whose plants were grown from seedlings procured in Beijing, is lovely to look at, but not nearly as fragrant, and the foliage is a duller dark green. In many instances, and no more so than with the 'August Lily,' the species is unsurpassed in beauty, resilience, and fragrance. And it is the only hosta to which we have observed a hummingbird nectaring.

The fabulously fragrant peacock orchids (*Acidanthera murielae*) are nearing the close of their florescence. Collected from the mountains of Ethiopia, *A. murielae* was introduced to western cultivation in the mid 1800s. The starry-white blossoms with violet eyes are borne along graceful arching stems, sometimes with as many as a dozen successively blooming flowers on a single scape. The expiring flower stalks are a thing of beauty in themselves. Where each flower had bloomed along the length of the scape, a seedpod develops, forming a roundly rhythmical stalk. The stiff, sword-like foliage is a lovely counterpoint to the delicate stems and lineal blossoms. Peacock orchids planted en masse are simply stunning, and even more so when the flowering scapes are caught bending and swaying in the seasonal breezes. Their gorgeous fragrance exhaled is intensified when they are grown in great drifts.

Emerging from dormancy very late in the growing season, by the end of the summer, the butterfly bushes (*Buddleia davidii*) are covered in panicles of fragrant blossoms, along with the welcome assortment of Lepidoptera they were planted to lure. Do not despair when there is no visible sign of life from the buddleia; by mid- to late-June you should expect to see new growth. Butterfly bushes take their sweet time coming to life, especially after a particularly long, cold winter.

The last of the sweet 'Belle of Georgia' white peaches are harvested as well as the D'Anjou pears, the pears stored away to ripen for several weeks. The Alpine strawberries, which began to bear fruit in early June, are still producing fine diminutive berries. There will be enough fruit to make several more tarts. Soon it will be time to harvest the herbs to insure a steady winter supply. Herbs such as tarragon, rosemary, and thyme maintain their flavors through drying, while the flavor of herbs with tender leaves, chives for example, are best preserved by wrapping tightly in a plastic bag and freezing immediately after harvesting.

Roses that continue to delight with much appreciated blossoms are two old Bourbons – 'Louise Odier' and 'Souvenir du Victor Landeau,' the hybrid teas – 'Fragrant Cloud' and 'Aloha,' and the Romantica – 'Frederick Mistral.' Then there is 'New Dawn.' Does 'New Dawn' ever stop? It must be the easiest rose to grow and one of the most carefree, as it is constantly in bloom, virtually disease free and even has the notable habit of continuing to flower while developing hips.

Forming a substantial clump (four feet wide and equally as tall) and nearly ready to bloom is a passalong from a generous friend. From a few cuttings of this heirloom chrysanthemum (*Chrysanthemum* 'Single Apricot Korean'), with apricot pink-tinted, daisy-like single flowers, we now have a patch of our own to share with friends. I am trying to ignore those bittersweet feelings of the season's end and rejoice in the scintillating warmth of sunlit September afternoons.

CHAPTER NINETEEN

Exquisite Flora in Autumn

GREEN LEAVES IGNITE, TRANSFORMED by a kaleidoscope of incinerating colors – devil-red, burnt tangerine, caramelized amber, searing saffron, and smoldering crimson-purple. The air is impregnated with the aromatic perfume of orchard fruits ripening in the fleeting flush of the sun's warm light. Hazy, slanting rays gild the late season glory in the garden. Surrounded by flowers of dissipating beauty and juxtaposed against the dazzling brilliance of autumn foliage, we are urged to spend every possible moment savoring our gardens before the onset of winter.

Autumn is the season to reflect upon our gardening successes and failures while they are still fresh in our minds. Whether recombining plants to create new associations of scents and colors, or replacing a tired plant that failed to thrive, early autumn is the ideal season to plant trees, shrubs, and perennials. The cooler weather directs the plant to put its energy into establishing strong root growth. Tender plants and newly planted trees, shrubs, and perennials benefit from being provided with an extra thick blanket by mulching with compost and newly fallen leaves, adding nutrients to the soil, and protecting the plant's roots against winterkill, particularly during severe winters.

The fiery, saturated hues of autumn are due in part not only to the blazing foliage of trees and shrubs but also to the copious members of the Compositae. Formerly called Asteraceae (Aster family), aster refers to a star, the Composite family of herbaceous perennials includes numerous native species attractive to butterflies as well as ornamental and late season flowering chrysanthemum and dendranthema. The composite flowers of sunflower (*Helianthus* spp.), coneflower (*Echinacea* spp.), goldenrod (*Solidago* spp.), and Joe-pye weed (*Eupatorium purpureum*) play host to myriad butterflies during the plants persistent florescence. Indigenous asters and Mexican sunflowers (*Tithonia rotundifolia*) are available for the southward migrating Monarchs and Ruby-throated Humming-birds.

With cheery, one-inch, button-shaped flowers borne along the lengths of the stalks, the pale-hued, lavender-blue ray flowers and yellow disk florets of the native New York aster (*Aster novi-belgii*) attract legions of butterflies. We have observed Common Sulphers, Pink-fringed Sulphurs, Monarchs, Painted Ladies, Red Admirals, and Cabbage Whites nectaring simultaneously on a clump growing in the sheltered border along our fragrant path. New York asters provide nourishing sustenance for transitory butterflies when many nectar-rich plants have finished blooming for the season. Our New York asters were obtained from gathering a stalk with ripened seeds growing in a nearby meadow. A quick shake of the stalk over a select sunny spot and there you go! We have rejoiced in New York asters coming up here and there ever since. This is a plant that has the potential to grow four to five feet in a single season. Pinch back the developing growth tips during the early part of the growing season (until roughly July fourth) to encourage a bushier and more compact plant.

Chrysanthemum 'Emperor of China' begins its lovely tableau in mid-fall and continues to bloom through the first hard frost. Plum rose with silvery high-lights, the quills shade paler toward the outer margins. When the plant is in full bloom, the rich green foliage shifts colors to vibrant hues of bronze to scarlet red. The 'Emperor of China' exudes a delicious lemon-spice fragrance notice-able from some distance.

As with New York asters, it is helpful to pinch the tips of each shoot to en-courage branching and more blossoms. Repeat this process at each four- to six-inch stage of new growth until the middle of July, or when the buds begin to develop. 'Emperor of China' is hardy through zone six and thrives in full sun to light shade in well-drained soil. This cultivar forms a 2½-foot mound in only a few years. Give the plant a top dressing of compost and mulch after the first hard frost.

An ancient variety of chrysanthemum originating from China, the 'Emperor of China' resembles and is thought to be the chrysanthemum depicted in early Chinese paintings. Chrysanthemums are also grown for their medicinal proper-ties, and their purported magic juices were an important ingredient in the life-prolonging elixir of the Daoist. Fragrant chrysanthemum tea was considered good for the health, and tonic wine was brewed from an infusion of their petals.[1] Although thought to be rich in healing properties and lovely in form, a more modest well-being was conferred by the vigorous blossoming of the chrysanthe-mum. Perhaps the late flowering chrysanthemum suggests their connection to a

CHRYSANTHEMUM TEA

Chrysanthemum tea is a tisane made from dried chrysanthemum flowers. The flowers are steeped in boiling water for several minutes, and rock sugar or honey is often added to heighten the sweet aroma. Popular throughout east Asia, chrysanthemum tea is usually served with a meal. In the tradition of Chinese medicine, the tisane is thought to be a "cooling" herb and is recommended for a variety of ailments including influenza, circulatory disorders, sore throats, and fever.

long life, for other plants have finished flowering just as the chrysanthemums begin.

The techniques for learning to paint the orchid, bamboo, plum blossom, and chrysanthemum comprise the basis of Chinese flower and bird painting. They are referred to as "The Four Gentlemen" and are thought to symbolize great intellectual ideas. The orchid is serene and peaceful, though sophisticated and reserved from the world. Bamboo is vigorous and survives throughout the seasons, forever growing upright. The plum blossom expresses *yin-yang* dualities of delicate and hardy, blooming through snow and ice to herald the arrival of spring. Chrysanthemums continue to flower after a frost, are self-sufficient, and require no assistance in propogating themselves.[2]

China owes its astonishing wealth of plant life to a combination of geographical incidents. The mountains escaped the ravages of the great ice caps and unlike much of Europe and North America, where many plants were wiped out, plant species in China continued to evolve. Additionally, the foothills of the Himalayas are moistened by soft winds from the south, creating an ideal climate for alpine plants. In this warm and moderate environment, three different floras – that of the colder, drier north; that of the sub-tropical south; and that of the alpine species – all mingled and crossed freely for thousands of years.[3]

Ernest Wilson, one of the world's greatest plant hunters, was not the first collector to explore this botanical paradise, but his determined efforts to push through to remote areas led him to the "richest temperate flora of the world."

From 1899 to 1911, Ernest "Chinese" Wilson sent the seeds of more than 1,500 different plants to the United States and England. Altogether his collection numbered 65,000 plants, representing about 5,000 species, all gathered from the wild. Through his exploration, and the work of the nurseries for which he collected, more than a thousand plants were established for Western cultivation.

Despite the wealth of flora collected by Ernest Wilson and his fellow plant hunters, Chinese gardens remained wholly unaffected. Although shiploads of plants were sent to London, St. Petersburg, Paris, and Cambridge, Massachusetts, Chinese horticulturists continued to develop plants their ancestors had loved and that had long since been domesticated. The tradition of conferring qualities of morality to plants and plants' allegorical to intellectual ideas made the newly collected wild plants unsuitable for the Chinese garden.

The fittingly named butterfly bush (*Buddleia davidii*) is just one of the now-common-to-every-garden introductions from Ernest Wilson, collected from western China for the Arnold Arboretum. Although the species name commemorates Armand David, the French missionary who first noted it growing in China in 1869, it was Ernest Wilson who collected several superior forms, and the great majority of cultivated *B. davidii* are derived from Wilson's collections. The elegant butterfly bush, with its willow-green elliptical leaves and sprays of arching canes is covered in fragrant blossoms from mid-summer through the first frost. *B. davidii* flower in a range of hues from purple to magenta to blue to rosy lavender and white. 'Nanho Blue,' a clear fresh blue and 'White Profusion,' with white florets and orange eyes, are both slightly more compact cultivars. The blossoms of 'Empire Blue' are similar in color to 'Nanho Blue,' although it grows several feet taller and tends to be leggy. 'Pink Delight' is covered in rose-pink florets, and the trusses of 'Black Knight' are a rich violet purple. All of these cultivars are potently fragrant with a luscious vanilla-honey-hay scent.

Plant butterfly bushes near a window, around the porch or along a walkway, not only to enjoy their traveling fragrance, but also to intimately observe the collection of butterflies that visit the shrubs. With persistent deadheading, the butterfly bushes continue to bloom through the late summer and early autumn months, just when the Japanese anemones are coming into flower. 'September Charm' is the first anemone to flower, and has an extended period of florescence, first opening during the last of the dog days of August and continuing through early October. The silvery lilac-rose flowers atop graceful slender stems blend exquisitely in the mixed border and they have the added ability to naturalize quickly. 'September Charm' is prolific and easily propagated by dividing the fibrous roots in early spring. Planted in the dappled shade cast by our 'Nanho Blue' butterfly bush, the two together create a lovely color association.

'Honorine Jobert' is a pure white cultivar of *A. japonica*, beginning to bloom a week later than 'September Charm.' The delicate white petals, with their apple green centers and bright orange stamens rising above the lush blue-green foliage, are a refreshing arrangement of colors. The foliage of the Japanese anemones makes an attractive plant in the border throughout the spring and summer months. *A. japonica* does not care much for dry shade, preferring a moist, rich soil in a semi-shaded spot. Provided with a mulch of decaying leaves, they require very little attention.

The little corner of the garden that shelters the 'Nanho Blue' butterfly bush and 'September Charm' anemones is a magnet for pollinators, with the butter-fly bush a mecca for swallowtails, Monarchs, Painted Ladies and fritillaries, and the anemones practically vibrating from the murmurings of the bumblebees.

Annually, in mid spring, before new growth begins to emerge, prune the stems back hard, leaving approximately six to ten inches above ground level. *B. davidii* is a shrub that breaks dormancy very late in the spring in northern gardens. The colder and lengthier the winter, the later the buddleias emerge. New growth may not be visible until the very last day of spring, literally June 20th! *B. davidii* blooms on the current year's growth, therefore flowering will not be affected by a spring pruning. The weeping butterfly bush (*B. alternifolia*) blooms in mid-spring on the growth of the previous season. Prune the weeping butterfly bush in early summer, after it has finished flowering.

And so the ripe year wanes. From turfy slopes afar the breeze brings delicious, pungent spicy odors from the wild Everlasting flowers, and mushrooms are pearly in the grass. I gather the seed-pods in the garden beds, sharing their bounty with the birds I love so well, for there are enough and to spare for us all.

Oh Garden of Fresh Possibilities!

Soon will set in the fitful weather, with fierce gales and sullen skies and frosty air, and it will be time to tuck up safely my Roses and Lilies and the rest for their long winter sleep beneath the snow, where I never forget them, but ever dream of their wakening in happy summers yet to be.

— from *An Island Garden* by Celia Thaxter

Exquisite Flora for
Late Summer and Autumn

SHRUBS AND SMALL TREES

Red chokeberry (*Aronia arbutifolia*) ~ *foliage, berries*
Black chokeberry (*Aronia melanocarpa*) ~ *foliage, berries*
Angel's trumpet (*Brugmansia* 'Charles Grimaldi', *Brugmansia suaveolens*) ~ *flowers*
Butterfly bush (*Buddleia davidii*) ~ *flowers*
Tea (*Camellia sinensis*) ~ *flowers*
Katsura tree (*Cercidiphyllum japonicum*) ~ *foliage*
Eastern redbud (*Cercis canadensis*) ~ *foliage*
Summersweet (*Clethra alnifolia*) ~ *foliage*
Dogwood (*Cornus*) ~ *foliage, berries*
American smoketree (*Cotinus obovatus*) ~ *foliage*
Ben Franklin tree (*Franklinia alatamaha*) ~ *flowers*
Rose of Sharon (*Hibiscus syriacus*) ~ *flowers*
Hydrangea (*Hydrangea macrophylla*) ~ *flowers*
'Peegee' hydrangea (*Hydrangea paniculata*) ~ *foliage, flowers*
Meserve holly (*Ilex meserveae*) ~ *foliage, berries*
'Winter Red' winterberry (*Ilex verticillata*) ~ *foliage, berries*
Spicebush (*Lindera benzoin*) ~ *foliage*
Honeysuckle (*Lonicera* 'Dropmore Scarlet') ~ *foliage*
Sargent crabapple (*Malus sargentii*) ~ *foliage, berries*
Honeysuckle Azalea (*Rhododendron viscosum*) ~ *foliage*
Repeat blooming roses (*Rosa* Souvenir de Victor Landeau, 'Louise Odier,' 'Aloha,' 'Mme. Alfred Carrière,' 'Fragrant Cloud,' and 'Frederick Mistral') ~ *flowers, hips*

Virginia rose (*Rosa virginiana*) ~ *hips*
Japanese stewartia (*Stewartia pseudocamellia*) ~ *foliage*
Highbush blueberry (*Vaccinium corymbosum*) ~ *foliage*
Arrowwood viburnum (*Viburnum dentatum*) ~ *foliage, berries*

PERENNIALS

Japanese anemone (*Anemone hupehensis* var. *japonica*)
New York aster (*Aster novi-belgii*)
New England aster (*Aster novae-angliae*)
Boltonia (*Boltonia asteroids*)
'Emperor of China' chrysanthemum (*Chrysanthemum*)
Montauk daisy (*Chrysanthemum nipponicum*)
Sheffield daisy (*Chrysanthemum rubellum* 'Sheffield Pink')
Korean daisy (*Chrysanthemum* 'Single Apricot Korean')
'Sweet Autumn' clematis (*Clematis paniculata*)
Coneflower (*Echinacea purpurea*)
Spotted Joe-pye weed (*Eupatorium purpureum*)
Crimson-eyed rosemallow hibiscus (*Hibiscus moscheutos ssp. lasiocarpos*)
'August Lily' and 'Aphrodite' (*Hosta*)
Sedum (*Hylotelephium spectabile* 'Meteor')
Seaside golden rod (*Solidago sempervirens*)
New York ironweed (*Veronia noveboracensis*)

ANNUALS

Cup-and-saucer vine, cathedral-bells (*Cobaea scandens*)
Cosmos (*Cosmos bipinnatus*)
Sunflower (*Helianthus*)
Jewelweed, spotted touch-me-not (*Impatiens capensis*)
Moonflower (*Ipomoea alba*)
Cardinal climber (*Ipomoea* x *multifida*)
Morning glory (*Ipomoea purpurea*)
Cypress vine (*Ipomoea quamoclit*)
Mexican sunflower (*Tithonia rotundifolia*)
Nasturtiums (*Tropaeolum majus*)
Verbena bonariensis
Zinnia (*Zinnia elegans*)

Oh Garden of Fresh Possibilities!

⌒

Just as autumn is the season to turn to look back on the year to plan improvements, I find myself also reflecting upon the moments in the garden for which I am especially grateful:

For the Ruby-throated Hummingbirds that arrived in early March and began calling our garden theirs, followed soon after by the advent of the stunning Baltimore Orioles. Migrating northward, the orioles herald the blossoming of fruit trees – upon arriving they take nectar from the cherry and plum and move on to the newly opening flowers of the pear trees. Brief encounters in the garden of wild creatures are enthralling and startling simultaneously. Cherishing these gifts, of the annual arrival of these two birds, with the flash of brilliant orange plumage of the oriole in flight and the Ruby-throated Hummingbirds hovering over a blossom is not meant to diminish the joy we derive from observing the small creatures that frequent our garden daily. Songbirds like the Black-capped Chickadees, foraging for seeds and insects day in and day out, winter, spring, summer, and autumn. We welcome the chickadees and chorus of songbirds enlivening the winterscape, along with the seasonal travelers.

With ongoing care we are harvesting an ever-increasing bounty of pears. I am thankful for one pear tree in particular. The branch of an Anjou pear had been grafted to the Beurre Bosc tree. From this tree we pick two different crops of pears, harvesting the Beurre Bosc approximately a month later than the Anjou. We have made a tradition of serving Beurre Bosc pears with a selection of cheese along with our Thanksgiving feast.

I give thanks for a particular fleeting moment of a steamy morning in late August. In the lingering haze of the silvery soft early morning light I walked through the garden down our narrow path taking in the sight and scent of every fragrant flower blooming. I put my face to the August lily, inhaling deeply the honeysuckle sweet fragrance. A footstep more, and leaning closer into the 'Moonlight of the Groves' jasmine, I breathed in the surrounding air suffused with the rich perfume evocative of distant destinations. Next to savor were the sublimely scented Oriental lilies, and then a few steps more to the white butterfly bush 'Profusion' with its fresh honey vanilla scent. Now and again I paused to breathe in the heavenly fragrance of the peacock orchids assembled in drifts along the walkway. Wending my way to the sunniest part of the garden, I stopped for a moment to become entwined with the perfume of the reblooming Japanese honeysuckle weaving its way through the trellis beneath the bedroom

window. Despite its tender size, the insinuating spicy fragrance of the foliage of the 'Lattarula' fig was impossible to ignore. Chinese gardenia had given us another bloom and the air surrounding the potted plant was impregnated with a sultry romance. I proceeded to take in each and every rose in bloom. Unforgettable was the demure fresh fragrance of 'Eden' and the deliciously fruity perfume of 'Aloha.' Then the sumptuous scent of the Bourbon rose 'Louise Odier,' in all of her exquisite camellia-like form. Perfect cupcake pink 'Frederick Mistral' and his delicious tea rose perfume, offset by a note of lemon, was cloaked in buds and newly opening blossoms. 'Fragrant Cloud' vibrates in waves of potent fragrance and vivid carmine vermilion hues. The last remontant rose of the morning was the luminous pearl-tinted 'Mme. Alfred Carrière,' with her intoxicating and far-flung Tea-Noisette perfume. The sun rose higher, the light grew sharper, and this transcendent moment was over.

For all of these moments in our garden, the celebrations of life in small spaces, the harmonies of light, flowers, and fragrances, the gifts of rhythm in renewal, I rejoice.

The morns are meeker than they were,
The nuts are getting brown;
The berry's cheek is plumper,
The rose is out of town.

The maple wears a gayer scarf,
The field a scarlet gown.
Lest I should be old-fashioned,
I'll put a trinket on.

— EMILY DICKINSON

CHAPTER TWENTY

A Note to Spring Signed Autumn

The narrow bud opens her beauties to
The sun, and love runs in her thrilling veins;
Blossoms hang round the brows of Morning, and
Flourish down the bright cheek of modest Eve,
Till clust'ring Summer breaks forth into singing,
And feather'd clouds strew flowers round her head.

The spirits of the air live in the smells
Of fruit; and Joy, with pinions light, roves round
The gardens, or sits singing in the trees.

—from *To Autumn* by WILLIAM BLAKE (1757–1827)

WHILE SMALL TREES AND SHRUBS are becoming established, the ground between them affords myriad places to plant spring flowers. Here bluebells, forget-me-nots, snowflakes, lily of-the-valley, narcissus and tulips make themselves at home. When the ground is left undisturbed for a year or two, the freely reseeding forget-me-nots yield a spring carpet of sweet blue florets. Provided with fertile and well-draining soil, jonquil and crocus naturalize readily. In a few short years, lily of-the-valley covers the ground with swaths of oval-shaped, spring-green foliage.

Autumn, with its cool weather and frequent rainfall, is the season to plant in anticipation of spring, whether planting trees and shrubs as part of the overall framework, organizing the borders, or planting the surrounding space to complement the flowering trees. Free and available for the taking is nature's beneficial mulch of newly fallen leaves. Amidst the flowering trees and shrubs and beds of perennials, the bulbs we sow in autumn illuminate the spring. What began as a short note on fragrant spring flowering bulbs, quickly took the form of a long letter addressed to the well-known and well-loved bulbs with scented flowers, as well as lesser-known fragrant species that deserve to be planted more abundantly.

Lily of-the-valley

With its incomparable perfume and snow-white flowers issuing forth in the bright hopeful season of spring, the lily of-the-valley has long been associated in literature with sweetness and the return of happiness.

> *No flower amid the garden fairer grows*
> *Than the sweet lily of the lowly vale,*
> *The queen of flowers.*

—JOHN KEATS (1795–1821)

The lily of-the-valley, known also as May lily and May bells, is native to northern Europe, the Allegheny Mountains of North America, and the British Isles. Between a pair of unfurling new-green leaves emerges a diminutive arching scape, covered in dangling pure white chubby bells. Their fabulous fragrance floats freely throughout the garden, unusual for a plant that grows close to the ground.

Beloved wherever it is grown, for its ineffable scent and sweet flowers, the lily of-the-valley is used extensively for perfumes, soaps, and toilet water, nowhere more so than in Europe. The French translation is *muguet des bois* (of the wood), the German translation is *mit Maiglockchen*, the Italian *al mughetto*, the Spanish say *lirio del valle*, the Finnish translation is *lehmakielo*, and the Swedish say *liljekonvalj*.

Convallaria majalis is the native species of northern Europe. The name *Convallaria* is from two Latin words meaning "with" and "valley," having reference to its habit of growing on mountain slopes. *Convallaria majuscula* is the species indigenous to North America. *C. majuscula* is found growing in remote woodland locations, along the mountainsides and ridges of Virginia, West Virginia, and south to Georgia. *C. majuscula* is nearly identical to *C. majalis*, with slightly smaller though equally fragrant flowers.

C. majalis is a vigorous perennial ground cover with a rhizomatic root structure that grows and spreads quickly. Thriving in nearly every light condition save full sun, lily of-the-valley never disappoints. Light, fertile, and preferably damp soil is the preferred growing medium of *C. majalis*. Provided with an annual mulch of compost or decaying leaves, lily of-the-valley multiplies rapidly. With its cold hardiness, ability to spread readily, and pervasively fragrant blossoms it is incomparable as a ground cover. The one drawback of lily of-the-valley is that, come late August, the foliage browns and becomes tattered. Grow with late season blooming perennials and bulbs, Japanese anemones and peacock orchids, for example, to draw your eye up and away from the messy foliage.

Set the pips, or bulblets, three inches deep and about four inches apart in a well-prepared bed. Water during dry periods and fertilize with fish fertilizer throughout the first season after planting to encourage strong root development. After it has become well established, the plant is easily propagated. A freshly dug clump, as a whole unit, can either be transferred and replanted in a newly dug and well-prepared location, or the bulblets can be carefully divided and spread more judiciously, allowing for a small section of roots for each one or two pips. Plunge a serrated-edge knife deeply into the ground. Cut out a plug six to eight inches in diameter. Refill the hole created by digging the clump with compost. Lily of-the-valley will soon recover and fill out the spot. Early spring and mid-fall are the best times of year to divide *C. majalis*, although they are not that fussy. If the plant has to be divided in the summer, water regularly to prevent the new division from drying out while becoming established in its new home. With regular thinning and transplanting, one's extra efforts will be rewarded with an ever-increasing treasure of scented flowers and sea of green groundcover, with many gifts to pass along to friends.

Not to be forgotten is the noteworthy *Convallaria majalis* var. *rosea*. Characteristic in form to the white lily of-the-vale, *rosea* has delicate, pendulous bells washed in shades of rosy pink. We have found it to be somewhat less hardy than *Convallaria majalis*.

A cautionary note is in order regarding *Convallaria*. All parts of the plant are highly poisonous. In old herbal guides, lily of-the-valley was recommended as a heart stimulant, and was used medicinally in ways similar to digitalis. The eye-catching, plump vermilion berries may be dangerously attractive to young children and can cause paralysis and severe respiratory disorders if ingested.

Crocus

One of the most ethereal scents of the early spring garden is the fragrant crocus. Within the genus, several of the species are scented, with fragrance also present in hybrids of the snow crocus (*C. chrysanthus*). Although the sweet, honeysuckle-like fragrance may be diminished out of doors in the cold air of late winter, a handful of crocuses brought inside and placed in a warm room will give one a hint of the scents to follow.

Crocuses show their best when planted closely together. Flowering in swirling ribbons under the diaphanous canopy of high-branched trees, and woven through the perennial and shrub borders, who could not be assured of spring's imminent arrival? Crocuses grow well in short grass, beneath trees, and tucked into crags and niches in the alpine garden. Wherever the soil is fairly fertile, loose, and noncompacted, they will endure and multiply. Given a nourishing and well-draining soil and a minimum of a half-day of sunlight, they will reward you with beautiful blooms for years and years.

To a Crocus

Welcome, wild harbinger of spring!
To this small nook of earth;
Feeling and fancy fondly cling
Round thoughts which owe their birth
To thee, and to the humble spot
Where chance has fixed thy lowly lot.

— BERNARD BARTON (1784–1849)

Snow crocus (*C. chrysanthus*), with smaller and a greater number of flowers than the more familiar Dutch crocus (*C. vernus*), generally blooms in late winter. By that virtue they have earned their nickname "snow crocus." The hardy and long-lived *C. chrysanthus*, with golden yellow flowers, is found growing in Bulgaria, Greece, and Asia Minor. 'Snow Bunting,' with white flowers stippled palest blue, is a sweetly scented hybrid of *C. chrysanthus* raised by E. A. Bowles, the celebrated English plantsman. The deliciously fragrant 'Cream Beauty,' with rounded flowers the color of pale butter-cream frosting, offset by bright orange stamens, is another cultivar of *C. chrysanthus*. Gerald Hageman of the Netherlands introduced 'Cream Beauty' in 1943. It is a "bunch" flowering crocus in that several flowers emerge from a single corm. 'Cream Beauty' and the luminous 'Blue Pearl' flower together, and both are among the most persistently blooming, readily naturalizing, and fragrant crocuses in our garden.

Crocus imperati is found growing around the Bay of Naples and southward of Calabria. Blooming earlier and with larger flowers than *C. chrysanthus*, it too, is one of the more sweetly scented crocuses. The petals are buff colored with delicate violet-purple feathering and yellow hearts accented with orange-scarlet anthers. The cultivar *C. imperatti* 'de Jager' is more widely available than the species. *Crocus imperati* was named after the sixteenth-century Italian botanist Ferrante Imperato. Roman women washed in toilet water made from the fresh flowers, and the petals were dried and used to fill pillows and cushions.[1]

Crocus suaveolens, known also as the Roman crocus, is a closely related species to *C. imperati*, blooming after both it and 'Cream Beauty.' The star-shaped flowers are smaller than *C. imperatti* with paler lilac shading washed over the buff colored petals, though what it lacks in size when compared to *C. imperati*, it more than compensates with a decidedly more pronounced fragrance.

Bluebells of England

After years of delighting in the beautiful display provided by our English bluebells (*Hyacinthoides non-scripta*), I was taken aback to see their loveliness slowly diminish. Our bluebells had become overcrowded, their blossoms dwindling in size and number. Pendulous lilac-blue bells rising above slender, apple-green foliage created an ethereal blue mist in our woodland border. The fragrance is similar, though lighter, than the heady fragrance of the large, hybridized Dutch hyacinths (*Hyacinthus orientalis*). I had waited at least a year too long to thin them, and their beauty was sorely missed.

The time of year to replant and divide the English bluebells is after the bulbs have gone dormant (indicated by foliage that has yellowed and withered). Patiently waiting until mid-summer, we were delighted to find a treasure trove of bulbs. From a handful planted some years earlier, we now had riches. I brushed off the soil and stored the full-sized and smaller offsets in a basket for several days while contemplating where to plant this unexpected largesse.

The splendid scent of English bluebells wafts through the garden and, ideally, they should grow where their fragrance can be enjoyed, along the garden path and in close proximity to the home. They multiply rapidly; we replanted sparingly, approximately eight inches apart, bearing in mind they would soon fill out. If one prefers a fuller look and can't wait for a year or two, plant the bulbs closer together.

H. non-scripta prefer a slightly damp, rich, and fertile soil, planted three inches deep. They are hardy to zone six and will grow in a range of light conditions from open areas to the dappled shade of deciduous trees. Bluebells are a fine companion to Magnolia *sieboldii*, flowering crabapples, and in particular *Malus sargentii*, *Paeonia rockii*, *Viola* 'Etain,' Virdiflora tulips, 'Snow Queen' iris, mid- to late-season jonquils, lily of-the-valley, and white bleeding heart (*Dicentra spectablis* alba). They provide an unobtrusive companion to the next wave of summer flowering plants. The bulbs retreat into dormancy relatively quickly, and the yellowed foliage should be removed for the remainder of the growing season. *Hyacinthoides non-scripta* is synonymous with *Endymion non-scriptus* and *Scilla non-scripta.*

Narcissus

The bee doth love the sweetest flower,
So doth the blossom the April shower.

Thinking of spring in autumn, I am reminded of the first time I smelled a fragrant jonquil. The diminutive, cupped-golden flowers were growing freely in an abandoned garden. I have no idea what variety of jonquil it was and can hardly give a good description, remembering more its scent than any distinguishing great beauty. This plain little jonquil was half the size of the more commonly grown big, brassy King Alfred trumpet types, and it (the dainty one) had a dreamy honeysuckle fragrance!

I have to laugh recounting a comment one of our children made after taking note of a border planted with soldier-like trumpet daffodils, forming neat perfect rows, face forward and at sentinel-like attention, growing in ground covered with bark mulch in that most peculiar shade of orange-red. She exclaimed, "Look, Mom, Lego daffodils!" I am sure everyone familiar with the plastic toy understands the allusion. Several of the sets come with miniature plastic flowers. Unlike their modern counterparts, the sweet and friendly species narcissus and early hybrids exude a lightness and grace of form, along with a delicious fragrance. Here is one species not improved by an ever more brazen variety of size and form.

Narcissus is named for the handsome youth in Greek mythology with whom Echo fell in love. Narcissus became so enamored of his own reflection in a pool, sitting and smiling at himself, that, on hearing Echo's repeated proclamations of love, he forgot to eat and drink until withering away and dying. Where he had been sitting, the lovely Narcissus flower sprang to life. Echo stood beside the

flower, pining and grieving, until she too withered away. Nothing was left of Echo but her voice, senselessly repeating the words of others.[2]

The following is a short list of favorite narcissus and jonquils, selected not only because they are fabulously fragrant, but also because these cultivars return reliably year after year. The list is arranged to create a cheery procession of scented blooms. By planting with nonscented narcissus that are either earlier blooming or later blooming, the daffodil season is extended typically from March to May.

Narcissus x *odorus* 'Campernelle' ~ Yellow perianth and corona, superb naturalizer, 10–12 inches, zone 4 to 9, early season.

Narcissus tazetta 'Martinette' ~ Golden petals and a vivid orange cup. Floriferous, blooming for several weeks, 14 inches, zone 4 to 9, early to mid-season.

N. jonquilla 'Sweetness' ~ Golden-yellow blossoms, 16–18 inches, zone 3 to 8, mid-season.

Narcissus tazetta 'Geranium' ~ Ivory white petals and a cheery vivid red-orange cup, floriferous, 16–18 inches, zone 4 to 9, mid-season.

N. 'Minnow' ~ Creamy white petals with a clear yellow cup. Many blooms on each 10-inch stem, zone 5 to 8, mid-season. 'Minnow,' along with 'Geranium,' are my current favorites for fragrance and their extended season of blooms.

N. 'Fragrant Breeze' ~ Apricot-orange, long cup daffodil juxtaposed against white petals, 14 inches, zone 3 to 8, mid-season.

N. poeticus 'Ornatus' ~ Pure white petals, the cup is similar to that of 'Actaea,' blooming two weeks earlier, 16 inches, mid-season.

N. 'Laurens Koster' ~ Creamy white perianth with deep cadmium yellow corona. Multiple flowers on many stems, 16–18 inches, zone 6 to 9, late-season.

N. poeticus 'Actaea' ~ Snowy white perianth with a picotee edging of red around the small yellow cup, 16 inches, zone 3 to 8, mid- to late season.

N. 'Fragrant Rose' ~ White overlapping petals combined with a long-cup shaped corona of rosy pink, 16 inches, zone 3 to 8, mid- to late season.

N. jonquilla ~ The species jonquil with two to three sunny yellow flowers on each stem, 5 inches, zone 5 to 9, late season.

N. 'Sinopel' ~ Sparkling, fresh white petals with short, light, bright green cup trimmed with yellow, 16 inches, zone 3 to 8, late season.

N. jonquilla 'Baby Moon' ~ Diminutive lemon-yellow jonquil with three to four blossoms on each stem, 8 inches, zone 3 to 8, late season.

N. jonquilla 'Bell Song' ~ Cups of rose pink surrounded by ivory white perianth, 12 inches, zone 3 to 8, late season.

N. 'Sir Winston Churchill' ~ Plump double daffodil, with pale orange petals swirled throughout the creamy white petals, 16 inches, late season.

In northern regions, daffodils are ideally planted from early September through early October to afford the plant ample time to establish their roots. Planted any later in the season and one is courting failure. Rich, nourishing soil, not too hot nor dry, nor too soggy, best suits their needs. Detach the flower head after blooming to encourage the daffodil to direct energy to increase bulb size rather than to producing seed. To insure blossoms for the following season, the foliage of the narcissus plants should not be removed immediately. Photosynthesis replenishes and restores the bulb. The leaves will eventually yellow and wither, whereupon the remains dug into the soil and the beds tidied-up.

Narcissus prefers a location out in the open with some dappled shade provided by a tree with high branches. A careless, scattered random effect is the desired result. Plant in gatherings, with little irregular groups trailing off here and there. Unlike crocuses, which present their best when planted closely together, daffodils need a little space to show off their joyful flowers and graceful foliage.

Tulipa

The sweet scents of May are rarely associated with the tulip. We are all familiar with scentless tulips available in the florist trade and gaily colored bedding tulips. Not usually realized is that numerous large flowered hybrids are sweetly scented, along with several of the more diminutive, though no less gay, species tulips.

Wild growing tulips are found "along a corridor which stretches either side of the line of 40 degrees north. The line, extending from Ankara in Turkey eastwards through Jerevan and Baku to Turkmenistan, then on past Bukhara, Samakand and Tashkent to the mountains of the Pamir-Alai, with neighbouring Tien Shan, is the hotbed of the tulip family."[3] The tulip takes its name from the Turkish headdress known as a turban or *tolipan*, which the flower resembles in form.

The Zurich botanist Conrad Gesner recorded the first known report of the tulip growing in western Europe, in the garden of John Harwart of Bavaria, in 1559. Upon visiting the garden Gesner describes not only the lily-like form and satiny red petals, but also fragrance " . . . a pleasant smell, soothing and delicate."[4] When describing a flower in the sixteenth century, fragrance was given as equal weight with the description of form and color. Tulips are one of the few flowers where scent is as pronounced in the *scarlet colors* as in those bearing pale yellow and white flowers.

The earliest cultivars to capture the imagination of the seventeenth-century European collectors were striped and streaked and feathered and flamed. This was due to a viral disease carried by aphids. Although benign, the virus caused the flowers to "break" into fancifully rich patterning in contrasting colors. The early collectors had no understanding of why the breaks occurred and each flower was unique unto itself. Once a bulb had "broken," its offsets could reproduce the characteristic patterning and colors, though the effect of the virus caused the bulb to weaken. The broken bulbs often commanded a stupendously high price, and if you could not afford the bulbs, you could always commission an artist to paint the flowers.

The early seventeenth century, including the brief mania of tulip collecting, speculating, and trading known as tulipomania (1634–1637), and the subsequent hundred years, was a period of great new wealth and prosperity in Holland. The developing importance of Amsterdam as a port city and the founding and the success of the Dutch East India Trading Company created a wealthy class of merchants, tradesmen, and professionals, doctors and lawyers. Art flourished, supported by the wealthy patrons. The Dutch floral painters mirrored the cultural prominence of flowers and society's burgeoning interest in botany.

Well worth seeking are the exuberant watercolor sketches of the van Huysum family. I first became enamored of their floral studies after stumbling upon one in the book *Flowers in Art from East to West* by Paul Hulton and Lawrence Smith. The sketch is attributed to Jan van Huysum. Jan and Jacob, and their less-well-known brothers Michael and Justus the Younger followed their father, Justice the Elder, by becoming artists. Jan (1682–1749) exceeded his brothers in prominence and fortune. During his lifetime, this Old Master commanded very high prices for his paintings and was patronized by kings and royalty throughout Europe. Although his oil paintings are rendered in the realistic style of the period, and are suffused with the symbols of morality that were an integral part of Dutch still-life paintings, he broke with the tradition of painting dark backgrounds. His later compositions, after 1720, are painted on a lighter ground with lively, loose, and less formalized compositions. Jan van Huysum was referred to by his contemporaries as the "phoenix of all flower painters" and he saw his work as an expression of a greater knowledge and awareness.

"Consider the lilies of the field, Solomon in all his glory was
not arrayed like one of these."
from an inscription on a flower vase painted by Jan van Huysum.

⌒

Unlike his brother, who lived and painted in Holland his entire life, Jacob van Huysum (1687–1740) moved to London in 1721 to the home of his patron Mr. Lockyear of South Sea House. He was subsequently patronized by other Englishmen to paint floral pieces. Best known today for providing the drawings for the majority of illustrations for the earliest botanical book with plates printed in color, John Martyn's *Historia Plantarum Rariorum* (1728–1738), Jacob van Huysum saw his drawings engraved, printed in quantity, and made available to a general public.

For the era in which they were painted, the watercolor drawings and sketches of the brothers Jacob and Jan have an unparalleled exuberance and luminosity. While not sacrificing botanical accuracy, the drawings resonate with an extraordinary light touch, managing to capture the essence of the flora. One would imagine, with the inexorable and highly profitable flow of trade between Holland and the East Indies that Jan van Huysum could not help but be influenced by paintings, ceramics, and textiles from east Asia. The few paintings that I have had the good fortune to encounter were of roses and tulips and belong to the permanent collection of the British Museum.

⌣

Fragrant Tulipa

SPECIES

T. celsiana synonymous with *T. persica* ~ The Persian tulip, with deep green, folded leaves tinged with crimson, bears star-like, clear yellow-orange flowers blushed bronze. 4 to 6 inches. Deliciously scented late-season bloomer.

T. humulis 'Alba Caurula Oculata.' ~ White flowers with violet blue hearts and black stamens. Sweetly fragrant. 3 to 4 inches. Synonymous with *T. pulchella*.

T. primulina ~ papery pale creamy yellow delicate bell-shaped flowers washed with green. Lavender-rose tint along the outer edges of the petal segments. Blooms early in the season with a lily of-the-valley perfume.

T. saxtalis ~ Pale lavender-pink and a large buttery yellow wash at the base of each petal. Early blooming with the sweet scent of primrose. Increases by underground stolens.

T. schrenkii synonymous with *T. suaveolens* ~ No taller than a crocus, cheerful scarlet-edged, golden yellow flowers appearing early in the season.

T. sylvestris ~ Narrow gray-green foliage with one to two nodding flowers atop slender stems. Graceful, rich golden yellow tulip shaded green on the outside, 6-12 inches. The tips recurve when in bloom as well as in bud. Increases by underground stolens. Sweetly scented of violets. Known also as the Florentine or wood tulip. Early.

T. turkestanica synonymous with *T. biflora* ~ Three creamy white flowers with cheery yellow hearts. Lightly scented.

SOME FRAGRANT HYBRIDS

Prince of Austria ~ Scented of orange blossoms and violets. Clear red shaded toward gleaming orange. Single Early and vigorous. 12 inches. 1860.

Bellona ~ Sun-golden yellow, egg shaped. Deliciously scented. Single Early. 14 inches. 1944.

General de Wet ~ Cups of brilliant cadmium red-orange shaded yellow at the base. Sweetly scented. Single Early. 12 to 14 inches. Early 1900s.

Murillo ~ White flushed with rose. The origin of most Double Earlies. Delicious honey scent. Mid-April. 1860.

Montreux ~ Ivory blossoms washed with rose-red. Richly scented. Double Early. 18 inches. Mid-April.

Purissima ~ Milky-white flowers with yellow centers borne on sturdy stems. Lightly scented of violets. Synonymous with 'White Emperor.' Fosteriana Group. April. 16 to 18 inches. 1943.

Apricot Beauty ~ Shades of lambent apricot and rose with a pale green star at the base. Light rose fragrance. Triumph Tulip. May. 16–18 inches.

Lightening Sun ~ Shimmering and radiant hues of marigold orange to rose-pink. Giant Darwin. May. 18 to 20 inches.

Ellen Willmott ~ Primrose yellow lily-flowered with a lovely honey perfume. Early May. 18 to 20 inches. 1900.

Ballerina ~ Sunset hues of vivid orange. Lily Flowered. May. 20 inches.

La Merveille ~ Exquisitely scented, lily-flowered petals scarlet-orange, flushed rose at the margins. Early May. 18–20 inches.

West Point ~ Clear beaming yellow lily flowering and lightly secented. May. 20 inches. 1943.

NOTE ~ For the most part, the Peony Flowering tulips, also known as Double Late, are scented. Peony tulips flower later than the Early Doubles, with long-lasting blooms. All grow to approximately 18 to 20 inches. One of the most popular tulips available, Angelique, is dressed in shades of warm rose pink. Hermione, in lilac-rose, growing with rose-red Maywonder and creamy white Tacoma creates a stunning arrangement for the border and indoor arrangements as well.

⌣

Although they may not be fragrant, there are many hundreds of worthwhile tulips as lovely in form, striking in color, and with extended periods of florescence as the scented varieties. Several of our favorites include the Viridiflora tulips, with prominent green striations combined with their primary color of pink or ivory-white (and which is one of those cultivars that does indeed bloom for several weeks); the Gregii tulips, with unusual purple-mottled foliage and a stubby stature; and in particular the scarlet blossoms of 'Red Riding Hood,' *Tulipa sprengeri* with starry clear red flowers and an amazing ability to naturalize through grass in full sun and dappled shade, and 'Zomerschoon,' from 1620. 'Zomerschoon' is a true broken tulip in the color division "roses," which is defined as red or pink on white. The luscious satiny petals are long and pointed, washed with a strawberries-and cream-patterning.

Here it is early autumn and I am dreaming of the sweet scents of the flowering bulbs of spring. Yet to plant are the just-arrived box of spring snowflakes (*Leucojum vernum*) with delicate pendulous bells dabbed with an apple-green dot at the tip of each petal. *Leucojum* is Greek for "white violet," characteristically describing its fragrance of violets, with a note of lily of-the-valley. A new bed has been prepared for the eagerly anticipated Parrot tulip 'Orange Favorite,' described by Roy Genders as ". . . the most striking tulip in existence. The orange-scarlet blooms being tinged with old rose and featherings of apple-green on the outside. It is scented of *white jasmine* [my italics]."[5]

Each treasure bundle is dug into a depth of three times the size of the bulb with a handful of bulb food swirled in the soil. The ground is then firmly packed around the bulb, not allowing for pockets of air, the bed watered thoroughly, and a shovelful of compost thrown on top for good measure. Weed around the bulbs by hand; do not use the hoe as you may unwittingly pull up the bundle of beauty.

Winter is but a brief interlude, a restorative time of year for our garden and for those who garden. Arriving in our garden last spring, the same time as the early jonquils, was the welcome sight of the Robin. She stayed for several weeks, initially attracted to the last of the winterberries and then moving on to the plump worms. Bellwethers of spring, the Robin and the early jonquil, and a welcome sight are they!

The Tulip

She slept beneath a tree —
Remembered but by me.
I touched her cradle mute —
She recognized the foot —
Put on her carmine suit
And see!

— EMILY DICKINSON

ENDNOTES

1. Roy Genders, *Scented Flora of the World* (London: England: Robert Hale Limited, 1977).

2. Ingri and Edgar Parin d'Aulaire, *Book of Greek Myths* (New York: Bantam Doubleday Dell Publishing Group, 1962).

3. Anna Pavord *The Tulip* (London: Bloomsbury Publishing, 1999).

4. Paul Hulton and Lawrence Smith, *Flowers in Art from East and West* (London: British Museum Publications, Ltd., 1979).

5. Roy Genders, *Scented Flora of the World* (London: England: Robert Hale Limited, 1977).

CHAPTER TWENTY-ONE

My Grandmother's Gardens

A SUMMER MORNING

I saw dawn creep across the sky,
And all the gulls go flying by.
I saw the sea put on its dress
Of blue midsummer loveliness,
And heard the trees begin to stir
Green arms of pine and juniper.
I heard the wind call out and say,
"Get up, my dear, it is today!"

— RACHEL FIELD (1884–1942)

THE FIRST GARDEN I RECALL was of my mother's childhood home in New Jersey, my grandmother Mimi's. Our grandparents' home was set back from the bustling thoroughfare down a green-shaded lane. The vegetable and cutting gardens were planted on either side of the winding driveway leading to the house. My grandmother's pottery studio and kiln were sited along the driveway, surrounded by the well-kept beds. This home of our grandparents was built in 1750 in a traditional colonial style, a side gable with a center entrance. When my husband and I were searching for a home of our own, I was immediately drawn to the house on Plum Street and realized only after purchasing it how similar in architectural style and sensibility ours is to theirs.

Their home had a commodious front porch, with space enough to accommodate a dining table for gatherings of our extended family. The porch furniture was painted Wedgwood china blue, her color. The magical Moravian star glowed amber gold while the children laughed and played after dinner, drawn like moths to the warmth of the adults lingering in conversation. Dinner was complete with silvery ice cream parlor bowls filled with perfect round scoops of pink raspberry sherbet, her favorite flavor, and therefore ours.

Oh Garden of Fresh Possibilities!

The enclosed garden behind my grandparent's house was entrancing, with lush viridissimus sheltering borders and countless secret places to hide. There was solace to be found in the enveloping green edging. Some of the small trees and larger shrubs growing there were pink flowering dogwood, the bee magnet—Japanese andromeda, cascades of spiraea and beauty bush, skin-piercing Japanese flowering quince, and ancient tree-like rhododendrons and mountain laurels. Her garden was made fragrant with ample plantings of lilacs, summersweet, honeysuckle, and mock orange. The silhouettes and colors of the flowering shrubs are permanently imprinted in my memory, as equally as are their alluring scents.

There were waves of orange tiger lilies undulating in summer winds. Freshly picked sweet asparagus was sampled when helping in the vegetable patch. Around back, behind the garage, we'd find wildly overgrown black raspberry bushes with endless ripe berries to snack on. I remember the thrill and the terror of watching my grandfather place his arms in a dark cloud of bees while tending his beehives. How brave and heroic he remains in my childhood memories.

In the early 1960s my grandparents purchased (for the amazing sum of seven hundred dollars!) a picturesque half-acre lot with private beach rights on Cape Cod. Their dream was to build a cottage on the tall bluff overlooking the bay.

Coincidentally, my grandmother continued to build their home in successive seven hundred dollar increments. Seven hundred dollars paid for digging the cellar, the next for pouring the cement for the foundation, and seven hundred dollars paid to frame the house. My grandfather finished the remaining work, and they were still building the cottage when we began to spend our summers there. He always had a hammer in one hand and a fistful of nails in the other, and I was thrilled to follow him about holding the nails.

My grandparents worked hard and created wonderful homes they generously shared. While still a young mother and throughout her life, my grandmother taught ceramics at the pottery studio our grandfather built for her. Working together, whatever they touched became transformed into something beautiful. Their homes had an enchanting and joyful atmosphere, or perhaps it just seems that way, recalled from a childhood of fond memories. When I was making plans to attend art school in Boston, my grandmother shared with me her portfolio from Parsons School of Design. I had come to spend the weekend, to help her close down the house for the winter. There, in her garage, tucked in an old cupboard, she carefully pulled out a well-worn, though neatly arranged, portfolio filled with her watercolors and sketches. Imagine, keeping her portfolio safe all those years, possibly with the hope of communicating some part of her earlier self to one of her grandchildren.

Eventually, their gray-shingled summer dream cottage was made inviting by a screened porch, blue painted shutters, and a white picket fence. A dooryard flower garden was planted in front, and around back a vegetable and flower garden were sited atop the cliff overlooking the bay. A narrow, sandy path bordered with deliciously fragrant wild beach roses led from the garden to the steep stairs descending to the beach. A weathered picket fence and rickety salvaged gate connected to a wooden archway enclosed the flower garden. By mid-summer the entryway to the garden was embowered with a cloud of sky blue morning glories. Situated in a haphazard manner outside the gated garden were wind- and weatherworn 1920s bamboo armchairs and matching comfy chaise lounge. On some days we would play imaginary children's games there in her garden overlooking the sea, and on other days we would draw and paint, make clay things from clay foraged from the bluff, and catch fat, helpless toads. I helped my grandmother plant hollyhocks and marguerites and marigolds. The colors, so vividly clear and fresh; flowers growing by the sea appear even more beautiful, perhaps from the ambient light reflected off the water.

Weather permitting, we usually served dinner on the porch. All the porch furniture was painted my grandmother's signature blue. We ate at a long table with a pretty white-on-white embroidered cloth and round crystal rose bowl full of whatever flowers we had collected that day. We would have family feasts in the fading rosy light, memorable diners of freshly boiled lobsters and mountains of steamed clams, buttery and sweet corn-on-the-cob, freshly picked vegetables and fruit, and ice cream.

Oh Garden of Fresh Possibilities!

Blissfully lying in bed early in the morning, I recall hearing the soft cries of the Mourning Doves and the cheery calls of the Bobwhites, mingled with the inviting sound of the surf. From my bedroom window I could look out across the garden to the bay and see the ships and sailboats coming and going in the sharply sparkling sea. The transcendent harmonies of the surrounding undulating sea-rhythms and shifting light, the blend of flower fragrances, and birdsongs created the desire to in turn provide similar experiences for our children.

Some years later and newly married, my husband and I were visiting my grandmother at her Cape house. We sat with her in the living room listening to her usual captivating tales, and told her our plans for our new life together. My husband later remarked to me how beautiful she looked. Mimi was wearing a summer shift in a lovely shade of French blue, seated in a chair slipcovered in a blue floral print, with the shimmering azure sea framed by the window behind her, her china blue eyes gazing serenely back at us.

My Garden — like the Beach —
Denotes there be — a Sea —
That's Summer —
Such as These — the Pearls
She fetches — such as Me

—EMILY DICKINSON

CHAPTER TWENTY-TWO

The Memorable Garden

Consult the genius of the place in all;
That tells the waters or to rise, or fall;
Or helps th' ambitious hill the heav'ns to scale,
Or scoops in circling theatres the vale;
Calls in the country, catches opening glades,
Joins willing woods, and varies shades from shades,
Now breaks, or now directs, th' intending lines;
Paints as you plant, and, as you work, designs.

— from *An Epistle to Burlington* by Alexander Pope (1688–1744)

I THINK OF THE STYLE OF GARDEN described in this book as a "new" cottage garden. Perhaps you will find the ideas in this book helpful when creating an inviting garden in the countryside or an informal seaside garden, a romantic rooftop garden, or an intimate garden room, planned within the context of a larger garden. The design style of the new cottage garden is linked to the more practical tradition of the Grandmother's garden, or to what the French typically call a *jardin de cure*, a country priest's garden. The idealized style of a cottage garden is meant to be an exuberantly planted intermingling of fragrant flowers and foliage, fresh fruit, and savory herbs – all at once very old and very new. This style of garden is designed to nurture and nourish, to provide an inviting place to dream and play, to draw and paint and write, and to share meals with family and friends. Imaginative disarray neatly complements an exuberantly planted cottage garden. Unconsciously, the formal armature becomes obscured and artful disorder reigns, while the blooms come pouring out one on top of another.

Whether one begins to plan the framework of a new garden or redesigns the borders of an existing garden, there are several principles well worth establishing from the onset and adhering to throughout the design process. The premier principle is to make a commitment to plant organically and sustainably. Do we really want our children to play in a chemically controlled environment? Along with providing a healthy environment for our children, and in turn our children's children, we are establishing a safe haven for the songbirds and pollinators that are instinctively drawn to an inviting array of plant material.

The second principle is to understand the individual plants' requirements for healthy growth. A beautiful garden is made by exploring and discovering how to help plants flourish. A love of plants is the foundation by which great gardens are built.

The third principle involves "consulting the genius of the place," the tangible and the intangible. I take this to mean the tangible features of borrowed landscape (and nowhere so is this key than in the small garden), sightlines created within the garden, sightlines created looking through the interior rooms of the home into the garden, and the potential flow of movement for practical and pleasurable activities in the garden. The intangibles are the poetic atmosphere created by changes in vacillating light and earthly rhythms and choice of planting material, which is in a state of continual flux through the seasons, transforming in hue and form, texture and mass.

Moving away from principled guidelines are the formal concepts of design needed to create the armature. The style of a new cottage garden is essentially romantic, but to be successful, the underlying structure of every romantic garden selectively borrows from the concepts of scale, volume, rhythm, and balance of classical garden design, whether classical western or eastern influences, or a combination of both.

⌣

Initiate the design for your garden by first envisioning what you wish to use your garden for and then ask yourself the following practical questions. What would you like to experience as you approach your home and then what would you like to experience as you move through the public to the more intimate spaces? Is recreational space for children required? What part of the garden is necessary for utilitarian purposes? Consider where one's family and guests would be most comfortable dining *al fresco* in the evening (and for convenience sake, in close proximity to the kitchen), and where you would enjoy a cup of tea in the morning

Assess one's own particular light conditions in choosing plant material intelligently. New England is approximately halfway between the equator and the

North Pole; therefore, tracking the path of the sun is critical. The arc of the sun is a great deal shallower in the winter, increasing in length as we move closer to the summer solstice. Along with the angle of available sunlight, there may be large trees casting shade, as well as instances where one's home or a neighbor's may obstruct sunlight.

Use our own lot as an example. The front borders of our home face southwest and receive the greatest amount of light. Sited here are sun-loving flowers, shrubs, and semi-dwarf fruit trees. The flowerbeds bordering the garden path on the southeast side of our home receive a fair amount of morning and midday sunlight, and are fully shaded later in the afternoon. I manage to keep these borders cheery with flowers. My sun-lovers thrive in the side borders, as they have a respite from the blazing sun later in the day. The following could be said of a wide variety of plants usually thought of as requiring full sun: the same flowering plants growing in the front borders become somewhat weary and do not flower as long into the summer as those planted in the side borders where they receive less light. In addition to the sun-loving plants growing on the side borders are plantings that tolerate greater degrees of shade.

Around to the back, the northeast side, both our home and our neighbors' voracious trees shade the garden. This area has pervasive dry shade. By greatly improving the soil, we have managed to overcome or at least mitigate these difficult growing conditions. We grow healthy shade-tolerant and shade-loving small trees, shrubs, and perennials here.

Practically speaking, recognizing the challenges and working within difficult circumstances allows one to create wonderfully varied results. We treasure the dappled sunlit areas in our backyard as equally as the sun-washed borders in the front.

The very practical concern of assessing the available sunlight is followed by careful consideration of the vertical framework (please refer to Part One ~ Creating the Framework). The well-designed framework is developed through thoughtful planning of living areas and corridors, framed and punctuated by plant material (small trees, shrubs, and vines), and man-made vertical structures (pergolas, fencing, trelliage, etc.). A good bone structure with an underlying sensibility to proportion and balance is necessary while simultaneously considering what to plant. Once satisfied with the bones, proceed to plant with less formality within the framework. Connect the interior rooms to the exterior garden rooms by training fragrant vines to climb vertical structures, surrounding windows that are open during the summer months and porch pillars, for example.

Bear in mind while planning the overall framework that the key elements of any well-designed project are scale and volume. Nowhere more so than in the small garden is this concept more critical. Do not plant a large tree on a small lot, or adjacent to a garden room; it will grow to forty feet or more, in time robbing the interior rooms of the home and the garden of light and circulation. (See Chapter Two for a list of recommended trees suitable for a small lot.) Trees that obtain a height of thirty feet or less, preferably with an airy canopy, are best suited for the small garden.

Thinking of traditional landscape paintings composed of a background, middle ground, and foreground, one can keep in the mind's eye this model to further develop the garden design. The house, fencing, small trees, and vines constitute the background; the mid-ground is comprised of rambling roses and larger shrubs such as lilacs and rhododendrons; the flowering perennials, herbs, and groundcover planted at their feet form the foreground. Not only is this traditional arrangement of planting the most sensible for viewing and maintaining plants, it is also easier for Lepidoptera to find nectar plants. In our small garden, where space is at a premium, each plant is appreciated for its unique beauty and also serves a purpose or possibly several. It may be sheltering and/or fragrant, edible, or provide flowers to cut for bouquets. Perhaps it is planted to disguise something we don't care to look at, or chosen to attract songbirds or pollinators.

Beyond the formal concepts of design, the soul of the garden begins to emerge in suggestions of fragrance, varied color associations, and rhythm in the repetition of forms and hues. One of the most delightful features of the garden is the sense of anticipation. With an evocation of memorable moments associated with the sight and scent of favorite flora and wildlife, the garden becomes a haven where the beauty of the physical world helps overcome the struggles of everyday life.

Color associations play an immediate role in either the success or failure of a garden. The forms and colors of the plantings are repeated to bring the viewer's eye into and through the garden. Green in all its infinite hues is the most prevalent color in any landscape. Plant silvery blue greens to create different harmonies and to soften hard edges, and vibrant chartreuse yellow-green to create more lively, contrasting arrangements.

When planning color arrangements for the garden, the primary idea to keep in mind is that flowers in the hot red to orange to yellow family will pop forward, whereas colors in the cooler spectrum – blue to purple to rose pink tend to recede. If one wishes to create the feeling of a greater depth of space, a useful concept for a small lot, plant flowers in the softer hues of violet, blue, and rose in the background.

As long as we are speaking of color choices for the borders, think also in terms of a relationship to the color schemes of your home's interiors. Perhaps a bowl of vibrant vermilion roses, 'Fragrant Cloud' comes to mind, would look stunning for your home. Blue flax, orange California poppies and white feverfew look delightful in our blue- and butter cream-colored kitchen. Rose pink and white cosmos loosely arranged in an iridescent green art glass vase and set atop our daughter's bird's-eye maple bureau, looks like the picture of a summer bouquet.

More often than not, white flowers are highly scented. For that reason and that reason alone I would plant them; they also comprise some of the most beautiful flowers in the world. Elegantly, white flowers illuminate the garden in the evening light or add a fresh note of light and air to the tabletop. They harmonize splendidly with the rose, purple, and blue hued flowers, and just as well with the hot orange to yellow family.

Frankly, I avoid dark blood-red flowers. Every time I have experimented with that shade of red, it simply looks harsh with my particular arrangement of color. On the other hand, vermilion, and its paler hue of rose doré, are two colors I could not live without.

Homes faced with stone, brick, or shingles will harmonize naturally with the colors of blossoms and foliage. When deciding colors to paint a home faced in wooden clapboards, bear in mind the differing hues of flowers and varying shades of green foliage. Plant to either complement the siding and trim, or paint to coordinate with your preferred palette of flora.

One of my favorite cookbooks from the south of France describes an apricot-colored house with hunter green shutters. As our garden began to take shape, I reluctantly (albeit fortunately) realized this color scheme would be a colossal failure, dramatically limiting our choice of planting material. Eventually, we decided on a more familiar creamy pale yellow with a touch of ochre for the clapboards and an ivory white for the trim and porch. I am very satisfied with this combination; the creamy warm tones harmonize well with all our flora, from pristine white blossoms to subtle shades of rose, silver, and blue, to the zesty yellows, and orange flowers. As Alexander Pope wrote, "Paints as you plant, and, as you work designs."

Oh Garden of Fresh Possibilities!

In the midst of writing this book, my husband and I were invited to partici-
pate in a home and garden tour to benefit the Sargent House Museum. Built in
1782, the Sargent House is the former home built for Judith Sargent Murray,
philosopher, writer, early champion of social justice, and wife of John Murray,
the minister responsible for transporting the Universalist religion from England
to America. We had the weather on our side that day, one of those crystal clear
and brilliant days in early June New Englanders dream of. Despite the unsea-
sonably long winter and freezing spring rains, our garden was *almost* to the point
of magnificence-in-early-summer-splendor.

We shared with our guests information about native plants to attract butterflies and songbirds, fragrance in roses, mock orange, and honeysuckle, and how
to create successive waves of blooming Shirley poppies. From both guests and
guides we heard we were among the favorites of the tour and I mention this to
neither boast nor brag, but to suggest that despite our modest means and very
small lot, our love of growing things had set the garden singing.

APPENDIX

Coaxing Winter Blooms

Living in New England the year round, with our tiresomely long winter stretching miles before us, and then a typically late and fugitive, fleeting spring, we can become easily wrapped in those winter-blues. Fortunately for garden-makers, our thoughts give way to winter scapes of bare limbs and berries, Gold Finches and Cardinals, and plant catalogues to peruse. If you love to paint and write about flowers as do I, winter is a splendid time of year for both, as there is hardly any time devoted to the garden during colder months. I believe if we cared for a garden very much larger than ours, I would accomplish little of either writing or painting, for maintaining it would require just that much more time and energy.

Coaxing winter blooms is yet another way to circumvent those late winter doldrums. Most of us are familiar with the ease in which amaryllis (*Hippeastrum*) bulbs will bloom indoors. Placed in a pot with enough soil to come to the halfway point of the bulb, and set on a warm radiator, in several week's time one will be cheered by the sight of a spring-green, pointed-tipped flower stalk poking through the inner layers of the plump brown bulbs. The emerging scapes provide a welcome promise with their warm-hued blossoms, a striking contrast against the cool light of winter. Perhaps the popularity of the amaryllis is due both to their ease in cultivation and also for their ability to dazzle with colors of sizzling orange, clear reds and apple blossom pink.

Oh Garden of Fresh Possibilities!

My aunt has a friend whose family has successfully cultivated the same bulb for decades. For continued success with an amaryllis, place the pot in the garden as soon as the weather is steadily warm. Allow the plant to grow through the summer, watering and fertilizing regularly. In the late summer or early fall and before the first frost, separate the bulb from the soil and store the bulb, on its side, in a cool dry spot – an unheated basement for example. The bulb should feel firm and fat again, not at all mushy. After a six-week rest, the amaryllis bulb is ready to re-pot and begin its blooming cycle again.

Paperwhites ('Ziva' blooms before the first of the year and 'Galilee' just after the holiday season) are another simple-to-force and necessary bulb. The 'Chinese Sacred Lily' (*Narcissus tazetta* var. *orientalis*) is almost as easy to force and has a sweeter, though no less potent fragrance, as do paperwhites. The scent is a dreamy blend of orange and honeysuckle. They are also a member of the tazetta group bearing multiple blossoms atop slender stalks, with white petals and cheery yellow cups. The 'Chinese Sacred Lily,' brought to this country by Chinese immigrants in the late 1800s, is traditionally forced to bloom for New Year's celebrations.

With both paperwhites and 'Chinese Sacred Lilies,' place the bulbs in bowl or pot and cover with stones. The emerging green tips should be poking though the stones. Water up to the halfway point of the bulb and place in a cool dark room; an unheated basement is ideal. Water periodically and within a few weeks, new growth will be visible. Place the bulbs in the room away from strong light, continue to water as needed, and once in bloom, they will flower and scent your home for a week or more. Beginning in November, we maintain a continuous flow of blooming narcissus by planting a new batch every two weeks or so.

Typically, spring flowering trees and shrubs develop their buds by fall. They can easily be coaxed into bloom after their required dormant period. We prune branches of flowering trees and shrubs during months when the branches can most easily be forced to bloom indoors. Rather than discard the branches, why not use them indoors?

After the first of the year we begin to poke around in our garden to observe more closely the shape and structure of the trees, shrubs, and vines. Mid- to late-winter is the perfect time of year to revisit the bones of your garden and plot improvements. While the trees and shrubs lie dormant and leafless, it is also an excellent time to look at individual plantings with a critical eye to improve their shape with careful pruning. In addition to modifying its silhouette, there are many sound reasons to annually prune a fruit-bearing tree. Removing vertically growing leaders permits the tree to mature with a manageable open center shape for easier harvesting of its fruit and general upkeep. Pruning competing lateral branches allows for healthier fruit to develop.

Begin with forsythia branches, the easiest of all flowers to force into earlier bloom. We planted our forsythia bush expressly to bring the branches indoors in January to bloom by February. Their cheery golden yellow bells are a welcome sight on dreary, sunless winter days.

From mid-February on is the recommended time to prune members of the copious Roseaceae (Rose family). Their cut branches are utilized to create stunning arrangements. The bare limbs dotted with five-petalled blossoms are particularly evocative juxtaposed against the cool, low light of winter. I am picturing the plum rose of *Prunus cerasifera* 'Thundercloud,' the warm peach-pink of *Prunus persica*, the elegant sparkling white blossoms of *Prunus armeniaca*, and the brilliant fiery red-orange 'Texas Scarlet' Japanese flowering quince illuminating the rooms in which they are placed. I have to say my favorite of favorites is *Chaenomeles speciosa* 'Toyo-Nishiki,' with buds swollen and ready to burst by mid-winter and flowering in multiple hues of white, rose, and apricot pink, the beauty of their blossoms emphasized by the sharply zigzagging branches.

March is the month to prune magnolia and dogwood trees for indoor blooms. A single, well-shaped branch in a suitable vase from either of these trees creates an elegant unstudied arrangement. Do not prune too much growth from either the dogwood or magnolia, as both have a naturally graceful shape; simply a stray branch here or there. Prune just enough to create a beautiful arrangement. Magnolias are a bit more difficult to force; wait until you see white or pink in the bud before pruning.

As you are deciding which branches to prune to maintain the aesthetic integrity of the tree, look for branches with more of the fat plump buds as opposed to the pointed buds, which will develop into leaves. When pruning, always keep in mind the overall desired silhouette of the tree or shrub.

To encourage branches out of dormancy, lay the cuttings in a bathtub full of tepid water and allow them to soak overnight. The following day, give the branches a fresh cut with a sharp knife, and either split the cut ends or peel the bark to several inches along the stem end. Place the branches in a container with very warm water in a cool, bright room (ideally 60–65 degrees). Refresh the water every three to four days, or sooner, as it becomes cloudy, and recut the stems periodically to encourage fresh water intake. When the buds begin to break, place the branch in a vase filled with fresh water.

Coaxing Winter Blooms

Dreaming of spring in winter, despite frigid temperatures and damp gray-clouded days, coaxing flowers to bloom indoors will refresh the heart and add a touch of light and grace to an otherwise drab-hued season. Vases arranged with bare limbs clothed in fresh-hued blossoms reminds one that yes, winter is nearing its end and our cherished springtime on beautiful Cape Ann will soon be arriving, just around that final cold front.

When to Cut Branches to Bloom Indoors

LATE JANUARY
Forsythia (*Forsythia* spp.)
Witch hazel (*Hamamelis mollis* 'Pallida, *H. mollis* 'Arnold's Promise')
Japanese flowering plum (*Prunus mume*)

FEBRUARY
Japanese flowering quince (*Chaenomeles speciosa*)
Apricot (*Prunus armeniaca*)
Plum (*Prunus cerasifera*)
Almond (*Prunus glandulosa*)
Peach (*Prunus persica*)
Cherry (*Prunus subhirtella, P. serrulata, P.* x *yedonsis*)
Pear (*Pyrus communis*)
'Korean Spice' viburnum (*Viburnum carlesii*)
Fragrant viburnum (*V.* x *carlcephalum*)

MARCH
Dogwood (*Cornus florida*)
Honeysuckle (*Lonicera*)
Magnolia (*Magnolia stellata, M. soulangiana*)
Apple (*Malus*)
Mock orange (*Philadelphus*)

Favorite Flowers for Butterflies

NECTAR PLANTS

Early Season

'Korean Spice' viburnum (*Viburnum carlesii*)

Arrowwood viburnum (*Viburnum dentatum*)

Forget-me-not (*Myosotis sylvatica*)

Wild columbine (*Aquilegia canadensis*)

Apple (*Malus*)

Phlox (*Phlox divaricata*)

Lilac (*Syringa vulgaris*)

Ox-eye daisy (*Leucanthemum vulgare*)

Blackberry (*Rubus alleghaniensis*)

Red Chokeberry (*Aronia arbutifolia*)

Lemon lily (*Hemerocallis lilioasphodelus*)

Lupine (*Lupinus perennis*)

Dame's violet (*Hesperis matronalis*)

Chive (*Allium schoenoprasum*)

Azalea (*Azalea* species)

Clover (*Trifolium repens*)

Rose verbena (*Verbena canadensis*)

Mock orange (*Philadelphus coronarius*)

Lavender (*Lavendula angustifolia*)

Feverfew (*Chrysanthemum parthenium*)

Mid-season

Honeysuckle (*Lonicera sempervirens, L. japonica, L. heckrotii*)

Virginia sweetspire (*Itea virginica*)

Meadowsweet (*Spiraea latifolia*)

Purple coneflower (*Echinacea purpurea*)

Mexican marigold (*Tagetes tenuifolia*)

Cosmos (*Cosmos bipinnatus*)

Blanket *flower* (*Gaillardia aristata*)

Lantana (*Lantana camara*)

Coaxing Winter Blooms

Bougainvillea (*Bougainvillea spectablis, B. glabra*)

Nasturtium 'Empress of India' (*Tropaeolum majus*)

Shasta daisy (*Chrysanthemum x superbum*)

Allwood's Alpine Pink (*Dianthus* x. 'Allwoodii')

Verbena (*Verbena bonariensis*)

Cardinal climber (*Ipomoea x multifida*)

Hollyhock (*Alcea rosea, Alcea rugosa*)

Black-eyed Susan (*Rudbeckia hirta, R. serotina*)

Zinnia (*Zinnia elegans*)

Yarrow (*Achillea millefolium*)

Catmint (*Nepeta faassenii*)

Mimosa tree (*Albizia julibrissin* 'Rosea')

Milkweed, butterflyweed (*Asclepias syriaca, A. incarnata, A. verticillata, A. tuberosa, A. speciosa*)

Bee-balm (*Monarda didyma*)

New Jersey tea (*Ceanothus americanus*)

Leadplant (*Amorphia fruticosa*)

Anise hyssop (*Agastache foeniculum*)

Phlox (*Phlox paniculata* ' David')

Gayfeather (*Liatris spicta*)

Blue pincushion (*Scabiosa columbaria* 'Butterfly Blue')

Meadow blazingstar (*Liatris ligulistylus*)

Butterfly bush 'Nanho Blue,' 'White Profusion,' 'Nanho Purple,' 'Empire Blue,' 'Pink Delight,' 'Black Knight' (*Buddleia davidii*)

Passionflower (*Passiflora incarnata*)

'Sailor's Delight', summersweet, sweet pepperbush (*Clethra alnifolia*)

Joe-pye weed (*Eupatorium purpurem, E. maculatum*)

Late Season

Spotted touch-me-not, jewelweed (*Impatiens capensis*)

Great blue lobelia (*Lobelia siphilitica*)

Ironweed (*Veronia noveboracensis*)

Sedum (*Hylotelephium spectabile* 'Meteor')

Boltonia (*Boltonia asteroides*)

Seaside goldenrod (*Solidago sempervirens*)

New England aster (*Aster novae-angliae*)

New York aster (*Aster novi-belgii*)

Korean daisy (*Chrysanthemum* 'Single Apricot Korean')

⌒

The nectar plants are arranged to create a garden of sequentially blooming butterfly attractants. Many of the early and mid season plants bloom continuously until the first hard frost. The caterpillar host plants are listed alphabetically by common name.

CATERPILLAR HOST PLANTS

Perennials and Annuals
    Aster (*Aster novae-angliae, A. novi-belgi*)
    Carrot (*Daucus carota sativus*)
    Cleome, spider flower (*Cleome hassleriana*)
    Curly-leaf parsley (*Petroselineum crispum*)
    Dill (*Anethum graveolens*)
    Fennel (*Foeniculum vulgare*)
    Hollyhock (*Alcea rosea*)
    Lupine (*Lupinus perennis*)
    Milkweed (*Asclepias syriaca, A. incarnata, A. verticillata, A. tuberosa, A. speciosa, A. curassavica*)
    Mint (*Mentha* spp.)
    Nasturtium (*Tropaeolum majus*)
    Ox-eye daisy (*Leucanthemum vulgare*)
    Queen Anne's lace (*Daucus carota*)
    Pansies (*Viola wittrickiana*)
    Pearly everlasting (*Anaphalis margaritacea*)
    Red clover (*Trifolium incarnatum*)
    Snapdragon (*Antirrhinum majus*)
    Strawberry (*Fragaria virginiana*)
    Turtlehead (*Chelone glabra*)
    Violet (*Viola* species including *pedata, striata, sororia, papilionacea*)
    Virginia snakeroot (*Aristolchia serpentaria*)
    White clover (*Trifolium repens*)

Small Trees, Shrubs and Vines
  Apple (*Malus* species)
  Azalea (*Azalea* species)
  Black cherry (*Prunus serotina*)
  Blueberry (*Vaccinium angustifolium laevifolium, V. corymbosum*)
Dogwood (*Cornus florida*)
  Dutchman's pipe (*Aristolochia macrophylla*)
  Golden hops (*Humulus lupulus* 'Aureus')
  Lilac (*Syringa vulgaris*)
  Meadowsweet (*Spiraea latifolia*)
Mountain laurel (*Kalmia latifolia*)
  New Jersey tea (*Ceanothus americanus*)
  Pawpaw (*Asimina triloba*)
  Plum (*Prunus* species)
  Redbud (*Cercis canadensis*)
  Rhododendron (*Rhododendron catawbiense*)
  Spicebush (*Lindera benzoin*)
  Sweetbay magnolia (*Magnolia virginiana*)
  Viburnum (*Viburnum* species)
  Wisteria (*Wisteria frutescens*)

Large Trees for Butterfly and Moth Caterpillars ~ Alder, American elm, aspen, ash, birch, black cherry, butternut, hackberry, hawthorn, hickory, oak, poplar, tulip-tree, walnut, willow.

My Mother's Garden

An exotic sunset-tinted rose
Intoxicating breath of a magnolia
The small windy brick path
Leading to a hidden paradise
Butterflies flutter their own petal-wings
Over the smiling face of a daisy
A hushed lullaby to the garden sings the stream
Honeysuckle vines twist their elegant tendrils,
Grasping the delicate lattice-work
Gorgeous, vibrant hollyhocks stretch their faces
Towards the radiant sun
Drinking in the soft yellow light
Soon the sweet mellow silence is broken
By a joyful cry of children,
Two, three, now four
Suddenly this garden is a place of singing and frolicking and dancing,
Youthful and inviting

This blessed garden's soul shines forth in each and every existence
From the flitting butterflies
To the smallest thriving plant
To the noisiest child that finds peaceful comfort,
In the gentle haven.

Written by our daughter, Olivia,
when she was twelve

Garden Design

Clayton, Virginia Tuttle. *The Once and Future Gardener*. Boston, Massachusetts: David R. Godine, Publisher, 2000.

Fearnley-Whittingstall, Jane. *Peonies*. London: Weidenfeld and Nicholson, 1999.

Fiala, Friar John L. *Lilacs: The Genus Syringa*. Portland, Oregon: Timber Press, Inc., 1988.

Freeman, Stan, and Mike Nasuti. *The Natural History of Eastern Massachusetts*. Florence, Massachusetts: Hampshire House Publishing Co., 1998.

Hayward, Gordon. *Garden Paths*. Charlotte, Vermont: Camden House Publishing, 1993.

Hill, Brawley May. *Grandmother's Garden: The Old-Fashioned American Garden 1865-1915*. New York: Harry N. Abrams, Inc., 1995.

Jacobson, Arthur Lee. *Purpleleaf Plums*. Portland, Oregon: Timber Press, Inc., 1992.

Kindersley, Dorling. *The American Horticultural Society Encyclopedia of Gardening*. London: Dorling Kindersley, Limited, 1993.

Martin, Tovah. *Old-Fashioned Flowers*. New York: Brooklyn Botanic Garden, Inc., 2000.

Michalak, Patricia. *Rodale's Successful Organic Gardening: Controlling Pests and Diseases*. Emmaus, Pennsylvania: Rodale Press, 1994.

Mitchell, Henry Clay. *The Essential Earthman*. Bloomington, Indiana: Indiana University Press, 1981, 2003.

The Organic Gardener's Handbook of Natural Insect and Disease Control. Emmaus, Pennsylvania: Rodale Press, 1996.

Bibliography

Otto, Stella. *The Backyard Orchardist*. Maple City, Michigan: Ottographics, 1993.

Pavord, Anna. *The Tulip*. London: Bloomsbury Publishing, 1999.

Peat, John, and Ted Petit. *The Daylily: A Guide for Gardeners*. Portland, Oregon: Timber Press, Inc., 2004.

Rogers, Allan. *Peonies*. Portland, Oregon: Timber Press, Inc., 1995.

Roses. Brooklyn, New York: Brooklyn Botanic Garden, Inc., 1980.

Smith, A. W. *A Gardener's Book of Plant Names*. New York: Harper & Row, 1963.

Stout, A. B. *Daylilies*. Sagaponack, New York: Sagapress, Inc., 1986.

Taylor's Guide to Fruits and Berries. New York: Houghton Mifflin Company, 1996.

Thaxter, Celia. *An Island Garden*. New York: Houghton Mifflin Company, 1894.

Thomas, Graham Stuart. *The Graham Stuart Thomas Rose Book*. Portland, Oregon: Sagapress, Inc./ Timber Press, Inc., 1994.

The Wise Garden Encyclopedia. New York: Harper Collins Publishers, 1990.

CHINESE AND JAPANESE GARDEN DESIGN

Cooper, Jean C. *Yin and Yan:g The Taoist Harmony of Opposites*. Wellingborough, Northamptonshire: The Aquarian Press, 1981.

Keswick, Maggie. *The Chinese Garden*. Cambridge, Massachusetts: Harvard University Press, 2003.

Museum of Fine Arts. Boston, Massachusetts.
Yin Yu Tang House. Peabody Essex Museum Salem, Massachusetts.
Metropolitan Museum of Art. New York.
Walters Art Museum. Baltimore, Maryland.
Huntington Botanical Gardens. San Marino, California.
Portland Classical Chinese Garden. Portland, Oregon.

CREATING THE FRAGRANT GARDEN

Genders, Roy. *Scented Flora of the World*. London: Robert Hale Limited, 1977.

Lawless, Julia. *The Aromatic Garden*. Great Britain: Kyle Cathrie Limited, 2001.

Wilder, Louise Beebe. *The Fragrant Garden*. New York: The Mcmillan Company, 1932.

ATTRACTING LEPIDOPTERA

Butterfly Gardens. Brooklyn, New York: Brooklyn Botanic Garden, Inc., 1995.

Mikula, Rick. *The Family Butterfly Book*. Pownal, Vermont: Storey Communications, Inc., 2000.

National Audubon Society. *Field Guide to Butterflies*. New York: Alfred A. Knopf, Inc. 1981.

Roth, Sally. *Attracting Butterflies and Hummingbirds to Your Backyard*. Emmaus, Pennsylvania; Rodale Press, 2001.

ILLUSTRATIONS

Blunt, Wilfred. *The Art of Botanical Illustration*. London: Collins, 1950.

Fong, Wen C. *Returning Home: Tao-chi's Album of Landscapes and Flowers*. New York: George Braziller, 1976.

Forrer, Matthi. *Hokusai: Prints and Drawings*. Munich, Germany: Prestel-Verlag, 1991.

Grandville, J. J. *The Court of Flora Les Fleurs Animees*. New York: George Braziller, 1847, 1981.

Guest, Coral G. *Painting Flowers in Watercolor*. Portland, Oregon: Timber Press, Inc., 2001.

Holden, Edith. *The Country Diary of an Edwardian Lady*. Exeter, England: Webb and Bower, Limited, 1977.

Hulton, Paul and Lawrence Smith. *Flowers in Art from East and West*. London: British Museum Publications, Limited, 1979.

Lei, Qui Lei. *Chinese Brush Painting*. London: Cico Books, 2004.

Mayer, Ralph. *The Artist's Handbook of Materials and Techniques*. New York: Viking Press, 1940.

Redouté, Pierre-Joseph. *Les Lilacees*. Cincinnati, Ohio: Collection of the Cincinnati Historical Society, early nineteenth century.

Redouté, Pierre-Joseph. Watercolors. Pittsburgh, Pennsylvania: Hunt Institute of Botanical Documentation, Carnegie-Mellon University, Catalogue available at the Arnold Arboretum, Boston, Massachusetts.

Sackville-West, Vita. *Some Flowers.* New York: Harry N. Abrams, Inc., 1993. Text Copyright 1937 Vita Sackville-West.

Saunders, Gill. *Picturing Plant:s An Analytical History of Botanical Illustration.* Berkeley, California: University of California Press, 1995.

Sherwood, Shirley. *Contemporary Botanical Artists.* London: Weidenfeld and Nicholson, Limited, 1996.

Skelding, Susie Barstow. *Flowers from Hill and Dale.* New York: White, Stokes, and Allen, 1883.

Wunderlich, Eleanor. *Botanical Illustration in Watercolor.* New York: Watson-Guptill Publications, 1991.

MISCELLANEOUS RECOMMENDED READING

Benfey, Christopher. *The Great Wave.* New York: Random House, 2003.

Capon, Brian. *Botany for Gardeners.* Portland, Oregon: Timber Press, Inc., 1990.

d'Aulaire, Ingri, and Edgar Parin. *Book of Greek Myths.* New York: Bantam Dell Publishing Group, Inc., 1962.

Dickinson, Emily. *Poems.* 1890.

Dickinson, Emily. *Poems, Second Series.* 1891.

Dickinson, Emily. *Poems, Third Series.* 1896.

Dictionary of Plant Names. Portland, Oregon: Timber Press, Inc., 1994.

Emboden, William A. *Leonardo Da Vinci On Plants and Gardens.* Portland, Oregon: Dioscorides Press, 1987.

Field, Rachel *Poems.* New York: Macmillan Publishing Company, 1924.

Lowell, Amy. *The Complete Poetical Works of Amy Lowell.* New York: Houghton Mifflin Company, 1955.

Petrie, W. M. Flinders. *Egyptian Decorative Art.* London: Methuen and Co. Limited, 1895.

Untermeyer, Louis. *Modern American Poetry.* New York: Harcourt, Brace and Howe, 1919.

Wong, Eva. *Taoism.* Boston, Massachusetts: Shambhala Publications, Inc., 1997.

ACKNOWLEDGEMENTS

To my husband Tom, without whose love and faith *Oh Garden of Fresh Possibilities!* would not have been possible. Thank you for reading and re-reading, for thoughtful suggestions given, and editing these many pages. *Oh Garden!* is dedicated to our children, Olivia and Alexander, whom, I hope, will one day make gardens of their own. With love to my parents, who encouraged me to grow my dreams. With love and thanks to Janet and Cornelius Hauck, my mother- and father-in-law, for their kind faith.

With thanks and deep appreciation to David R. Godine for his advice and fine editing, and for the vision to see in the earliest manuscript, notebooks and illustrations, a book worthy of becoming a Godine title. With thanks to Carl W. Scarbrough, Sue Ramin, and Jennifer Delaney for their good work. With thanks to Dan Pritchard for help in sorting through the details.

With grateful appreciation to Dede Cummings for her artistry and guidance given, from our very first meeting through all the stages of bringing *Oh Garden!* to fruition. Along with addressing all the many complicated elements of design envisioned, I am particularly appreciative of her beautiful text wraps. Dede's superb selection of typography, coupled with her facility in, added an exquisite dimension to the book's overall design. With thanks and gratitude to both she and her assistant, Carolyn Kasper, for their thoughtful work.

With thanks to George Laws for his modern calligraphy. I first saw George's calligraphy on the jacket of *A Flight of Butterflies*, a book of Japanese woodcuts by Kanzaka Sekka. We found George through Paul Shaw of The Typophiles, an educational association dedicated to the appreciation and production of fine typography and bookmaking. We were elated when George agreed to share his talents.

A NOTE ON THE TYPE

The Monotype Janson font family is based on types originally cut by the Hungarian punch-cutter, Nicolas Kis, *circa* 1690, and was named after Anton Janson, a Dutch printer. The original matrices came into the hands of the Stempel Foundry in Germany in 1919. New type was cast and proofs made: these were used as the source for Monotype's version of Janson. The original hand-cut Janson types have a number of small design irregularities that give the typeface its unique charm. These have been carefully incorporated into the new version. The overall effect is of an easy readability that makes Monotype Janson most at home in book and publishing work.

Typography by Dede Cummings and Carolyn Kasper
DCDESIGN

Calligraphy by George Laws
Binding design by Carl W. Scarbrough

Printed & bound by South China Printing Company, Singapore